# COMMON ENTRANCE MAT



# COMMON ENTRANCE 13+
# REVISION AND PRACTICE

## Introduction

*This workbook is designed to be used as a revision tool to help you prepare for your Common Entrance examination. It covers the syllabus for paper 1, 2 and 3*
*It consists of:*

*revision notes*
*methods and formulae*
*examples for you to complete*
*practice questions.*

*We suggest you write in this book in pencil. There should be plenty of room in the example and answer boxes for your answers, but you can correct your work if necessary if you have used pencil. There are hints in the right hand column of some problems which you can cover up if you wish to complete the problems unaided.*
*There are suggested solutions in the answers section at the back of the book.*
*Do not think you can work through this book in one attempt. It will be far more useful to attempt one section at a time and ensure you have all the rules and methods secure before attempting the next section.*

***Remember there are restrictions on the use of calculators in the exams. Only use a calculator with this workbook where you see the calculator sign otherwise do not use one except to check your answers. You need to be able to do most questions with or without a calculator.***

*You should use this workbook in conjunction with past papers and consult with your Mathematics tutor to revise effectively.*

***N. Dawson and P.Thorns***

***Alpha Workbooks***
Published by Alpha Workbooks
www.alphaworkbooks.co.uk
phil@alphaworkbooks.co.uk

# CONTENTS




ISBN: 978 1 903406 73 1

# Arithmetic

**Numbers:**

Place value - you should be able to write down the value of any digit in a number.

| | millions | hundreds of thousands | tens of thousands | thousands | hundreds | tens | units | In words |
|---|---|---|---|---|---|---|---|---|
| 52438 | | | 5 | 2 | 4 | 3 | 8 | fifty two thousand, four hundred and thirty eight |
| 109605 | | 1 | 0 | 9 | 6 | 0 | 5 | one hundred and nine thousand, six hundred and five |
| 2594713 | 2 | 5 | 9 | 4 | 7 | 1 | 3 | two million, five hundred and ninety four thousand, seven hundred and thirteen |

You may need to state the value of any particular digit, for example in the last number the 7 digit stands for 7 hundred and the 5 digit stands for 5 hundred thousand.

1. Write the number 720208 in words.
2. Write forty thousand and fifty seven in figures.
3. What does the 2 digit represent in the number 562147.

**Even and odd numbers:**

Even numbers are numbers that can be divided exactly by 2. They are numbers that end in 2, 4, 6, 8 and 0

Odd numbers are numbers that cannot be divided exactly by 2. They are numbers that end in 1, 3, 5, 7 and 9

4. Write down whether the following are odd or even

(a) 254 (b) 359 (c) 123 (d) 798 (e) 247 (f) 256

**Multiples:**

Numbers that appear in the times table.

Example: Multiples of 3 are 3, 6, 9, 12, 15, 18,……… and 201, 204,… and 300, 303,….and so on.

5. Write down the first eight multiples of 7.
6. Write down the first five multiples of 13.
7. Write down the multiples of 9 that are between 60 and 80.

**Factors:**

These are numbers that divide exactly into a given number.

Example: Factors of 24 are 1, 2, 3, 4, 6, 8, 12, 24

8. Write down the factors of 30.
9. Write down the factors of 50.
10. From the list below ring the numbers that are factors of 72.

3 5 15 9 42 144 720 18 1 16

**Prime numbers:**

A prime number has exactly two factors (1 and itself). No other numbers divide exactly into a prime number.

Examples: The first 6 prime numbers are 2, 3, 5, 7, 11, 13. (1 is not a prime number)

11. Which of these numbers are prime? (Check: See if 2, 3, 5, 7, ....etc divide into them with no remainder.)

15 23 42 49 17 19 99 91 79 121

12. Write down the prime numbers that are between 80 and 90.

Mixed questions:

13. 40, 100, 60, 65, 81, 97, 25, 2, 39, 24, 6, 200

From the list of numbers above write down any that are

a) odd numbers

b) prime numbers

c) multiples of 12

d) factors of 100

14. Write down the prime numbers that are between 50 and 60.

15. 7 4 6 9 Using all these digits once only write down
a) the largest number
b) the smallest odd number
c) the smallest even number

**Product of primes, highest common factor and lowest common multiple:**

1. Complete: Write 300 as the product of prime numbers.

2 | 3 0 0
|
| 7 5
|
|
1

Keep dividing **by** the prime numbers starting with 2s then 3s then 5s and so on. Stop when you reach 1.
Divide by 2 to give 150.
Then divide by 2 again.
This gives 75.
2 does not divide in so try the next prime number, 3.
Write down the answer. Then see what divides into this.
Try 5.
Then 5 again.
Stop at 1

OR

300
$2 \times 150$
$2 \times 2 \times$
$2 \times 2 \times \quad \times$
$2 \times 2 \times \quad \times \quad \times$

See what two numbers multiply to give 300. (There is more than one way)
Then keep trying to break up the numbers into two other numbers that multiply.
Keep going until you cannot break up the numbers any further.

So $300 = 2 \times 2 \times 3 \times 5 \times 5$ or, using index notation, $300 = 2^2 \times 3 \times 5^2$

2. Write 450 as the product of prime numbers.

3. If $200 = 2^a \times 5^b$ find $a$ and $b$

4. Find the highest common factor (HCF) of 420 and 196.
Complete: 420 196

*Write both numbers as the product of primes.*

$420 = \quad \times \quad \times \quad \times \quad \times$ $196 = \quad \times \quad \times \quad \times$
The HCF is $2 \times 2 \times 7 = 28$

*The factors and repeated factors in both.*

5. Find the lowest or least common multiple (LCM) of 30 and 36.

The LCM is $2 \times 2 \times 3 \times 3 \times 5 = 180$

*Write both numbers as the product of primes.*
*You want the most of every prime factor from* ***both*** *numbers.*
*(Or write down multiples of 30 and 36 until you find the first number that appears in both)*

6. Find the HCF and the LCM of 54 and 36.

*The same as Q4 and Q5*

**Powers and roots:**

**Squares:** Examples: $2^2 = 2 \times 2 = 4$, $3^2 = 3 \times 3 = 9$ and in words 2 squared $= 2 \times 2 = 4$, 3 squared $= 3 \times 3 = 9$

**Square roots:**

$\sqrt{4}$ *means* $+\sqrt{4}$

A positive number times itself to give 4

When said or written in words:
the square root of 4 means 'a number times itself to give 4'.
As $2 \times 2 = 4$ **and** $(-2) \times (-2) = 4$ the answer is 2 or -2.
When written $\sqrt{4}$ it means the positive square root.

You should know $\sqrt{4} = 2$ $\sqrt{9} = 3$ $\sqrt{16} = 4$ and in words the positive square root of 36 = 6

Squares and square roots that you should know. Try to remember all these - they will turn up later.

1. $1^2 = 1 \times 1 =$ $2^2 = 2 \times 2 =$ $3^2 = 3 \times 3 =$ $4^2 = 4 \times 4 =$ $5^2 =$
   $6^2 =$ $7^2 =$ $8^2 =$ $9^2 =$ $10^2 =$
   $11^2 =$ $12^2 =$ $13^2 =$ $14^2 =$ $15^2 =$

2. $\sqrt{1} = 1$ $\sqrt{4} = 2$ $\sqrt{9} =$ $\sqrt{16} =$ $\sqrt{25} =$ $\sqrt{36} =$ $\sqrt{49} =$ $\sqrt{64} =$
   $\sqrt{81} =$ $\sqrt{100} =$ $\sqrt{121} =$ $\sqrt{144} =$ $\sqrt{169} =$ $\sqrt{196} =$ $\sqrt{225} =$

**Cubes:** $2^3 = 2 \times 2 \times 2 = 8$ and in words 2 cubed $= 2 \times 2 \times 2 = 8$

**Cube roots:** $\sqrt[3]{8} = 2$ $\sqrt[3]{27} = 3$ and in words the cube root of 125 = 5

A number times itself and times itself again to give 8

Cubes and cube roots that you should know. Try to remember all these - they will turn up later.

3. $1^3 = 1 \times 1 \times 1 =$ $2^3 = 2 \times 2 \times 2 =$ $3^3 = 3 \times 3 \times 3 =$
   $4^3 =$ $5^3 =$ $10^3 =$

4. $\sqrt[3]{1} =$ $\sqrt[3]{8} =$ $\sqrt[3]{27} =$ $\sqrt[3]{64} =$ $\sqrt[3]{125} =$ $\sqrt[3]{1000} =$

**Powers or Indices:** *Squares and cubes are also powers*

You should know $2^2 = 2 \times 2 = 4$ $2^3 = 2 \times 2 \times 2 = 8$ $2^4 = 2 \times 2 \times 2 \times 2 = 16$
$3^2 = 3 \times 3 = 9$ $3^3 = 3 \times 3 \times 3 = 27$ $3^4 = 3 \times 3 \times 3 \times 3 = 81$

and a mix $5^2 = 5 \times 5 = 25$ $7^2 = 7 \times 7 = 49$ $10^5 = 10 \times 10 \times 10 \times 10 \times 10 = 100\,000$

and in words 2 to the power 3 = 2 cubed $= 2^3 = 2 \times 2 \times 2 = 8$ 2 to the power 4 $= 2^4 = 2 \times 2 \times 2 \times 2 = 16$
3 to the power 4 $= 3^4 = 3 \times 3 \times 3 \times 3 = 81$ 2 to the power 5 $= 2^5 = 2 \times 2 \times 2 \times 2 \times 2 = 32$

A mix of questions:

5. Complete: a) $2^4 = 2 \times 2 \times$ b) $\sqrt{25} =$
   c) $4^2 =$ d) $\sqrt[3]{1000} =$
   e) $9^2 =$ f) $10^4 =$
   g) $10^6 =$ h) $20^3 =$

6. a) Work out 4 cubed.

   b) Find the positive square root of 100.

   c) Work out 5 to the power 4.

   d) What is the cube root of 27.

   e) Work out 3 squared plus 4 squared.

   f) Work out 5 squared minus 4 squared.

**Order of operations - BIDMAS:**

**Brackets first, then powers, then do multiplications and divisions before addition and subtraction**

Using brackets: Always work out the brackets first. $5(2 + 3)$ means $5 \times (2 + 3)$

Examples: $2 \times (5 + 3) = 2 \times 8 = 10$ Work out the bracket and **write it down**. Then do 2 times this answer.

$(9 - 6) \times (3 + 6) = 3 \times 9 = 27$ Work out both brackets and **write them down**. Then do the multiplication.

Write down complicated fractions with brackets then you will be able to work them out correctly.

So $\frac{12-4}{9-5} = \frac{(12-4)}{(9-5)} = \frac{8}{4} = 8 \div 4 = 2$ (Remember: a fraction is a division sum)

After brackets work out any powers. Then do multiplications and divisions before addition and subtraction.

Examples:

$3 \times 2^2 = 3 \times 4 = 12$ Work out the power and **write it down**. Then do the multiplication.

$5 + 4 \times 3^2 = 5 + 4 \times 9 = 5 + 36 = 41$ Work out the power and **write it down**. Then do the multiplication and **write it down.** Then do the addition to give the answer.

Examples:

$10 - 3 \times 2 = 10 - 6 = 4$ Do the multiplication first. (**NOT** 10 minus 3 is 7 times 2 is 14 .This is wrong!)

$5 \times 4 + 2 \times 6 = 20 + 12 = 32$ Do both multiplications first. **Write them down.** Then Add.

$5 + \frac{8}{4} = 5 + 8 \div 4 = 5 + 2 = 7$ Remember $\frac{8}{4}$ means $8 \div 4$ Do the division first. Then Add.

$(4 \times 3 + 2) \times (12 \times 4 - 3 \times 14) = (12 + 2) \times (48 - 42) = 14 \times 6 = 84$ Work out both brackets first remembering to do multiplication before addition or subtraction.

1. Work out the following

(a) $7 \times (9 - 3) =$ (b) $19 + 11 \times 11 =$ (c) $9 \times 8 + 7 \times 8 =$

(d) $(11 + 4) \times (18 - 3) =$ (e) $(6 \times 3 + 2) \times (13 \times 13 - 12 \times 12) =$

(f) $100 - 9 \times 2^2 =$ (g) $\frac{16-4}{8-5} =$

(h) $5 + \frac{8}{4} =$ (i) $\frac{56}{7} + \frac{42}{6} =$

(j) $9 \times (3^2 - 2^2) =$ (k) $(5 \times 2^2) + (4 + 2^3)$

(l) $\frac{5 \times 3 + 6}{25 - 8 \times 3} =$ (m) $2 \times 3^2 =$

(n) $100 \times 60 - 50 \times 80 =$ (o) $\frac{80 \times 70}{20 \times 20} =$

(p) $3(15 - 7) =$ (q) $2 \times (6.7 + 4.3)^2$

(r) $9^2 + 3^3 =$ (s) $15^2 - 13^2$

Some calculators allow you to enter the complete expression in one go. ***Make sure that you know how your calculator works.*** If not sure then you must use the order of operations. When using your calculator and order of operations, **always** write down the values after each calculation - you will then make fewer errors. e.g. For 1a work out 85 - 27 and **write it down**. Then do the multiplication to give the answer. (DO NOT do $16 \times 85 - 27$ as it is wrong!)

2. Work out the following using your calculator

(a) $16 \times (85 - 27) =$ (b) $459 + 21 \times 21 =$

(c) $19 \times 8 + 17 \times 7 =$ (d) $(174 + 329) \times (531 - 489) =$

(e) $32 \times 13^2 =$ (f) $7870 - 19 \times 12^2 =$

(g) $\frac{8456 - 5894}{705 - 425} =$ (h) $489 + \frac{872}{4} =$

(i) $19 \times (16^2 - 7^2) =$ (j) $(15 \times 14^2) + (54 + 9^3)$

(k) $\frac{15 \times 13 + 446}{79 - 18 \times 3} =$ (l) $(16 \times 13 + 482) \times (128 \times 5 - 52 \times 9) =$

(m) $414 \times 6 - 155 \times 7 =$ (n) $\frac{810 \times 17}{20 \times 25} =$

(o) $35(4195 - 3257) =$ (p) $28(42.7 + 0.3)^2 =$

(q) $12^3 \times 25^2 =$ (r) $2^2 \times 13^2 + 15^2 =$

**Using positive and negative numbers:**

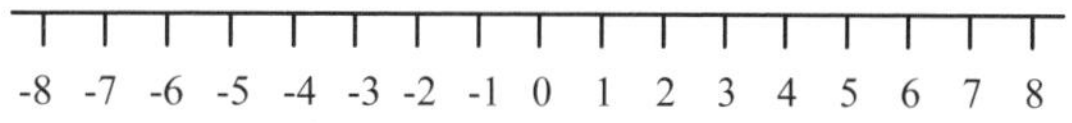

Using the number line to help you (horizontally or vertically)
5 is greater than 3
2 is greater than 1
-2 is greater than - 6 etc.

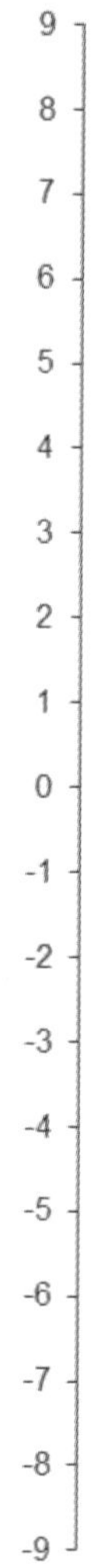

> To put a mix of positive and negative numbers in order think about where they would be on a number line

| 1. Arrange these numbers in ascending order. 3 , -3 , -5 , 7 , -1 |
|---|

- 6 + 9 = 3 (start at the -6 and go up 9)
5 - 7 = - 2 (start at the 5 and go down 7)
For signs that are <u>together</u> use the rules for multiplying and dividing positive and negative numbers.

> If the signs are the same then it is a +
> If the signs are different then it is a -

3 - -5 = 3 + 5 = 8 (- - together makes a + so start at 3 and go up 5)
-2 - 4 = - 6 (Signs not together so start at -2 and go down 4)
-5 + -2 = -5 - 2 = -7 (+ - together makes a - so start at -5 and go down 2)

Complete:

| | | |
|---|---|---|
| 2. a) -5 + 4 = | (b) 6 - (-2) = | (c) 7 - 12 = |
| 3. a) -7 - (-1) = | (b) -5 - 2 = | (c) 1 - -3 = |
| 4. a) 8 - 9 = | (b) -8 + (-2) = | (c) 1 - (-7) = |

Check that you can do these questions above on your calculator (using the +/- key)

The rules for <u>multiplying and dividing</u> positive and negative numbers.

> If the signs are the same then it is a +
> If the signs are different then it is a -

So

$3 \times 2 = 6$ (no sign means a + number, so the 3 is really (+3) and the 2 is (+2))
$(-2) \times 5 = -10$ ( a - number times a + number gives a - number and $2 \times 5$ is 10 so the answer is -10)
$7 \times (-4) = -28$ (a + number times a - number gives a - number and $7 \times 4$ is 28 so the answer is -28)
$(-6) \times (-9) = 54$ (a - number times a - number gives a + number and $6 \times 9$ is 54 so the answer is +54)
$42 \div (-6) = -7$ (a + number divided by a - number gives a - number and $42 \div 6$ is 7 so the answer is -7)
Check that you can do these questions above on your calculator (using the +/- key)

Complete the following:

| | | | |
|---|---|---|---|
| 5. a) $(-7) \times 5 =$ | (b) $32 \div (-4) =$ | (c) $(-6) \times (-8) =$ | (d) $(-72) \div (-8) =$ |
| 6. a) $(-3) \times (-7) + 2 \times (-5) =$ | | (b) $(121) \div (-11) + (-225) \div (15) =$ | |
| 7. a) $3 \times (-7) - 2 \times (-5) =$ | | (b) $(-42) \div (-6) + (-56) \div (8) =$ | |

| 8. If $a = 4$ $b = -2$ $c = -3$ and $d = 6$ work out the values of | |
|---|---|
| i) $ab =$ | *ab means a × b. The a is 4 which is really (+4) and the b is (-2)* |
| ii) $3a =$ | *3 a means 3 × a. The 3 is really (+3) and the a is 4 really (+4)* |
| iii) $2a + 3c =$ | *2 × a plus 3 × c. Work out each one first then add.* |
| iv) $5a - 3b =$ | *5 × a minus 3 × b. Work out each one first then subtract.* |
| v) $abc + c^2 =$ | *a × b × c + c × c. Work out each one first then add.* |
| vi) $\frac{a}{b} =$ vii) $\frac{2bd}{c} =$ | *vi) a ÷ b vii) Work out 2 × b × d first then ÷ by c.* |
| viii) $\frac{a - 2d}{2b} =$ | *Work out the top and bottom first. Then the top ÷ by the bottom.* |
| ix) $(a + b)^2 =$ | *Work out a + b first then square (see order of operations).* |
| x) $a^2 + b^2 =$ | *Work out a × a and b × b first then add.* |
| xi) $a^2 - c^2 =$ | *Work out a × a and c × c first then subtract.* |

**Multiplying and dividing numbers:**

You must know your tables!

You must be able to multiply and divide numbers and decimals without a calculator. Practise with these.

<table>
<tr><td>

1. $496 \times 7$

Complete:

$$\begin{array}{r} 4\ 9\ 6 \\ \times\ \ \ \ 7 \\ \hline 2 \\ \hline \end{array}$$

4

</td><td>

*1. $7 \times 6 = 42$ write down the 2 and carry 4.*<br>
*2. $7 \times 9 = 63$ plus the carried 4 is 67. Write down the 7 and carry 6.*<br>
*3. $7 \times 4 = 28$ plus the carried 6 is 34. Write down 34.*<br>
*You should have 3472.*

</td></tr>
<tr><td>

2. $273 \times 48$

Complete:

$$\begin{array}{r} 2\ 7\ 3 \\ \times\ \ 4\ 8 \\ \hline {}_2\ 4 \\ \hline \\ \hline \end{array}$$

</td><td>

*Multiplying 273 by 8.*<br>
*1. $8 \times 3 = 24$ write down the 4 and carry 2.*<br>
*2. $8 \times 7 = 56$ plus the carried 2 is 58. Write down the 8 and carry 5.*<br>
*3. $8 \times 2 = 16$ plus the carried 5 is 21. Write down 21.*<br>
*You should have 2184 in the first row.*<br>
*Multiplying 273 by 4 (really 40).*<br>
*1. Write down a 0. (this is the ten part of the 40).*<br>
*2. $4 \times 3 = 12$ write down the 2 and carry 1.*<br>
*3. $4 \times 7 = 28$ plus the carried 1 is 29. Write down the 9 and carry 2.*<br>
*4. $4 \times 2 = 8$ plus the carried 2 is 10. Write down 10.*<br>
*You should have 10920 in the second row.*<br>
*Add the two rows together. You should get 13104.*

</td></tr>
<tr><td>

3. $739 \times 65$

Complete:

$$\begin{array}{r} 7\ 3\ 9 \\ \times\ \ 6\ 5 \\ \hline \\ \hline \\ \hline \end{array}$$

</td><td>

*First multiply 739 by 5.*

*Then write down a zero and multiply 739 by 6.*

*Add the two answers together.*

</td></tr>
<tr><td>

4. $3704 \div 8$

Complete:

$$\begin{array}{r} 4\ \ \ \ \ \ \ \ \\ 8\overline{)3\ 7\ {}^{5}0\ 4} \end{array}$$

</td><td>

*8 into 3 does not go.*<br>
*8 into 37 goes 4 times. Write down the 4, above the 7.*<br>
*$4 \times 8 = 32$. $37 - 32 = 5$ carry the 5.*<br>
*8 into 50 goes 6. Write down the 6.*<br>
*$6 \times 8 = 48$. $50 - 48 = 2$. Carry the 2.*<br>
*8 into 24 goes 3. Write down the 3.*<br>
*$3 \times 8 = 24$. $24 - 24 = 0$. Answer 463.*

</td></tr>
<tr><td>

5. $2571 \div 3$

$$\overline{)2\ 5\ 7\ 1}$$

</td><td>

6. $863 \div 5$ (You will have to go into decimal places here.)

</td></tr>
<tr><td>

7. $2571 \times 3$

</td><td>

8. $863 \times 25$

</td></tr>
</table>

**Inverse operations:**

$8 + ? = 13$ You can find ? by working out $13 - 8 = 5$ $\therefore\ ? = 5$ That is using the inverse of + which is -

$? - 4 = 16$ Using the inverse of - which is + So $16 + 4 = 20$ $\therefore\ ? = 20$

$18 - ? = 11$ which is the same as $11 + ? = 18$ Using the inverse $18 - 11 = 7$ $\therefore\ ? = 7$

$6 \times ? = 48$ Using the inverse of $\times$ which is $\div$ So $48 \div 6 = 8$ $\therefore\ ? = 8$

$? \div 6 = 4$ Using the inverse of $\div$ which is $\times$ So $4 \times 6 = 24$ $\therefore\ ? = 24$

$56 \div ? = 8$ which is the same as $8 \times ? = 56$ Using the inverse of $\times$ which is $\div$ So $56 \div 8 = 7$ $\therefore\ ? = 7$

Use your calculator to work out the following:

9. Fill in the missing numbers

| | | |
|---|---|---|
| a) .......... + 25 = 254 | (b) ......... - 58 = 27 | (c) 62 + .......... = 184 |
| d) 345 - .......... = 176 | (e) .......... × 25 = 675 | (f) ......... ÷ 5 = 24 |
| g) 27 × ........... = 540 | (h) 171 ÷ ........ = 57 | (i) ........ × 18 = 144 |

## Rules and number:

You may be given rules to follow with or without a flow chart and/or a table. Sometimes the number that you start with is called the **input** number and the number that you end up with the **output** number.

For example: Use the rules [ × 3 ] followed by [ +4 ] with the number 6. So 6 × 3 = 18 then 18 + 4 = 22

or input → [ × 3 ] → [ +4 ] → output     Input 5   output 5 × 3 = 15 then 15 + 4 = 19

To find an input number given an output number just go from right to left using the inverse operation.
So instead of + use - and instead of × use ÷
So for this example given an output number 16 the input number would have been 16 - 4 = 12 then 12 ÷ 3 = 4

This flow chart changes miles to kilometres (an approximation)

miles → [ × 8 ] → [ ÷ 5 ] → kilometres

> For 30 miles
> 30 × 8 = 240 then 240 ÷ 5 = 48
> So 30 miles is approximately 48 kilometres

To change kilometres to miles you work backwards and use the inverse operation.
So for 80 km   80 × 5 = 400 then 400 ÷ 8 = 50   80 km is approximately 50 miles
You could redraw the flowchart going from left to right using the inverse operations.

kilometres → [ × 5 ] → [ ÷ 8 ] → miles

1. The cost of hiring a mixer is £9 per day plus £42.
   a) How much would it cost to hire the mixer for 7 days?
   b) If Jo had to pay £150 how many days did she hire the mixer?

*a) Number of days ×9 then add 42.*

*b) Use the inverse operations. First subtract 42 then divide by 9.*

2. Here is a table using the rule × 2 - 3.
   Complete the table

| rule × 2 - 3 | |
|---|---|
| Input | Output |
| 3 | |
| 5 | |
| | 9 |
| | 17 |

3. Complete the table using this flow chart.

input → [ × 5 ] → [ + 2 ] → output

| Input | Output |
|---|---|
| 1 | |
| 5 | |
| | 37 |
| | 47 |

4. Fill in the missing numbers
   a) 3 × .......... + 4 = 22   (b) 3 × 4 + ......... = 20   (c) 3 × ......... - 8 = 13

## Distance/time charts:

The approximate distance by road in miles between some towns is shown on the chart

| Brighton | | | | | | |
|---|---|---|---|---|---|---|
| 170 | Bristol | | | | | |
| 80 | 200 | Dover | | | | |
| 260 | 230 | 260 | Hull | | | |
| 260 | 210 | 270 | 60 | Leeds | | |
| 55 | 120 | 80 | 180 | 200 | London | |
| 280 | 225 | 280 | 40 | 25 | 210 | York |

> To read a distance/time chart:
> Example
> For Hull to all the towns above you go across.
> So Hull to Bristol is approximately 230 miles.
> For Hull to all the towns below you go down.
> So Hull to York is approximately 40 miles.

5.a) Work out the approximate distances between
i) Bristol and London

ii) Leeds and Brighton

b) Work out the total distance to go from Brighton to Bristol to Leeds to Hull

| Brighton | | | | | | |
|---|---|---|---|---|---|---|
| 170 | Bristol | | | | | |
| 80 | 200 | Dover | | | | |
| 260 | 230 | 260 | Hull | | | |
| 260 | 210 | 270 | 60 | Leeds | | |
| 55 | 120 | 80 | 180 | 200 | London | |
| 280 | 225 | 280 | 40 | 25 | 210 | York |

## Order of decimals

| | hundreds | tens | units | | tenths | hundredths | thousandths | In words |
|---|---|---|---|---|---|---|---|---|
| 425.9 | 4 | 2 | 5 | • | 9 | | | four hundred and twenty five point nine |
| 38.46 | | 3 | 8 | • | 4 | 6 | | thirty eight point four six (**NEVER**: thirty eight point forty six) |
| 5.387 | | | 5 | • | 3 | 8 | 7 | five point three eight seven |

To put a mix of decimals in order it is best to write them down under each other with the decimal point lined up. Put them in descending order (going down in value) by looking for the largest digit in each value position going from left to right
Then write them in order, descending (going down in value) or ascending (going up in value) according to the question.
Example: Write down these decimals in ascending order 12.591 , 52.6 , 12.59 , 0.908 , 0.958 , 9.8
Line them up

| | | | | | |
|---|---|---|---|---|---|
| 1 | 2 | • | 5 | 9 | 1 |
| 5 | 2 | • | 6 | | |
| 1 | 2 | • | 5 | 9 | |
| | 0 | • | 9 | 0 | 8 |
| | 0 | • | 9 | 5 | 8 |
| | 9 | • | 8 | | |

Look at the first **column** with a number in it. Choose the largest. here 5 so 52.6 is the largest number. Then pick the next largest. Here both the same so for these two numbers only go to the next column until one has a digit that is bigger than the other. Here in the last column 1 is bigger than nothing so 12.591 is bigger than 12.59
So far in descending order 52.6 , 12.591 , 12.59
For the remaining numbers: look at the first **column** with a number in it and pick the largest. Here 9 so 9.8 is the next largest number.
For the remaining numbers: look at the first **column** with a number in it and pick the largest. Here both the same so for these two numbers only go to the next column until one has a digit that is bigger than the other. Here in the hundredths column the 5 is bigger than 0 so 0.958 is bigger than 0.908
So in descending order 52.6 , 12.591 , 12.59 , 9.8 , 0.958 , 0.908
The question asks for **ascending order** so the answer is:
0.908 , 0.958 , 9.8 , 12.59 , 12.591 , 52.6

*If not sure - think 'where would the numbers be on a number line'.*

1. Arrange the following numbers in ***descending*** order 3.65 , 4.7 , 2.152 , 3.6 , 3.649 , 4.699

2. Arrange the following numbers in ***ascending*** order 12.5 , 9.999 , 8.9 , 8.095 , 9.9 , 9.10

## Working with Decimals without a calculator:

### Addition and subtraction

3. Complete: 1.27 + 0.8

| | | | |
|---|---|---|---|
| 1 | • | 2 | 7 |
| 0 | • | 8 | |
| | • | | |

*For addition of decimals you must line up the decimal point and write in the decimal point in the answer line. Then just add using your normal method. There may be some spaces - these are just zeros.*

4. Complete: 1.2 - 0.87

| | | | |
|---|---|---|---|
| 1 | • | 2 | 0 |
| 0 | • | 8 | 7 |
| | • | | |

*For subtraction of decimals you must line up the decimal point and write in the decimal point in the answer line. Then just subtract using your normal method. There may be some spaces - these are just zeros - **write them in**.*

5. 8.75 + 12.6

6. 18.65 - 9.7

| 7. 4.5 + 8.26 | 8. 7 - 2.56 |
|---|---|
| 9. 0.68 + 3.6 + 2.48 | 10. 25.1 - 12.47 |
| 11. 0.58 + 0.0068 | 12. 0.321 - 0.0146 |

**Multiplication and division of decimals:**

Multiplying and dividing by 10, 100, 1000

| 13. 34.865 × 10 = | *Move the decimal point one place to the right. (Digits move one place to the left)* |
|---|---|
| 14. 5.875 × 100 = | *Move the decimal point two places to the right. (Digits move two places to the left)* |
| 15. 67.9871 × 1000 = | *Move the decimal point three places to the right.* |
| 16. 34 × 1000 = | *The decimal point is after the 4. Move the decimal point three places to the right. You will need to add some zeros.* |
| 17. 54.83 ÷ 10 = | *Move the decimal point one place to the left. (Digits move one place to the right)* |
| 18. 8532.7 ÷ 100 = | *Move the decimal point two places to the left. (Digits move two places to the right)* |
| 19. 456 ÷ 100 = | *The decimal point is after the 6. Move the decimal point two places to the left.* |
| 20. 3456.5 ÷ 1000 = | *Move the decimal point three places to the left.* |
| 21. 6.84 ÷ 100 = | *Move the decimal point two places to the left. You will have to add zeros. Best to write 0.…….* |
| 22. 5.9 × 1000 = | *Move the decimal point three places to the right. You will need to add some zeros.* |

Multiplying and dividing by multiples of 10, 100, 1000

| 23. 3.48 × 20 = | *Multiply 3.48 by 2 Then move the decimal point one place to the right.* |
|---|---|
| 24. 5.8 × 500 = | *Multiply 5.8 by 1000 then divide by 2.* |
| 25. 67 × 3000 = | *Multiply 67 by 3 The point is after the last digit. Then move the decimal point three places to the right. You will need to add some zeros.* |
| 26. 34 × 2000 = | *Multiply 34 by 2 The point is after the last digit. Then move the decimal point three places to the right. You will need to add some zeros.* |
| 27. 54 ÷ 20 = | *Divide 54 by 2 The point is after the last digit. Then move the decimal point one place to the left.* |
| 28. 8532.3 ÷ 300 = | *Divide 8532.3 by 3 Then move the decimal point two places to the left.* |
| 29. 755 ÷ 500 = | *Divide 755 by 5 The point is after the last digit. Then move the decimal point two places to the left.* |
| 30. 6456.4 ÷ 2000 = | *Divide 6456.4 by 2 Then move the decimal point three places to the left.* |
| 31. 6.84 ÷ 300 = | *Divide 6.84 by 3 Move the decimal point two places to the left. You will have to add zeros. Best to write 0.…….* |

Multiplication and division of other decimals:

| | |
|---|---|
| 1. $1.2 \times 0.6$<br>Complete: $12 \times 6 =$<br>$1.2 \times 0.6 =$ | *Ignore the decimal point and multiply.*<br>*Count the total number of decimal places (after the point) in BOTH numbers in the question and count back this number of places in the answer. Put the decimal point back in. Write 0.72*<br>*Check whether the answer looks about the right size.* |
| 2. Work out $0.1 \times 0.3$ | *Ignore the decimal point and multiply.*<br>*Count the total number of decimal places (after the point) in BOTH numbers in the question and count back this number of places in the answer and put the decimal point back in. Here you will have to add extra zeros.*<br>*Check whether the answer looks about the right size. Here one tenth* ***of*** *three tenths.* |
| 3. Calculate $0.34 \times 0.2$ | *Ignore the decimal point and multiply.*<br>*Count the total number of decimal places (after the point) in BOTH numbers in the question and count back this number of places in the answer. Put the decimal point back in.*<br>*Check whether the answer looks about the right size. Here two tenths* ***of*** *0.34* |
| 4. Work out $1.2^2$ | 5. Work out $0.2^3$ |
| 6. Work out $1.1 \times 1.2$ | 7. Work out $5.65 \times 0.1$ |
| 8. Work out $25 \times 0.5$ | 9. Work out $0.5 \times 0.6$ |
| 10. Work out<br>a) $863 \times 0.1$ (b) $86 \times 0.1$ (c) $8 \times 0.1$ | 11. Work out<br>a) $1248 \times 0.001$ (b) $124 \times 0.001$ (c) $12 \times 0.001$ |
| 12. Work out<br>a) $350 \times 0.01$ (b) $35 \times 0.01$ (c) $3 \times 0.01$ | 13. Work out<br>a) $0.1 \times 92.5$ (b) $0.1 \times 9.25$ (c) $0.1 \times 0.925$ |
| 14. $38.5 \times 0.62$<br>$\begin{array}{r} 3\ 8\ 5 \\ \times\quad 6\ 2 \\ \hline \end{array}$<br>Complete:<br>______<br>______<br>$38.5 \times 0.62 =$ | *Ignore the decimal point and multiply.*<br>*Here you need to set out a 'long multiplication'.*<br><br>*Count the total number of decimal places in BOTH numbers in the question and count back this number of places in the answer and put the decimal point back in.* |
| 15. Work out $2.5 \times 7.6$ | 16. Work out $27.5 \times 1.2$ |
| 17. $46.97 \div 8$<br>Complete: $\overline{)4\ 6.9\ 7}$ | *If the number you are dividing by is a whole number then the decimal point stays in the same place in the answer line of the division.*<br>*Keep dividing - add some zeros. You should get 5.87125* |

| | |
|---|---|
| 18. $86.28 \div 1.2$ Complete: $86.28 \div 1.2 = \frac{86.28}{1.2} = \frac{86.28 \times 10}{1.2 \times 10} =$ | *Here we need to make the number you are dividing by into a whole number without changing the division. Write as a fraction. Multiply top and bottom by 10.(To make the bottom number whole) (Equivalent fractions so they are the same) You do not need to write this down but it helps to understand what you are doing. You can just remember –* ***move the point over the same number of places in BOTH numbers and do the division*** *862.8 ÷ 12* *There is no need to move the decimal point back as this is an equivalent division.* |
| 19. Work out $9 \div 40$ | *Here you will need to add a decimal point (and don't forget to put one in the answer) and also add zeros.* |
| 20. $3.876 \div 0.06$ | 21. $86.32 \div 0.2$ |

Check that you are familiar with using you calculator for decimal work by checking your answers above.

**Decimals with a calculator:**

Some calculators allow you to enter the complete expression in one go. ***Make sure that you know how your calculator works.*** If not sure then you must use the order of operations. As you work out each bit write down your answer. So for example write down $2(3.8 - 2.54) = 2 \times 6.34 = 12.68$

| | | |
|---|---|---|
| 22. $\frac{1}{0.5} =$ | 23. $\frac{1}{0.2^2} =$ | *remember a fraction is the same as a division. So Q22 is 1 ÷ 0.5 and Q23 square the 0.2 first and write down your answer. Then 1 ÷ this answer* |
| 24. $\frac{35.6 + 19.9}{12.4 - 4.9} =$ | 25. $2\sqrt{0.0144} =$ | *Q24 Work out the top and work out the bottom and write down your answers. Then divide. Q25 root 0.0144 first. Write it down. Then 2 times this answer.* |
| 26. $\frac{5(2.65 + 3.8)}{0.7 + 6.8} =$ | | *Work out the bracket first and write it down. 5 outside the bracket means 5 times the bracket. Write it down. Add the bottom two numbers and write it down. Then a fraction is the same as a division so divide the top by the bottom.* |
| 27. $\frac{3.24 \times 2.2}{5} =$ | | 28. $\frac{7.7 + 3.85}{2.2 \times 2.5} =$ |
| 29. $\frac{3(2.36 - 1.25)}{5} =$ | | 30. $\frac{1.2(2.3 + 5.53)}{6.45 - 2.1} =$ |

**Money:**

Just use the decimal methods but remember to write answers to 2 decimal places.
For an answer of £2.4 you should write £2.40
For five pound and four pence you should write £5.04

Note: You may say six pounds fifty two for £6.52 but you should **never** say six point fifty two for the decimal number 6.52 (as fifty means five tens and you have five tenths - you say six point five two).

| | |
|---|---|
| 31. What is the total cost of two items costing £3.67 and £4.56? | 32. What change do I get from £20 if I buy three items at £2.24 each? |
| 33. Jon is paid £9 per hour. a) How much does he earn in a week where he works 20 hours? b) How many hours did he work in a week where he was paid £72? | 34. Find the total cost of two ticket at £13.25 and three tickets at £7.15 |
| 35. Work out (a) $8 \times £2.65$ (b) $£985.20 \div 24$ | 36. Work out $£17.20 \times 8 + £12.23 \times 12$ |

**Changing decimals into fractions:**

Count the number of decimal places. This will be the number of zeros you put in the denominator. Always cancel your answer into its simplest form.

e.g. $0.9 = \frac{9}{10}$ (One decimal place ∴ one zero) $0.38 = \frac{38}{100} = \frac{19}{50}$ (Two decimal places ∴ two zeros) $0.125 = \frac{125}{1000} = \frac{5}{40} = \frac{1}{8}$ (Three decimal places ∴ three zeros)

1. Write the following decimals as fractions in their simplest form:
(a) $0.4 =$ (b) $0.48 =$ (c) $0.95 =$ (d) $0.132 =$ (e) $0.1228 =$

**Changing fractions into decimals:**

Remember: 'a fraction is a division' - the top(numerator) divided by the bottom(denominator).
Fractions in which the bottom numbers have only prime factors of 2 and/or 5 end up as *terminating decimals* when you change them. (Terminating means that the division will stop)

Examples: $\frac{1}{2} = 1 \div 2 = 0.5$ $\frac{2}{5} = 2 \div 5 = 0.4$ (Working $5\overline{)2.0}$ = 0.4) $\frac{7}{10} = 7 \div 10 = 0.7$ $\frac{5}{8} = 5 \div 8 = 0.625$ (Working $8\overline{)5.0^20^40}$ = 0.6 2 5)

2. Write the following fractions as decimals (a) $\frac{4}{5}$ (b) $\frac{7}{8}$ (c) $\frac{3}{20}$ (d) $\frac{13}{40}$ (e) $\frac{8}{100}$

Some fractions when you divide to change to a decimal, give you *recurring decimals*.(The division keeps going) You should be able to change these.

3. Complete: Change these fractions to decimals a) $\frac{1}{3}$ b) $\frac{2}{7}$

a) $3\overline{)1\,.\,0\,^10\,^10}$ = 0 . 3 3 3 do it yourself here $\overline{)\qquad\qquad}$

We write this answer as $0.\dot{3}$

*3 into 1 does not go. Add a decimal point and a zero after the 1. Put 0. in the answer line.*
*3 into 10 goes 3. Write down the 3.*
*3 × 3 = 9 10 - 9 = 1. Carry the 1.*
*3 into 10 goes 3. Write down the 3.*
*3 × 3 = 9 10 - 9 = 1. Carry the 1.*
*3 into 10 goes 3. Write down the 3.*
*3 × 3 = 9 10 - 9 = 1. Carry the 1. And so on.*

b)

$7\overline{)2\qquad\qquad\qquad}$

$\frac{2}{7} = 0.\dot{2}8571\dot{4}$ (the dots show that the numbers in between keep repeating themselves)

Note: If you obtain $\frac{2}{7}$ as the answer to a problem, this is the **exact** answer.
Whereas writing it as 0.29 to 2 d p is not exact.

*b) 7 into 2 does not go. Add a decimal point and a zero after the 2. Put 0. in the answer line.*
*7 into 20 goes 2. Write down the 2 above the 0*
*2 × 7 = 14. 20 -14 = 6. Carry the 6. Add a 0*
*7 into 60 goes 8. Write down the 8 above the 0*
*8 × 7 = 56. 60 - 56 = 4. Carry the 4. Add a 0*
*7 into 40 goes 5. Write down the 5 above the 0*
*5 × 7 = 35. 40 - 35 = 5. Carry the 5. Add a 0*
*Keep going until the numbers start repeating themselves.*
*You should obtain 0.28571428571428……*

4. Write as decimals (a) $\frac{5}{6}$ (b) $\frac{3}{8}$ (c) $\frac{3}{11}$

Do not use a calculator (except to check). Show all working and write down whether the resulting decimal is terminating or recurring.

**Approximations:**

Rounding numbers:

| | |
|---|---|
| 1. Round to the nearest whole number<br>a) 23.4<br>b) 46.495<br>c) 176.84 | 2. Round to the nearest ten<br>a) 346<br>b) 8 751<br>c) 999 |
| 3. Round to the nearest 100<br>a) 568<br>b) 4 032<br>c) 945 554 | 4. Round to the nearest 10 000<br>a) 45 499<br>b) 25 874<br>c) 244 569 |
| 5. Round to the nearest million<br>a) 2 587 634<br>b) 35 062 444<br>c) 44 999 999 | 6. Round to the nearest hundred<br>a) 2 564<br>b) 807<br>c) 256 873 |

**Decimal places and Significant figures:**

Examples:

3.4839 is 3.5 to 1 decimal place ( look at the $2^{nd}$ decimal place: if 5 or more add 1 to the figure before it)
is 3.48 to 2 decimal places ( look at the $3^{rd}$ decimal place: if 5 or more add 1 to the figure before it)
is 3.484 to 3 decimal places ( look at the $4^{th}$ decimal place: if 5 or more add 1 to the figure before it)

34762 is 30000 to 1 significant figure (if the $2^{nd}$ figure is 5 or more add 1 to the $1^{st}$ figure , write it down and add zeros to make the number the same length)
is 35000 to 2 significant figures (if the 3rd figure is 5 or more add 1 to the $2^{nd}$ figure , write down two figures and add zeros to make the number the same length)
0.0427 is 0.04 to 1 significant figure (DO NOT COUNT LEADING ZEROs - the zeros in front. You must NOT add zeros to make it the same length).
is 0.043 to 2 significant figures. (DO NOT COUNT LEADING ZEROs. The third figure is 5 or more so add 1 to the $2^{nd}$ figure.DO NOT add zeros to make it the same length).
0.06 is 0.0600 to 3 significant figures. (DO NOT COUNT LEADING ZEROs. Add zeros on the right to make the correct amount of significant figures).

7. Write the following to the number of decimal places given in the brackets:

| | |
|---|---|
| a) 25.553 (1 dec pl) | 25.553 (2 dec pl) |
| b) 67.497 (2 dec pl) | 67.497 (1 dec pl) |
| c) 34.342 (1 dec pl) | 34.342 (2 dec pl) |
| d) 24.5827 (2 dec pl) | 24.5827 (3 dec pl) |
| e) 6.3499 (1 dec pl) | 6.3499 (3 dec pl) |

8. Write the following to the number of significant figures given in the brackets:

| | |
|---|---|
| a) 45 678 (1 sig fig) | 45 678 (2 sig fig) |
| b) 23 415 (1 sig fig) | 23 415 (2 sig fig) |
| c) 524 (1 sig fig) | 524 (2 sig fig) |
| d) 1 983 (1 sig fig) | 1 983 (3 sig fig) |
| e) 6 184 945 (1 sig fig) | 6 184 945 (4 sig fig) |
| f) 45 (1 sig fig) | 45 (3 sig fig) |
| g) 56.73 (1 sig fig) | 56.73 (2 sig fig) |
| h) 0.005274 (1 sig fig) | 0.005274 (2 sig fig) |
| i) 0.128 (1 sig fig) | 0.128 (2 sig fig) |

Significant figures are often used in estimating. You will have to be able to multiply and divide multiples of 10, 100, 1000 and 0.1, 0.01, 0.001 etc. without using a calculator.

Multiplying multiples of 10, 100, 1000 and 0.1, 0.01, 0.001 etc

| | |
|---|---|
| Examples a) $30 \times 500 = 3 \times 10 \times 5 \times 100$<br>$= 3 \times 5 \times 10 \times 100$<br>$= 15 \times 10 \times 100 = 15000$<br>b) $600 \times 0.4$<br>$600 \times 4 = 2400$<br>so $600 \times 0.4 = 240.0 = 240$ | *You can miss out these lines as you just multiply the 3 and the 5 and add the same number of zeros on the end.*<br>*Ignore the decimal point and multiply.*<br>*Count the number of decimal places in BOTH numbers in the question and count back this number of places in the answer.*<br>*Put the decimal point back in.* |
| Examples c) $6000 \div 30 = 6000 \div 3 \div 10$<br>$= 2000 \div 10 = 200$<br>d) $500 \div 0.02 = \frac{500}{0.02} = \frac{500 \times 100}{0.02 \times 100}$<br>$= \frac{50000}{2} = 25000$ | *This is the same as $6000 \div 3$ then $\div 10$*<br>*Write the division as a fraction.*<br>*Multiplying the top and the bottom of the fraction to get rid of the decimal point (here × 100).* ***Still the same division as the fractions are equivalent.***<br>*You do not need to do this line but it helps to understand what you are doing.*<br>*You can just remember –* ***move the point over the same number of places in BOTH numbers and do the division.***<br>*Just $50000 \div 2$* |
| 1. Complete:<br>$800 \times 3\,000 = 8 \times \quad \times \quad \times$<br>$=$ | *For practice write each number as a single digit times a power of 10 i.e. 10 or 100 or 1000 or.....*<br>*Write down the answer.*<br>*You can check on your calculator.* |
| 2. Complete $50 \div 0.5 = \frac{50}{0.5}$<br>$= \frac{50 \times}{\times} = \frac{\quad}{\quad} =$ | *Write the division as a fraction.*<br>*Multiply top and bottom by 10.*<br>*You do not need to do this line but it helps to understand what you are doing.*<br>*You can just remember –* ***move the point over the same number of places in BOTH numbers and then do the division.***<br>*Work out the top and bottom. Then you should be able to divide the top by the bottom to give you the answer.* |

| | |
|---|---|
| 3. $600 \times 300$ | 4. $90 \times 7000$ |
| 5. $40 \times 50$ | 6. $300 \times 0.04$ |
| 7. $900 \div 30$ | 8. $8000 \div 40$ |
| 9. $5000 \div 0.5$ | 10. $30 \div 0.02$ |

Estimating (no calculator - except to check your answers)

| | |
|---|---|
| 11. Estimate: a) $4.9 \times 105$ (b) $96 \times 8.3$<br>c) $267 \times 52$ (d) $3499 \times 7.95$<br>e) $846 \times 0.127$ (f) $0.56 \times 8.74$ | *Round both numbers to one significant figure and multiply. Show working.*<br>*Remember to ignore leading zeros.*<br>*0.127 to 1 sig.fig. is 0.1* |
| 12. Estimate: a) $76.3 \div 2.41$ (b) $78945 \div 430$<br>c) $638 \div 0.134$ (d) $\frac{4673}{789}$ | *Show all working.*<br>*d) A fraction is the same as a division. So this is $4673 \div 789$.* |
| 13. Estimate:<br>a) $\frac{234 \times 38}{3.6}$ (b) $\frac{27 \times 891}{284}$<br>c) $\frac{7834 \times 57}{0.187}$ (d) $\frac{45 \times 0.37}{13 \times 0.019}$ | *Write each number to one sig. fig. Then multiply the top together and then divide by the bottom.*<br>*d) Work out the top and bottom separately before doing the top divided by the bottom.* |
| 14. Estimate the cost of:<br>a) 2643 units of electricity at 7.145 pence per unit<br>b) 22 tickets at £11.75 per ticket<br>c) 783 litres at 84 p per litre. | *Answer in pence. Change to pounds.*<br>*You could use £10 or £12 for your estimate here.* |

**Square roots without a calculator:**

| Question | Hint |
|---|---|
| 1. Without a calculator find $\sqrt{7}$ to 1 decimal place. | *This is a 'trial and error' question. Try working out numbers times themselves and see how far away from 7 you are. You will have to do some long multiplication. Good practice!* |
| Complete: $2 \times 2 = 4$ too small | |
| $3 \times 3 =$ too big so the answer is between and | |
| $2.5 \times 2.5 =$ too small | |
| $2.6 \times 2.6 =$ too small | |
| $2.7 \times 2.7 =$ too big so the answer is between and | |
| $2.65 \times 2.65 =$ too big | *All numbers between 2.6 and 2.65 round down to 2.6 - so this is the answer.* |
| Answer $\sqrt{7}$ = to 1 decimal place. | |
| 2. Without a calculator find $\sqrt{50}$ to 1 decimal place. Show your working. | |

**Index laws:**

When multiplying or dividing numbers raised to powers and the base numbers (the big numbers) are the same you can use the following

$2^3 \times 2^4 = 2^{3+4} = 2^7$ (as $2^3 \times 2^4 = 2 \times 2 \times 2 \times 2 \times 2 \times 2 \times 2 = 2^7$)

If the ***base number is the same*** AND you are **multiplying** **add** the powers.

$2^6 \div 2^4 = 2^{6-4} = 2^2$ (as $2^6 \div 2^4 = 2 \times 2 \times 2 \times 2 \times 2 \times 2 \div 2 \div 2 \div 2 \div 2 = 2^2$

If the ***base number is the same*** AND you are **dividing** **subtract** the powers.

| Question | Hint |
|---|---|
| 3. Write as a power of 10 | |
| a) $10^5 \times 10^6 =$ b) $10^7 \div 10^4 =$ | *a) Add the powers. (b) Subtract the powers.* |
| c) $10^6 \times 10^2 =$ | *Add the powers.* |
| d) $\frac{10^9}{10^5} =$ | *A fraction is a division. Subtract the powers.* |
| 4. Write as a power of 2 | |
| a) $2^3 \times 2^4 \times 2^3 =$ | *Add the powers.* |
| b) $\frac{2^8}{2^5} = 2^8 \div 2^5 =$ | *Subtract the powers.* |
| c) $2^6 \times 2^2 \times 2^5 =$ | *Add the powers.* |
| Careful with questions on powers - not all questions require you to add/subtract powers. | |
| 5. Work out | |
| a) $2^3 + 5^2 =$ | *a) Work out the value of each term and then add. (see order of operations)* |
| b) $3^2 \times 2^4 =$ | *b) Multiplying but not the same base number. Work out the value of each term and then multiply.* |
| c) $5^2 \times 10^3 =$ | *c) as b* |
| d) $2^2 \times 2^3 =$ | *d) Yes - the same base and multiplication - you can add the powers and the work out the value OR you can work out each part and multiply.* |

**Fractions:**

Simplifying fractions:

When simplifying fractions try to find a number that divides into the top and bottom of the fraction. If stuck try 2, 3, 5, 7,……(sometimes more than once).

Example: Simplify $\frac{24}{108}$ $\qquad \frac{24}{108} = \frac{12}{54} = \frac{6}{27} = \frac{2}{9}$ Dividing the top and bottom of the fraction by 2, then by 2 and then by 3

*These are equivalent fractions*

| | |
|---|---|
| 1. $\frac{28}{36} = —$ 2. $\frac{45}{100} =$ 3. $\frac{36}{102} =$ 4. $\frac{105}{120} =$ 5. $\frac{60}{84} =$ 6. $\frac{27}{90} =$ 7. $\frac{72}{168} =$ 8. $\frac{56}{336} =$ 9. $\frac{66}{198} =$ 10. $\frac{32}{72} =$ | *Cover this up first and try them without help.* *1. Top and bottom ÷ 2, then ÷ 2 (or ÷ 4)* *2. Top and bottom ÷5* *3. ÷2, then ÷3 (or ÷6)* *4. ÷5, then ÷3* *5. ÷2, ÷2, then ÷3* *6. ÷3, then ÷3(or ÷ 9)* *7. ÷2, ÷2, ÷2, then ÷3 (or other factors)* *8. ÷2, ÷2, ÷2, then÷7 (or other factors)* *9. ÷2, ÷11, then ÷3 (or other factors)* *10. ÷2, ÷2, then ÷2 (or other factors)* |
| 11. Write 24 as a fraction of 60. | *Just 24 over 60 and simplify.* |
| 12. The receipts from a football match increase from £232 000 to £340 000. Find the fractional increase. | *Find the actual increase. Then write this as a fraction of the original value. Then simplify.* |

Other equivalent fractions

Just multiply the top and bottom numbers by the same number

e.g. $\frac{3}{5} = \frac{6}{10} = \frac{9}{15} = \frac{12}{20}$ Here the top and bottom of $\frac{3}{5}$ has been multiplied by 2, then by 3 and then by 4

*These are equivalent fractions*

You may need to do this so that you can compare fractions to see which is larger. Also required for addition and subtraction of fractions.

Example: Put these fractions in order of size (smallest first)

$$\frac{5}{6}, \frac{7}{8}, \frac{3}{4}, \frac{2}{3}$$

Write equivalent fractions for each fraction using the same denominator $\frac{5}{6} = \frac{20}{24}, \frac{7}{8} = \frac{21}{24}, \frac{3}{4} = \frac{18}{24}, \frac{2}{3} = \frac{16}{24}$

From here it is easy to see the order from the 24ths $\frac{2}{3}, \frac{3}{4}, \frac{5}{6}, \frac{7}{8}$

You can get these 24ths by finding a number that 6, 8, 4 and 3 divide into (i.e. 24) and then working out the equivalent fractions directly.

You could divide each fraction to obtain a decimal. It would then be easier to order the fractions. The best method if allowed a calculator.

| | |
|---|---|
| 13. Arrange in order of size ( smallest first) $\frac{1}{3}, \frac{2}{5}, \frac{3}{10}$ | *Do not use your calculator.* |
| 14. Use your calculator to help you arrange these numbers in order of size with the smallest first. 3.14 , $\frac{22}{7}$ , $\pi$ , 3.1 | *Divide the fraction.* *If not sure - think 'where would the numbers be on a number line'.* |

15. Put into ascending order $\frac{2}{3}$, $\frac{3}{4}$, $\frac{7}{12}$

16. Put into descending order $\frac{5}{8}$, $\frac{11}{16}$, $\frac{13}{24}$

17. $\frac{7}{12} > \frac{9}{15}$ True or false?(You must explain how you know)

18. Which is larger $\frac{4}{9}$ or 0.45 ?

Fractions of an amount:

To find $\frac{1}{2}$ divide by 2 To find $\frac{1}{3}$ divide by 3 To find $\frac{1}{4}$ divide by 4 etc.

To find $\frac{2}{3}$ divide by 3 to find $\frac{1}{3}$ and then multiply by 2

To find $\frac{3}{5}$ divide by 5 to find $\frac{1}{5}$ and then multiply by 3

etc.

Now complete these (try working without a calculator - show working):

19. Find $\frac{1}{4}$ of 360 $360 \div 4 =$ $\overline{)3\,6\,0}$

20. Find $\frac{1}{8}$ of £936

21. Find $\frac{1}{5}$ of 24785m

22. Find $\frac{1}{10}$ £3456

23. Find $\frac{3}{5}$ of £867

24. Work out $\frac{3}{4}$ of 426 km

25. Work out $\frac{7}{10}$ of £289

**Shading fractions:**

26. Shade ⅓ of this shape.
12 equal parts
⅓ of 12 = 12 ÷ 3 = 4
So shade 4 parts.

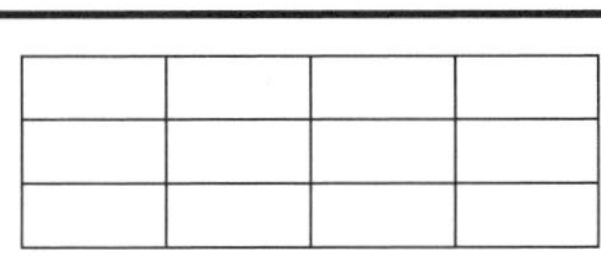

27. What fraction of this shape is shaded?

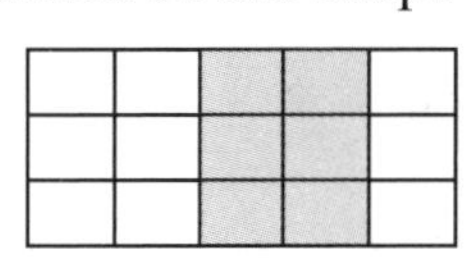

Give answer in its lowest terms.
(Cancel down if possible)

28. Shade ⅝ of this shape

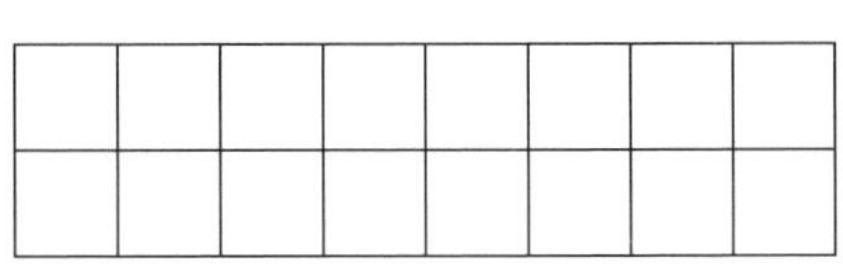

29. Shade $\frac{7}{12}$ of this shape

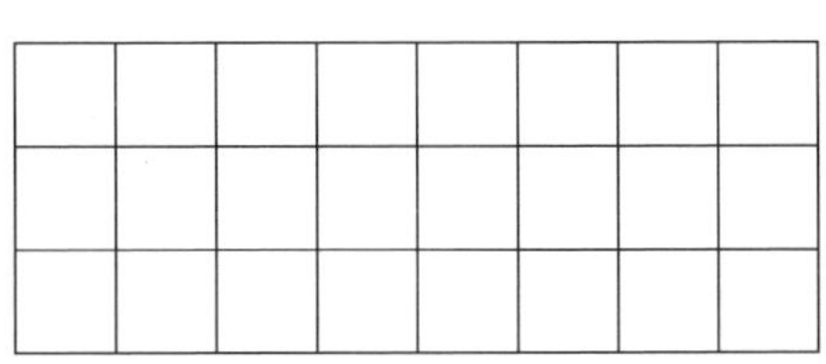

30. What fraction of this shape is not shaded?

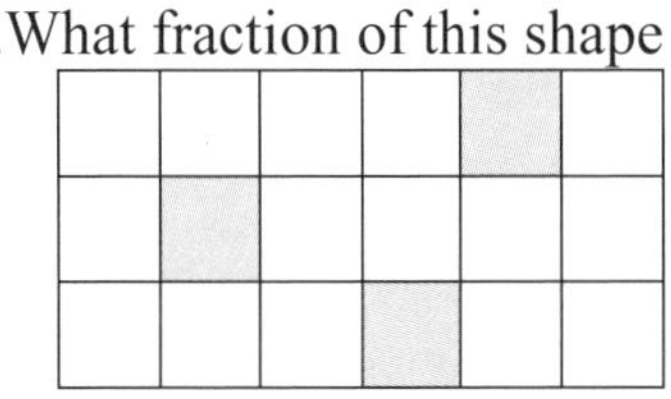

**+ - × ÷ of fractions:**

Easy for the calculator paper - you must know how to use the fraction key on your calculator [ $a\,^b/_c$ ] or [ $\frac{\square}{\square}$ ]

Example: To work out $\frac{2}{5}+2\frac{3}{4}$ use these keys [2] [$a\,^b/_c$] [5] [+] [2] [$a\,^b/_c$] [3] [$a\,^b/_c$] [4] [=]

The calculator shows 3 ⌋ 3 ⌋ 20 which **you must write** as $3\frac{3}{20}$

Without a calculator. (Check your answers on a calculator - then you will be familiar with using it for fractions.)

| | |
|---|---|
| 1. Complete: $\frac{4}{5}+\frac{2}{3}=\frac{\quad + \quad}{15}$ <br> $=\frac{\quad}{15}$ <br> $=$ | *First find a number that 5 and 3 divide into, a common denominator.Here it is 15. Now make equal fractions:* <br> *5 × 3 = 15 so multiply the 4 by 3.* <br> *3 × 5 = 15 so multiply the 2 by 5.* <br> *Just add the top numbers together.* <br><br> *A 'top heavy' fraction so change it to a mixed number.(How many 15s in 22 and how many left over)* |
| 2. Complete: <br> $\frac{7}{8}-\frac{3}{10}=\overline{\qquad\qquad}$ <br> $=$ | *First find a number that 8 and 10 divide into. You could use 40 or 80.* <br> *Say we use 40 then* <br> *8 × 5 = 40 so multiply the 7 by 5.* <br> *10 × 4 = 40 so multiply the 3 by 4.* <br> *Then just subtract the top numbers.* |
| 3. Complete: $\frac{4}{5}\times\frac{2}{3}=\frac{\quad\times\quad}{\quad\times\quad}=\overline{\quad}$ | *Just multiply the top numbers together and the bottom numbers together.* |
| 4. Complete: <br> $\frac{5}{6}\div\frac{3}{4}=\overline{\quad}\times\overline{\quad}=\frac{\quad\times\quad}{\quad\times\quad}=\overline{\quad}=\overline{\quad}$ | *Write down the first fraction.Change the ÷ to ×.Turn the second fraction upside down and write it down.* <br> *Then multiply the top numbers together and the bottom numbers together and tidy up the answer.* |

If you have mixed numbers e.g. $2\frac{1}{4}$ you can use the above methods if you change them to 'top heavy' fractions (improper fractions) e.g. $2\frac{1}{4}=\frac{9}{4}$ (You **must** use 'top heavy' fractions for × and ÷ ) Do not use your calculator - except to check your answers.

Obtained by $2 \times 4 + 1 = 9$

To write a whole number as a fraction just put it over 1. So $5=\frac{5}{1}$, $8=\frac{8}{1}$, etc.

5. Fill in the missing numbers for this mix of improper fractions and mixed numbers

a) $3\frac{1}{4}=\frac{\quad}{4}$ (b) $5\frac{2}{3}=\frac{\quad}{3}$ (c) $4\frac{3}{5}=\frac{\quad}{5}$ (d) $\frac{20}{3}=6-$ (e) $\frac{34}{8}=\quad-$

6. Work out: a) $\frac{4}{5}+\frac{1}{8}=$ (b) $\frac{3}{10}+1\frac{3}{4}=$

c) $\frac{1}{3}+\frac{2}{9}=$ (d) $\frac{7}{8}-\frac{2}{3}=$ (e) $2\frac{1}{4}-\frac{1}{3}=$

f) $4\frac{3}{5}-1\frac{7}{8}=$ (g) $5\times\frac{2}{3}=$ (h) $\frac{4}{5}\times 12=$

i) $\frac{3}{4}\times\frac{2}{3}=$ (j) $\left(\frac{3}{4}\right)^2=$ (k) $1\frac{2}{5}\times 2\frac{3}{4}=$

l) $\frac{3}{8}\div\frac{6}{7}=$ (m) $\frac{5}{9}\div 3\frac{1}{3}=$ (n) $2\frac{7}{10}\div 1\frac{1}{4}=$

Now check your answers on a calculator - then you will be familiar with using it for fraction work.

**Cancelling or simplifying fractions:**

You can use equivalent fraction work to simplify some awkward fractions

You know $\frac{3\times5}{2\times3} = \frac{15}{6} = \frac{5}{2} = 2\frac{1}{2}$

Instead of multiplying here we could divide top and bottom by 3 (you may have called this cancelling down or simplifying). This then gives $\frac{1\times5}{2\times1} = \frac{5}{2} = 2\frac{1}{2}$.

You should think 'Top and bottom divided by the same number'.

If there are **only × signs** on top and bottom then one number on the top and one number on the bottom can be divided by the same number.

7. Complete: Without using a calculator evaluate

a) $\frac{15\times24}{5}$ = ____________ =

b) $\frac{24\times45}{2.4}$ = ____________ =

c) $\frac{16\times9\times49}{2\times7}$ = ____________ =

d) $\frac{2.5\times1.2}{5\times10}$ = ____________ =

*Divide top and bottom by 5.*

*This is then just 3 × 24 ÷1.*

*Work out 24 ÷ 2.4 (× top and bottom by 10 to give 240 ÷ 24)*
*Then work out the × 45.*

*See if you can work out c) and d) without help.*

**Word Problems:**

Many Common Entrance fraction questions are given in the form of a problem. The key to answering this type of question is firstly to decide what type of problem it is (addition, subtraction, multiplication or division) and then to apply the correct fraction methods. You may find that drawing diagrams helps you to understand what is happening.

Examples:

A. John and his friends Alfie and Gaurav share a pizza. John eats ¼ of the pizza, Alfie eats $^1/_3$ of the pizza. What fraction of the pizza does Gaurav get?

John and Alfie together ( ie. add) eat $\frac{1}{4} + \frac{1}{3}$

$= \frac{3+4}{12}$

$= \frac{7}{12}$

| J | J | J | A |
|---|---|---|---|
| A | A | A | |
| | | | |

$\frac{7}{12}$ eaten so Gaurav gets $\frac{5}{12}$ ( since $\frac{7}{12} + \frac{5}{12}$ make $\frac{12}{12}$ i.e. the whole pizza)

B. John and his friends Alfie and Gaurav share a pizza. John eats ¼ of the pizza. If Alfie and Gaurav share the rest of the pizza how much does each get?

After John has eaten ¼ there is ¾ of the pizza left

| J | | | |
|---|---|---|---|

Alfie and Gaurav each get half of what is left so cut the ¾ in half giving $^3/_8$ for each of Alfie and Gaurav.

| J | A | A | A |
|---|---|---|---|
| J | G | G | G |

8. Jack buys 2 cakes. He eats eats ¾ of one of the cakes and Shares the rest of the cakes equally between his three friends. What fraction of a cake does each friend get?

*What fraction is left?*
*2 -¾ = ….*

*Divide this by 3.*

*Hint: To divide a fraction by three simply multiply the denominator by three.*

**Fractions of an hour:**

There are 60 minutes in an hour therefore 45 minutes is $\frac{45}{60}$ hour

So 2 hours 45 minutes is $2\frac{45}{60}$ hours = 2.75hours (as 45 ÷ 60 = 0.75)

15 minutes = $\frac{15}{60}$ hour = $\frac{1}{4}$ hour = 0.25 hour

10 minutes = $\frac{10}{60}$ hour = $\frac{1}{6}$ hour = 1 ÷ 6 = 0.16666..... hour = $0.1\dot{6}$ hour = 0.17 hour (to 2 decimal places)

25 minutes = $\frac{25}{60}$ hour = $\frac{5}{12}$ hour = 5 ÷ 12 = 0.416666.... hour = 0.42 hour (to 2 decimal places)

7 hours 25 minutes = $7\frac{5}{12}$ = 7.416666...hour = $4.41\dot{6}$ hour

> When doing calculations with hours **always** use fractions or the full decimal - **never** the hours shortened to 2 or 3 decimal places.

| |
|---|
| 1.Change these times to decimal hours:<br>a) 2 hours 15 minutes    b) 8 hours 12 minutes    c) 6 hours 18 minutes |
| 2. Change these decimal hours to hours and minutes<br>a) 4.75 hours    b) 6.2 hours    c) 3.4 hours |

**Fractions, decimals and percentages:**

You should know $\frac{1}{2} = 0.5 = 50\%$ $\frac{1}{4} = 0.25 = 25\%$ $\frac{3}{4} = 0.75 = 75\%$ $\frac{1}{3} = 0.\dot{3} = 33\frac{1}{3}\%$ $\frac{1}{10} = 0.1 = 10\%$ $\frac{1}{5} = 0.2 = 20\%$

Decimal→Fraction e.g. $0.7 = \frac{7}{10}$ $0.45 = \frac{45}{100} = \frac{9}{20}$ $0.365 = \frac{365}{1000} = \frac{73}{200}$

One decimal place ∴ one zero | Two decimal places ∴ two zeros | Three decimal places ∴ three zeros

Fraction→Decimal e.g. $\frac{3}{5} = 3 \div 5 = 0.6$ $\frac{7}{20} = 7 \div 20 = 0.35$

> Remember a fraction is the same as a division

Decimal→Percentage e.g . 0.36 = 36 % 0.4 = 40 % 0.235 = 23.5 %

> Just multiply by one hundred (move the decimal point two places to the right to make it bigger).

Percentage→Decimal e.g. 23 % = 0.23 6 % = 0.06 12.5 % = 0.125

> Just divide by one hundred (move the decimal point two places to the left to make it smaller).

Percentage→Fraction e.g. $45\% = \frac{45}{100} = \frac{9}{20}$ $8\% = \frac{8}{100} = \frac{2}{25}$

> Per cent means out of 100. So just write the number over 100 and simplify if possible.

Fraction→ Percentage e.g. $\frac{4}{5} \times 100 = 4 \div 5 \times 100 = 80$

> Just divide the fraction and multiply by 100 (or 4 × 100 and then ÷ 5).

Now try these:

| |
|---|
| 3. Write as decimals a) 60% = b) 35% = c) 3% = d) $\frac{3}{10}$ = e) $\frac{27}{100}$ =<br>f) $\frac{9}{100}$ = g) $\frac{1}{4}$ = h) $\frac{4}{5}$ = i) $\frac{2}{3}$ = j) $\frac{5}{8}$ |
| 4.Write as percentages: a) 0.2 = b) 0.84 = c) 0.07 = d) 0.735 =<br>e) $\frac{7}{10}$ = f) $\frac{9}{100}$ g) $\frac{27}{100}$ h) $\frac{7}{8}$ = |
| 5. Write as a fraction in its simplest form (this means 'cancel down' if you can):<br>a) 0.6 = b) 0.02 = c) 0.95 = d) 0.165 = e) 5% =<br>f) 16% = g) $12\frac{1}{2}\%$ =<br>Write over 100 and multiply top and bottom by 2 or 10 . Then simplify. |

**Percentages:**

You may have learnt different methods - use your method for the examples and check the answer to ensure you are doing it correctly - if not seek help.

Finding a percentage of an amount

| | |
|---|---|
| Example: Find 20% of £360<br>$\frac{20}{100} \times 360 = 0.20 \times 360 = 72$ **or** $20 \times 360 \div 100 = 72$<br>Answer £72 | *'of' means times.*<br>*You could find 10% (divide by 10) and double it.*<br>*Use the method that you find easiest to remember - and remember it!* |
| 1. Find 5% of £540<br>27 | *Quick method here is to find 10% (divide by 10) and halve it.* |
| 2. Find 12% of 240kg<br>2880kg | *Simply 12 × 240 ÷ 100 or your method. Again try to do this calculation without a calculator.* |
| 3. A printer costs £160 before VAT is added. How much VAT is added and what is the total cost of the printer for each of the following VAT rates?<br>i) VAT at 15%<br>184<br>ii) VAT at 20%<br>192<br>iii) VAT at 17½%<br>189 | *VAT or Value Added Tax is a tax levied on most goods and services. It is subject to variation.*<br><br>*i) Work out 15 % of £160*<br>*OR 15% is 10% + 5%*<br>*So find 10% halve it for 5%*<br>*Then add it to £160 for the total cost.*<br>*(or 160 × 1.15 see below)*<br>*ii) Work out 20 % of £160*<br>*OR 20% is 10% + 10%*<br>*So find 10% and double it.*<br>*Then add it to £160 for the total cost.*<br>*(or 160 × 1.20 see below)*<br>*iii)Work out 17 ½ % of £160*<br>*OR 17½% is 10% + 5% + 2½%*<br>*So find 10% halve it for 5%. Halve again for 2½% and add the answers.*<br>*Then add it to £160 for the total cost.*<br>*(or 160 × 1.175 see below)* |

Percentage increase or decrease

Example: A woman earns £18 000 per annum. She receives an increase of 4%. How much does she earn after the increase?

Either: to calculate a 4% increase multiply by 1.04
$1.04 \times 18\,000 = 18720$

OR Find 4% and add it on.
$\frac{4}{100} \times 18000 = 720$ $(4 \times 18000 \div 100)$
$18\,000 + 720 = 18720$

Answer £18 720 per annum

Example: Decrease £2 500 by 5%

Either: find 95% (100 - 5)
$\frac{95}{100} \times 2500 = 2375$ $(95 \times 2500 \div 100)$

OR Find 5% and take it away
$\frac{5}{100} \times 2500 = 125$ $(5 \times 2500 \div 100)$
$2500 - 125 = 2375$

Answer £2 375

| | |
|---|---|
| 4. Increase £6780 by 15%<br>£7797 | *Multiply by 1.15 OR find 15% and add it on.* |
| 5. Decrease £1765 by 12%<br>£1500.25 | *Multiply by 0.88 OR find 12% and take it away.* |
| 6. In 2010 a computer costs £1250 plus VAT at 17.5%. Find the total cost.<br>£1468.75 | *Multiply by 1.175 OR find 17.5% and add it on.* |
| 7. A gas bill is £76.60 plus VAT at 5%. Find the total charged.<br>£80.43 | *Multiply by 1.05 OR find 5% and add it on.* |

| | |
|---|---|
| 8. A car is bought for £9 500. It depreciates by 8% each year. How much is it worth after 2 years? | *100 - 8 = 92. Multiply by 0.92 and by 0.92 again.*<br>*OR Find 8% and take it away - then find 8% of the new amount and take it away.*<br>*DO NOT find 16% and take away! It will be wrong.* |
| 9. Igor invests £600 in an account which pays 4% interest per year. The interest being added at the end of each year. If Igor does not withdraw any money, how much does he have in the account at the end of two years? (to the nearest penny) | *Here it is easiest to multiply by 1.04 and then by 1.04 again.*<br><br>*This is* ***compound interest****.* |
| 10. James earns £ 16 000 per annum. If he receives a 3% increase each year, how much does he earn per annum after three years? | *Easiest to × 1.03 × 1.03 × 1.03*<br><br>*Round to the nearest penny.* |
| 11. The cost of essential goods is £3400 in a particular year. The price of these goods rises each year by 4.2%. Find the cost of these goods after 2 years. | *Round to the nearest penny.* |

**Finding a percentage:**

First write as a fraction

and then change to a percentage (× 100)

> If question says 'out of' write like an exam mark ( e.g. 23 out of 40 is $\frac{23}{40}$ )
> If question gives increase/decrease/change write this over the **original** amount

| | |
|---|---|
| Example: 57 students out of 300 had passed their driving test. Write this as a percentage.<br>First write as a fraction $\frac{57}{300}$ then × 100 $\frac{57}{300} \times 100 = 19\%$ (57 ÷ 300 × 100 or 57 × 100 ÷ 300) | |
| 1. Parimal earns £125 per week. He receives a £4 increase. What percentage increase is this? | *First write as a fraction. Increase over original amount and then × 100* |
| 2. A camera normally costs £320. In a sale it is reduced to £280. Calculate the percentage reduction. | *First find the actual reduction.*<br>*Then this amount over the original (320) is the fraction. × 100 to give a percentage.* |
| 3. Peter bought a car for £9000 and later sold it for £6000. What percentage of his money did he lose? | *First find the actual reduction.*<br>*Then this amount over the original (9000) is the fraction. Simplify and make a percentage – it is one you should know!* |

**Reciprocals:**

A number times its reciprocal equals 1.

To find the reciprocal of a number, make it into a fraction and then turn it upside down.

Examples: The reciprocal of $\frac{1}{4}$ *is* $\frac{4}{1} = 4$ $\left(as\ \frac{1}{4} \times 4 = 1\right)$ The reciprocal of $\frac{2}{3}$ *is* $\frac{3}{2}$ $\left(as\ \frac{2}{3} \times \frac{3}{2} = 1\right)$

The reciprocal of 5 *is* $\frac{1}{5}$ $\left(as\ 5\ is\ the\ same\ as\ \frac{5}{1}\ and\ 5 \times \frac{1}{5} = 1\right)$ The reciprocal of 8 *is* $\frac{1}{8}$ $\left(as\ \frac{8}{1} \times \frac{1}{8} = 1\right)$

4. Write down the reciprocals of the following

First make 'top heavy'

| | | | | |
|---|---|---|---|---|
| a) 2 | (b) ½ | (c) ¾ | (d) $\frac{6}{5}$ | (e) $2\frac{1}{2}$ |
| f) $3\frac{3}{4}$ | (g) $\frac{1}{9}$ | (h) 9 | (i) 15 | (j) $\frac{1}{15}$ |

**Ratio:**

Lemon squash can be made with 1 part undiluted lemon to four parts water. This is the ratio 1 : 4
1 : 4 is the same ratio as 2 : 8 , and 3 : 12 and 4 : 16 etc.
You multiply up ratios and simplify ratios like fractions. Just multiply both figures by the same number or divide both figures by the same number.

| | |
|---|---|
| 1. Complete: Simplify<br>a) 3 : 24 = b) 6 : 15 = c) 300 : 360 = | *Just find a number/s that divides into both.* |
| 2. Write the ratio 4 : 5 in the form 1 : n. | *This just means that you have to find n. The 4 has been ÷ 4 to give 1, so just ÷ the 5 by 4. You end up with a decimal in the ratio.* |

Dividing an amount in a given ratio.

| | |
|---|---|
| 3. Complete: Divide £4800 between Suresh and Laura in the ratio 5 : 7<br>5 + 7 =<br>4800 ÷ =<br>Suresh 5 × =<br>Laura 7 × = | *The money has to be divided into 5 + 7 equal parts so that Suresh can have 5 parts and Laura can have 7 parts.* |
| 4. Divide £7650 between A, B and C in the ratio 2 : 3 : 5.<br>(*Show your working*) | *Just 2 + 3 + 5 parts.*<br>*Try this one without a calculator.* |
| 5. A sum of money is divided in the ratio 2 : 3. If the smaller sum is £84 , find the total amount of money. | *Here the £84 is 2 parts. So ÷ 2 to find 1 part and then × 5 to find the total sum (all 5 parts).* |

**Proportion:**

Most of these problems are usually solved by finding the value of 'one' of the quantity.
Example: 3 plants cost £4.05. Find the cost of 5 of the same plant.
3 plants cost £4.05
1 plant costs £4.05 ÷ 3 = £1.35
5 plants cost £1.35 × 5 = £6.75

| | |
|---|---|
| 6. A car uses 50 litres of petrol to travel 320 miles.<br>a) How far will it go on 12 litres?<br>b) How many litres would it use to go 100 miles? | *Find the distance travelled using 1 litre. Then 12 litres.*<br>*Find how many litres it would use to go 1 mile (or here you could use 10 miles). Then 100 miles.* |
| 7. Nine identical cans hold 4.5 litres of liquid. How many litres would five of these cans hold? | *Find the amount of liquid in 1 can. then × 5* |
| 8. If the exchange rate for the USA is \$1.62 = £1, find the cost in £ of a toy marked \$28.95 | *Find out how many 1.62 there are in 28.95 Give answer to the nearest penny.* |

# Test Yourself

Try these questions. If you are unable to do a question go back and revise the relevant section.

1. Write down the prime numbers between 40 and 50

2. 3, 4, 5, 18, 24, 46, 54, 134, 450

   Write down, from the list above, the numbers that are (a) factors of 36. (b) multiples of 6.

3. Write 440 as the product of primes.

4. Find the highest common factor and the lowest common multiple of 108 and 60.

5. Find a) $\sqrt{49}$ b) 12 squared c) 5 cubed d) $0.6^2$ e) cube root of 1000

6. Work out $\dfrac{2.5\ (5.8 - 2.9)}{6.3 + 2.2}$ to two decimal places.

7. If $x = 4$, $y = -3$ and $z = 6$ evaluate:

   (a) $x + y$ (b) $x - y$ (c) $2z$ (d) $5y$ (e) $xy$ (f) $xyz$ (g) $y^2$ (h) $2x - 3y$ (i) $\dfrac{xz}{y}$

8. Work out (a) $3.67 \times 10$ (b) $34.78 \times 10\ 000$ (c) $45.92 \div 1\ 000$ (d) $34 \div 10$

9. Work out (a) $238 \times 74$ (b) $6754 \div 5$ (c) $38 \times 429$ (d) $1904 \div 14$

10. Work out a) $1.7 \times 8$ b) $6.48 \times 0.3$ c) $\dfrac{8.22}{0.03}$

11. Write a) 35689 to 1 significant figures

    b) 0.04567 to 1 significant figure

    c) 34.497 to 1 decimal place.

12. Work out a) $300 \times 80$ (b) $40^2$ (c) $600 \div 0.3$ (d) $4 \div 0.005$

13. Estimate (a) $389 \times 42$ (b) $\frac{341 \times 568}{94}$ (c) $\frac{25.8 \times 82.9}{0.173}$

14. Work out (a) $\frac{12 \times 9 \times 2}{4 \times 2}$ (b) $\frac{1.4 \times 9}{7 \times 3}$

15. Work out (a) $\frac{7.6 + 6.89}{4}$ (b) $\frac{2.5\,(4.3 - 2.86)}{5.84 - 3.59}$ (c) $\frac{35.16 - 5.4}{3.1 \times 2.5}$

16. What is the value of a) $4^3$ (b) $2^4 \times 2^2$

17. What is the value of a) $\sqrt{144}$ (b) $\sqrt[3]{64}$

18. If $x^2 = 25$ what are the two values of $x$?

19. Find $\sqrt{17}$ to 1 decimal place (*Without a calculator*)

20. Write as a power of 10 a) $10^{11} \times 10^7$ (b) $10^{13} \div 10^7$

21. Calculate $3.42 \times 41.682$ and write your answer correct to 3 significant figures.

22. Calculate $(356.234 + 127.9823) \times 22.34$ and write your answer correct to 2 decimal places.

23. Evaluate (a) $(2.36 \times 10^2) \times (7.5 \times 10^3)$ (b) $\frac{4.2 \times 10^{15}}{2.5 \times 10^8}$ (c) $(6 \times 10^3) \times (2.7 \times 10^2)$ (d) $(4.8 \times 10^6) \div (6 \times 10^4)$

24. Simplify a) $\frac{18}{48}$ b) $\frac{256}{880}$

25. Write in order of size ( smallest first) $\frac{2}{5}, \frac{4}{7}, \frac{3}{10}$

26. Work out $\frac{3}{5}$ of £378

27. Work out (*Without a calculator*)

a) $\frac{2}{5} + \frac{3}{4}$ b) $2\frac{1}{4} - 1\frac{2}{5}$ c) $\frac{2}{9} \times 1\frac{3}{4}$ d) $\frac{5}{6} \div \frac{3}{10}$

Now check with a calculator.

28. a) Write 26.5% as a decimal b) Write 0.045 as a percentage

c) Write 0.35 as a fraction d) Write $\frac{3}{40}$ as a decimal

e) Write $\frac{7}{20}$ as a percentage f) Write 24% as a fraction

29. Write $\frac{6}{7}$ as a recurring decimal.

30. Find 15% of £425

31. Increase £268 by 24%

32. A car costing £9800 depreciates by 10% each year. How much is it worth after 3 years?

33. A sideboard costing £345 is offered in a sale at £293.25. What is the percentage reduction?

34. In a test Sam scored 18 out of 20. What percentage did he get?

35. Ronak bought a vase for £240 and sold it for £300. What was his percentage profit?

36. Write the following percentages as fractions in their simplest form.

a. 10% b. 20% c. 25% d. 75% e. $33^1/_3$ %

37. Write down the reciprocal of 8.

38. What is the reciprocal of $^2/_3$ ?

39. What is the reciprocal of $4\ ^1/_4$ ?

40. Simplify the ratio 27: 36

41. Divide £12 480 in the ratio 3 : 5

42. Chris and Ivan share £36 in ratio 7 : 5 respectively. How much does each get?

43. Two stones have masses 1235g and 1.45kg. Write the ratio of their masses in its simplest form.

44. If 4 bags of sugar cost £3.24, how much would 7 bags cost?

45. The exchange rate for changins £s into euros is £1 = 1.14 euros. How many euros would I get for £22?

46. A shopkeeper can buy 48 identical items for £32.60. What would he pay for 120 such items?

# GRAPHS AND STATISTICS

**Averages:**

Mean: Add up all the values and divide by the number of values.

Median: Put the values in order of size. The median is the middle value. If there are two values in the middle add them together and divide by 2.

Mode: The value that occurs most often.

| Question | Hint |
|---|---|
| 1. Complete: Find the mean, median and mode of the following set of numbers. 2, 8, 5, 4, 7, 3, 4, 9, 4, 5<br>2 + 8 + 5 + 4 + 7 + 3 + 4 + 9 + 4 + 5 =<br>mean =<br>Numbers in order: 2, 3,<br>median =<br>mode = | *Add up the values.*<br>*Divide by 10.*<br>*Write the numbers in order.*<br>*Work out the number/s in the middle.*<br>*Two numbers in the middle, so add them up and divide by 2.*<br>*Use the ordered numbers to see which number occurs most often.* |
| 2. If the mean of four numbers is 5.5, what is the sum of the four numbers? | *The sum is the total of the four numbers added up. To find the mean you sum the numbers and divide by 4. So if you have the mean and you want the sum multiply by 4.* |
| 3. The mean of seven scores in a test is 12. Another score of 6 is now included. What is the mean of the eight scores? | *Find the sum of the seven scores (see question 2). Add the eighth score.*<br>*This is the sum of the eight scores -so divide by 8 to find the mean of the eight scores.* |
| 4. The temperature in Brighton (in °C) during a particular week was as follows: 21 24 23 23 22 20 23<br>Find a) the mean temperature to 2 decimal places<br>b) the median temperature<br>c) the mode | |
| 5. Find the mean of the numbers 105, 107, 104, 108, 107, 105 | *No calculator! Use a quick method: Ignore the 'one hundred' on each number and find the mean of 5 7 4 8 7 5 and add the 'one hundred'.* |
| 6. Four students have a mean score of 55 for a test and six students have a mean score of 45 for the same test. What is the mean score for all ten students? | ***DO NOT** add the two means together and divide by 2. Your answer of 50 would be wrong!*<br>*Find the total score for the four students.*<br>*Find the total score for the six students.*<br>*Add them to find the total score for all ten.*<br>*Divide by 10 to find the mean score for all ten students.* |
| 7. The mean weight of five packets of food is 1.6 kg. The mean weight of four of the packets is 1.8 kg. What is the weight of the fifth packet? | *Find the total weight of the five packets.*<br>*Find the total weight of the four packets.*<br>*Subtract to find the weight of the fifth packet.* |
| 8. The mean of five numbers is 134. Find $a$ if the five numbers are 130,156,121,132, $a$ | *Find the total of the five numbers.*<br>*Find the total of the four given numbers.*<br>*Subtract to find the fifth number.* |

**Range:**

Range = Highest value - lowest value

This is a measure of how spread out the data is.

Example: Find the range of the numbers 2, 8, 5, 4, 7, 3, 4, 9, 4, 4

Range = 9 - 2 = 7 ← Notice the answer is 7 NOT 2 - 9 or 2 to 9

| |
|---|
| 9. Find the range of the numbers 12, 18, 15, 14, 17, 13, 14, 19, 14, 15 |
| 10. Find the range of the numbers 21, 24, 23, 23, 22, 20 |

**Pie Charts:**
Pie charts show us the proportions (fractions) for each of the categories.

**Drawing pie charts**

There are $360^\circ$ in a circle. This must represent the total.

Example: Thirty students were asked how they travelled to college on a particular day. 8 said by car, 7 said by bus, 3 said cycle and 12 said that they walked. Represent this information in a pie chart.
First we need to find the angle for one person.

Easiest to show by using a table. (This may be given to you)

| Type of transport | Frequency |
|---|---|
| Car | 8 |
| Bus | 7 |
| Cycle | 3 |
| Walk | 12 |
| TOTAL | 30 |

$360^\circ \div 30 = 12^\circ$

Therefore $12^\circ$ represents one person. multiply the each frequency by $12^\circ$ to obtain the angle for each type of transport as shown here.

| Type | Frequency | Angle |
|---|---|---|
| Car | 8 | $8\times12^\circ = 96^\circ$ |
| Bus | 7 | $7\times12^\circ = 84^\circ$ |
| Cycle | 3 | $3\times12^\circ = 36^\circ$ |
| Walk | 12 | $12\times12^\circ = 144^\circ$ |
| TOTAL | 30 | $360^\circ$ |

Draw the pie chart. **Label the angle and each sector.**

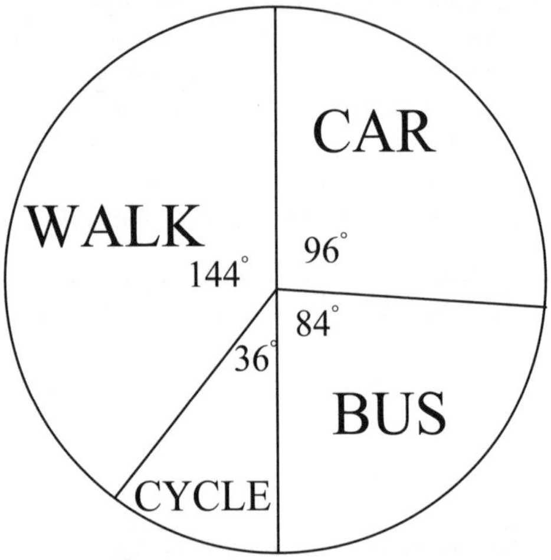


***Pie chart showing how 30 students came to college.***

1. Complete: Draw a pie chart from the information in the table to show how a university student spent his weekly allowance of £150 in a particular week.

| Item | Amount | Angle |
|---|---|---|
| Rent | 65 | $65\times \quad = 156^\circ$ |
| Food | 40 | $40\times \quad =$ |
| Saving for bills | 10 | |
| Entertainment | 20 | |
| Other | 15 | |
| | | |

$360^\circ \div \qquad =$

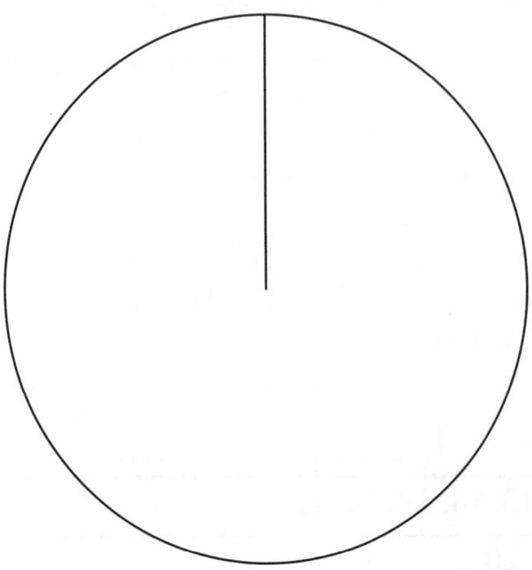

*Find the angle for each pound.*
*$360^\circ$ represents £150*
*Use this answer to find each angle in the table above.*

*Draw the Pie chart.*
*Measure the angles carefully. You will lose marks if you do not.*

*Label the angles as well as the sector.*

2. This table shows the proportions of different drinks sold in a cafe

| Tea | Coffee | Orange | Lemon | Water |
|---|---|---|---|---|
| 35% | 25% | 15% | 5% | 20% |

Draw a clearly labelled pie chart to represent this information.

*Here percentages are given instead of the actual numbers.*

*Whole circle is $360^\circ$.*
*You need 35% of $360^\circ$ etc.*

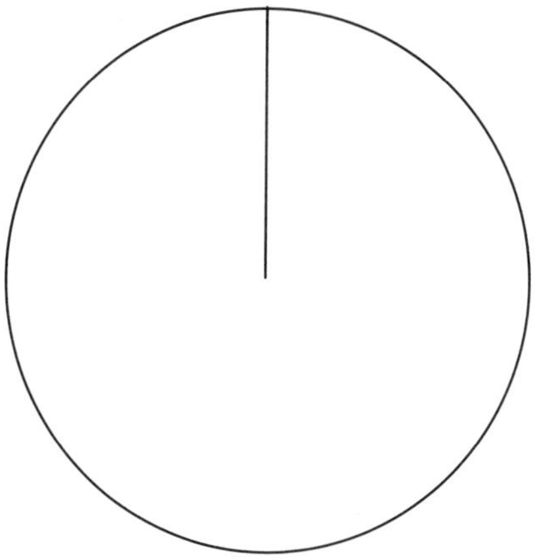

35% of $360^\circ$ = $35 \times 360 \div 100 =$

25% of $360^\circ$ =

**Interpreting pie charts:**

If you are given a pie chart you are often asked to find out some information.

***Pie chart showing the loaves of bread sold in a supermarket***

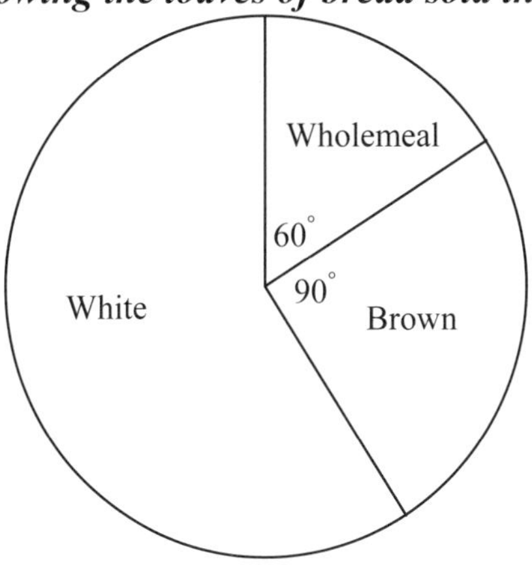


Some information may seem obvious to you but that is what the examiners are expecting you to comment on.
e.g.
The most popular was white bread - the mode .

Over half the bread sold was white.

A quarter of the loaves sold were brown.

The least popular was wholemeal.

You may be given other information that you need to use to calculate some values.
e.g. The total number of loaves sold was 120. How many white loaves where sold?

The angle for white is $360^\circ - (90^\circ + 60^\circ) = 210^\circ$

| Find the angle for each loaf | OR | Find the amount of loaves for each $1^\circ$ |
|---|---|---|
| $360^\circ \div 120 = 3^\circ$ | | $120 \div 360 = 0.333333...$ |
| Then - how many $3^\circ$ in $210^\circ$ | | $210^\circ$ will be $210 \times 0.333333... = 70$ |

i.e. $210^\circ \div 3^\circ = 70$ CHECK THAT YOUR ANSWER IS SENSIBLE (It is easy to divide the wrong numbers)

3. Pie chart showing the colours of cars in an airport car park.

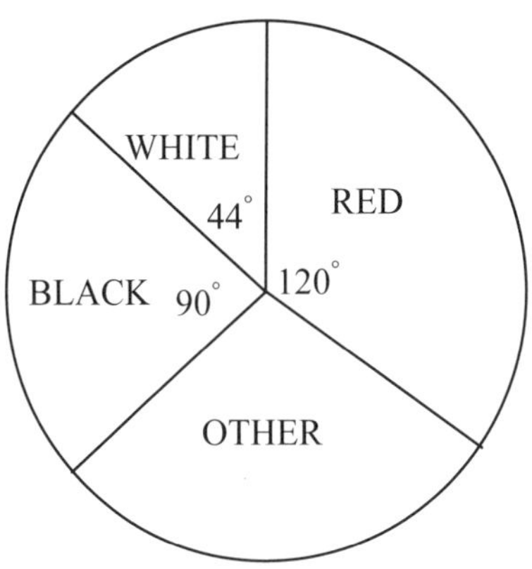


If there are 154 white cars, how many cars are there altogether?

*This time $44^\circ$ represents 154 cars.*
*Find out how many cars for $1^\circ$.*
*Then $\times 360$ to give the total number of cars.*

## Pictograms:

In this diagrammatic form data is represented by the repeated use of a simplified picture.
Line up the separate pictures so that the whole diagram is easy to read. Normally you choose a key so that whole or half pictures are used (occasionally quarters are used). It is too difficult to draw other fractions of small pictures and make it easy to understand.
YOU MUST HAVE A KEY.

1. The number of different types of drink bought in a shop over a period of time are displayed in the pictogram below.

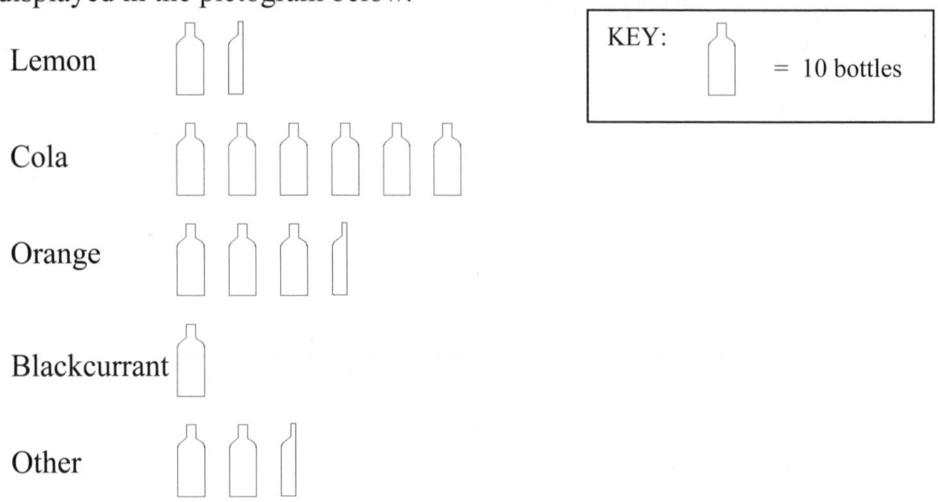


a) How many bottles of orange were bought in this period?

b) How many bottles of drink were bought altogether in this period?

c) Which drink is the most popular?

2. The results of a survey of the number of trees in particular areas of a town are shown in the table below. Represent this data in the form of a pictogram.

| Area | Number of trees |
|---|---|
| North | 40 |
| East | 80 |
| South | 90 |
| West | 120 |
| Centre | 10 |

## Bar graphs and vertical line graphs:

You should be familiar with different types of bar graphs and be able to answer questions about them as well as being able to draw them. Bar graphs are most suitable for categorical data (that is data that can be put in categories e.g. colour of cars, type of mobile phone) or discrete data (that is data that can only have certain values e.g. shoe size, goals scored, score on a die).
Bar graphs

- usually have gaps between the bars
- are easy to understand
- show the values for each category

A vertical line graph is just a bar graph where a vertical line is drawn instead of a bar.

Here are some questions for you to complete on different types of graphs.

1. The colours of a number of cars passing a junction at a particular time of day were recorded and a vertical line graph was drawn as shown.
Find the total number of cars recorded.

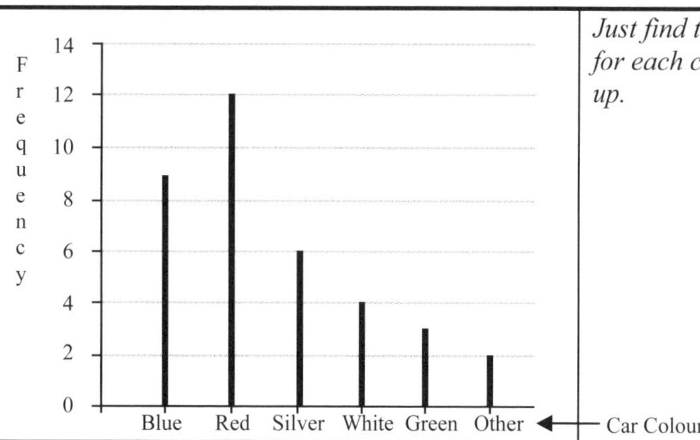


*Just find the number of cars for each colour and add them up.*

2. Here is a sectional bar graph showing the number of students that studied Mathematics A level at a particular college over a number of years.

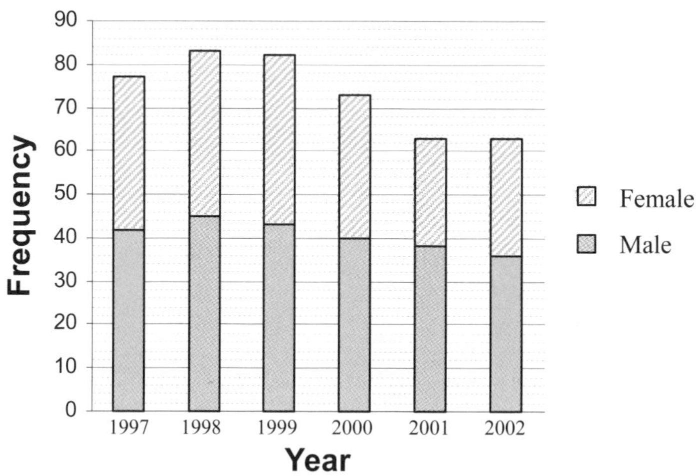


a) How many students studied Mathematics in 1999?

b) How many female students studied Mathematics in 2001?

c) In 2002, what percentage of the mathematics students were male?

*c) For 2002 How many male students studied Maths? How many students altogether? Write this as a fraction, number of male Maths students over total number of students. Then multiply by 100.(Work it out on your calculator)*

**Mean median and mode from a frequency table:**

Example: The following is a frequency table showing the number of scores obtained in a game.

| Score | Tally | Frequency |
|---|---|---|
| 1 | /// | 3 |
| 2 | //// | 4 |
| 3 | ~~////~~ | 5 |
| 4 | / | 1 |
| 5 | / | 1 |

This means that there were three scores of 1
four scores of 2
five scores of 3
one score of 4
one score of 5

Remember that the each tally mark is 1 and when you get to 5 you put a line through the 4 strokes to make counting the tallies easier.

In full you could write them down as 1, 1, 1, 2, 2, 2, 2, 3, 3, 3, 3, 3, 4, 5
To find the mean you could work out the mean of this set of numbers but notice you have 3 ones which is 3, 4 twos which is 8, 5 threes which is 15, 1 four and 1 five. So, to find the total you can multiply and add them up.

| Score | Frequency | Score×frequency |
|---|---|---|
| 1 | 3 | $1 \times 3 = 3$ |
| 2 | 4 | $2 \times 4 = 8$ |
| 3 | 5 | $3 \times 5 = 15$ |
| 4 | 1 | $4 \times 1 = 4$ |
| 5 | 1 | $5 \times 1 = 5$ |
| Total | 14 | 35 |

The quick way is to do this on the table with an extra column and an extra row as shown (you may be given them in your exam).

Mean score = $35 \div 14 = 2.5$

Remember to divide by the total of the frequency column.

The mode is the most frequent i.e.

The mode = 3

Careful: a common error is to write down the frequency 5

The median - The scores are in order in the table - as there are 14 of them you want the $7^{th}$ and $8^{th}$ (there are two numbers in the middle). Using the frequency column and counting down you can see that the $7^{th}$ number is a 2 and the $8^{th}$ number is a 3. So

median score = $(2 + 3) \div 2 = 2.5$

1. Complete: Find the mean, median, mode and range for the shoe size of children at a club given in the frquency table as follows:

| Shoe size, $x$ | Tally | Frequency, $f$ | $f \times x$ |
|---|---|---|---|
| 2 | // | 2 | $2 \times 2 = 4$ |
| 3 | 卌 | | |
| 4 | 卌 /// | | |
| 5 | /// | | |
| 6 | // | | |
| TOTALS | | | |

Mean =

Mode =

Median =

Range =

*Complete the frequency column from the tallies.*

*Mean:*
*Total of $f \times x$ divided by total frequency.*
*The mean is a mathematical value - do not round to a whole number just because the shoe sizes are whole numbers.*

*Mode:*
*The most frequent (NOT 8)*

*Median:*
*Frequency is even - so two numbers in the middle - the $10^{th}$ and the $11^{th}$.*

*Range:*
*Largest shoe size - smallest shoe size*

2. The following table shows the number of goals scored by 24 teams in a league on a particular Saturday.
   Calculate (a) the total number of goals scored
   (b) the mean and mode for the number of goals scored.

| Goals | Number of teams | |
|---|---|---|
| 0 | 5 | |
| 1 | 9 | |
| 2 | 5 | |
| 3 | 3 | |
| 4 | 2 | |
| | | |

Total number of goals scored =

Mean =

Mode =

*This means*
*5 teams scored 0 goals*
*9 teams scored 1 goal*
*etc.*

3. Here is a bar graph showing the results when a spinner labelled 1, 2, 3, 4, 5 and 6 was spun a number of times.

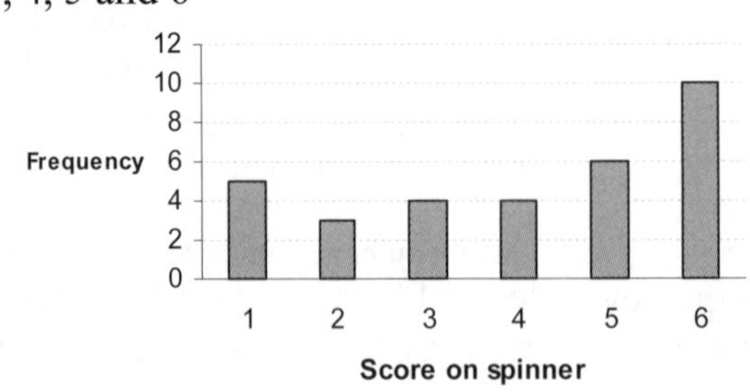


a) What is the modal score?

b) Calculate the mean score.

c) How would you check whether the spinner is fair (not biased)?

*The most frequent.*

*You may find it easier to draw up a frequency table to work out the mean. You need to obtain from the bar graph the frequency for each score. Then work out the mean as for frequency tables.*

4. This dual bar graph shows the sales of tea and coffee in a café over a week.

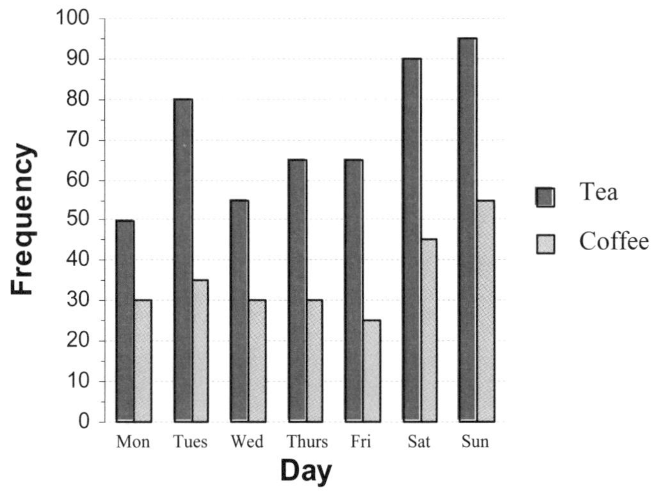


a) How many drinks were sold on Saturday?

b) How many teas were sold in the week?

c) What is the mean number of teas sold per day (to 1 decimal place)?

*Show your working even if you use a calculator.*

**Grouped Data:**

The classes or groups that you are given can be set out in different ways

| Height (cm) | Frequency |
|---|---|
| 10 - 19 | 5 |
| 20 - 29 | 8 |
| 30 - 39 | 6 |

Here you should assume that the measurements were to the nearest cm. Any data item from 9.5 up to 19.5 would go in the first group 10 - 19 and so on.
The boundaries between the groups are 19.5 and 29.5

| Height, h (cm) | Frequency |
|---|---|
| $10 \leq h < 20$ | 5 |
| $20 \leq h < 30$ | 8 |
| $30 \leq h < 40$ | 6 |

Here the first group boundaries are from 10 up to but not including 20. So a data item of 20 would be in the second group, 20 up to but not including 30.
$20 \leq h < 30$ means h is greater than or equal to 20 but less than 30.

**Histograms also called frequency graphs:**

Histograms are most suitable for continuous data (that is data that can take any value - usually measurements e.g. heights, lengths, weights, temperatures etc).

Histograms

- have **NO** gaps between the bars
- have a scale on the horizontal axis (like the frequency axis, go up in ones or twos or fives or tens etc.)
- show the frequency for each group
  (as long as you have equal group widths)

Note: **<u>DO NOT</u>** use the groups to label the bars

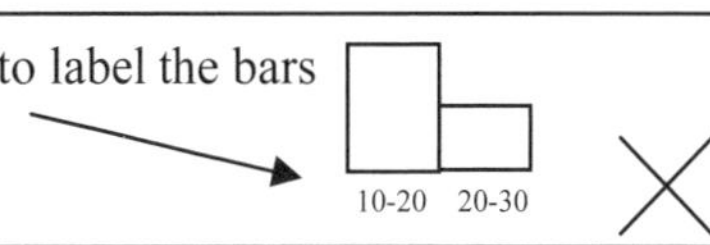

1. The time to complete a task given to some students is shown in the following table

| Time in minutes | Frequency |
|---|---|
| 5 and under 6 | 4 |
| 6 and under 7 | 6 |
| 7 and under 8 | 9 |
| 8 and under 9 | 3 |
| 9 and under 10 | 2 |

Draw a frequency diagram below to represent this data.

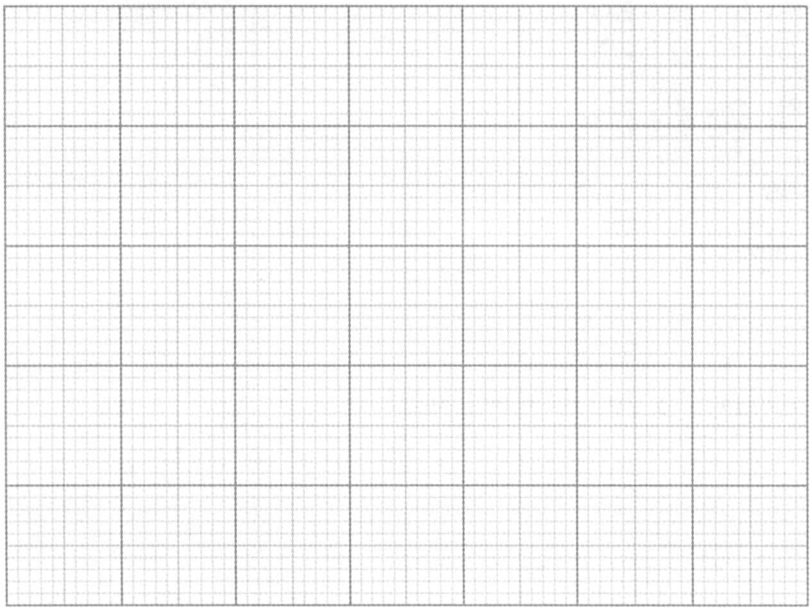

a) How many students altogether?

b) What fraction of the students took less than 7 minutes?

c) What is the modal class of the distribution?

*A frequency diagram is a histogram.*

*Axes:*
*Frequency always up.*
*Maximum is 9 so go up to 10 in twos.*
*Time then goes across.*
*Here you can start at 4 and go across in ones.*

*Look at the question below.*
*No gaps between bars.*
*Notice how the axes are labelled. DO NOT use 5-6,6-7 etc to label your histogram.*

*The modal class is the group with the highest frequency.*

2. The following frequency diagram shows the height of some particular plants, six weeks after sowing.

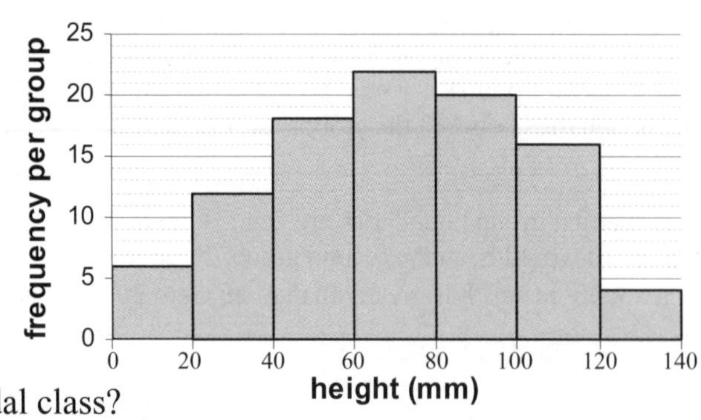


a) What is the modal class?

b) How many plants altogether?

c) Work out an estimate of the mean height by using the mid-points of each group.

*The modal class is the group with the highest frequency.*

*Just read off the frequencies and add them together.*

*You may wish to draw up a table with mid points and frequencies.*

**Scatter Diagrams, Correlation and Line of Best Fit:**

A scatter diagram shows two sets of data. From the diagram you can see if there is a linear correlation (straight line connection) between the two sets of data.

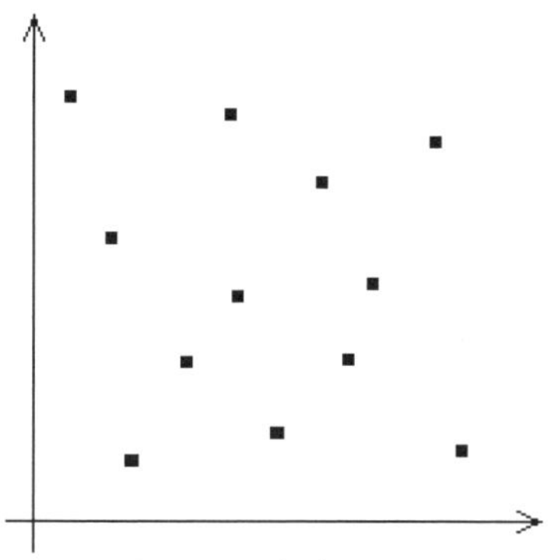
No correlation
No linear (straight line) correlation.

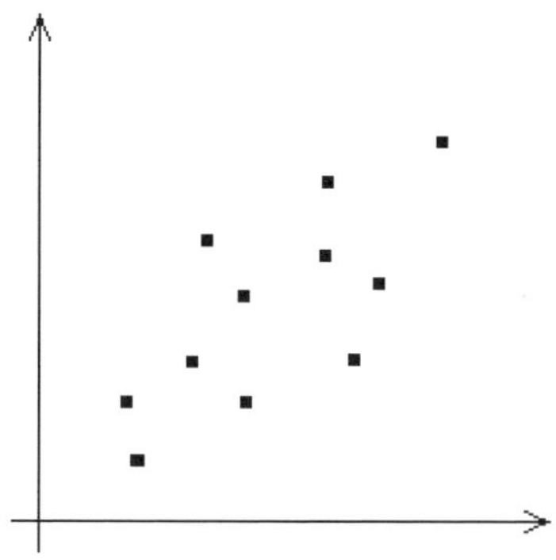
Positive correlation

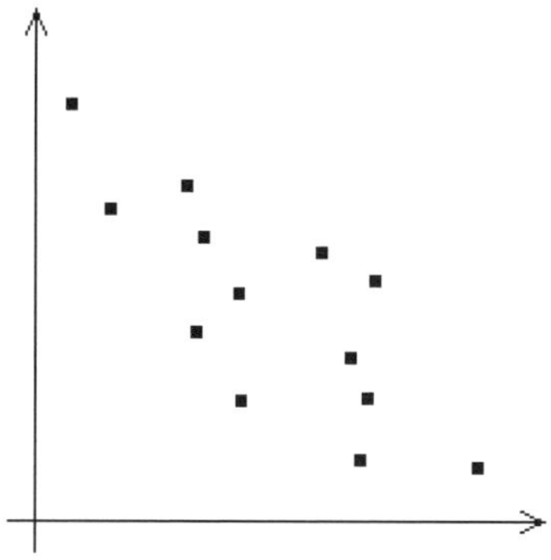
Negative correlation

1. The marks of 10 students in two mathematics examination papers are:

| Student | A | B | C | D | E | F | G | H | I | J |
|---|---|---|---|---|---|---|---|---|---|---|
| Paper1 | 30 | 37 | 44 | 44 | 45 | 52 | 59 | 65 | 72 | 75 |
| Paper2 | 36 | 36 | 45 | 49 | 56 | 62 | 64 | 76 | 79 | 86 |

Complete the scatter diagram of the marks and draw a line of best fit.

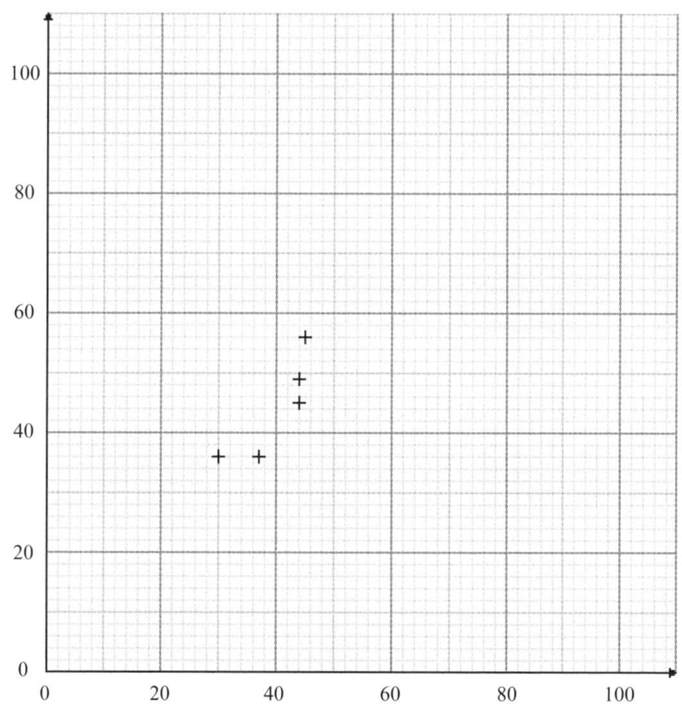


a) Explain the relationship between the marks for Paper 1 and the marks for Paper 2.

b) What type of correlation does this scatter diagram show?

Use your line of best fit to estimate:

c) the mark on Paper 2 corresponding to a mark of 40 on Paper 1.

d) the mark on Paper 1 corresponding to a mark of 75 on Paper 2.

*Plot your points as* ***accurately as possible****. It is easier to be accurate if you draw your crosses like this + rather than like this ×.*

*The line of best fit is the best straight line that you can draw through the points.*
*The line should go in the general direction of the crosses and you should try to have as many points above the line as below it.*
*Extend the line a little way past the region of the crosses at either end.*

*You can use the line to estimate the mark on Paper2 given a mark on Paper1 (and vice versa).*

***You should not use the line outside the region of the crosses as you do not know whether the marks in these areas follow the same pattern.***

*'As the mark for Paper1 increases the mark for .....'*

*Which of the above does this scatter most look like?*

*c) Draw a vertical line from 40 on the Paper1 axis up to your line of best fit. Then draw a horizontal line to the Paper2 axis. Read off this value* ***as accurately as you can****. This is what an examiner would do on* ***your*** *graph.*
*d) Start at 75 on the paper2 axis.*

2. The table below shows petrol consumption and engine size for 8 cars.

| Car | A | B | C | D | E | F | G | H |
|---|---|---|---|---|---|---|---|---|
| Engine size (cc) | 4800 | 3900 | 3200 | 2400 | 3400 | 2500 | 1400 | 1800 |
| Petrol consumption (km/litre) | 5.8 | 8.6 | 8.9 | 10.9 | 11.2 | 13.4 | 13.4 | 16.0 |

Draw the corresponding scatter diagram below

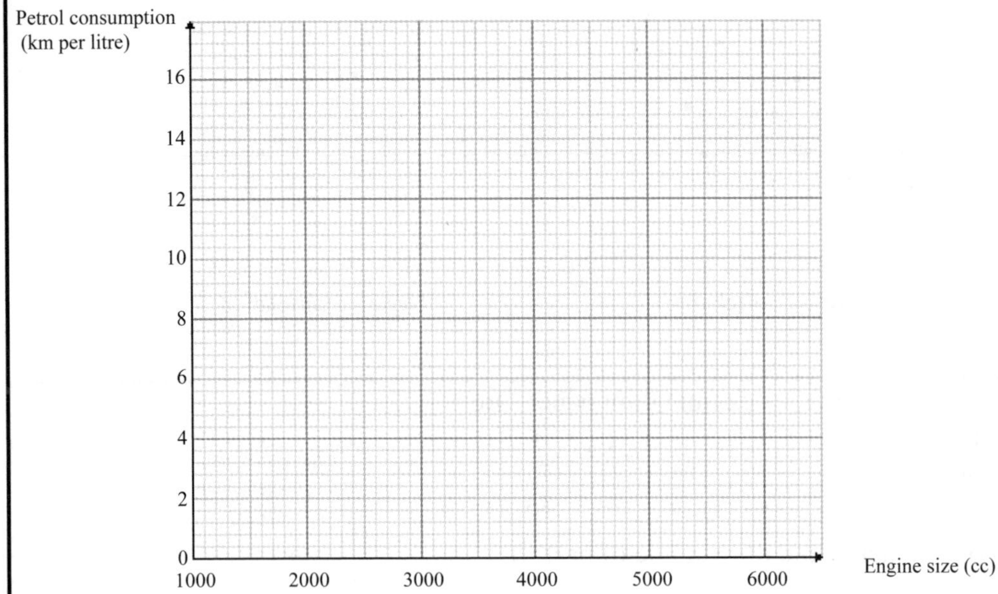


*Plot the points as accurately as you can.*

*Be careful of the scales.*

*For engine size - Each 10 small squares is worth 1000 so each small square is worth 100*

*For petrol consumption - Each 10 small squares is worth 4 so each small square is worth 0.4*

a) Explain the relationship between engine size and petrol consumption.

*'As the .......increases the ..........*

b) What type of correlation does the graph show?

Draw a line of best fit on the scatter diagram.

A new car is made with an engine size of 2000 cc.

c) Estimate the petrol consumption for this car.

*Use the line of best fit. Draw a line from 2000 up to the line and then across. Read off this value.*

3. The table below shows father's height and son's height (when fully grown) for a sample. Draw the corresponding scatter diagram on the graph below (the axes have been done for you).

| Father's height (cm) | 157 | 178 | 167 | 165 | 172 | 168 | 160 | 180 | 162 | 175 |
|---|---|---|---|---|---|---|---|---|---|---|
| Son's height (cm) | 155 | 172 | 170 | 162 | 170 | 173 | 165 | 178 | 166 | 178 |

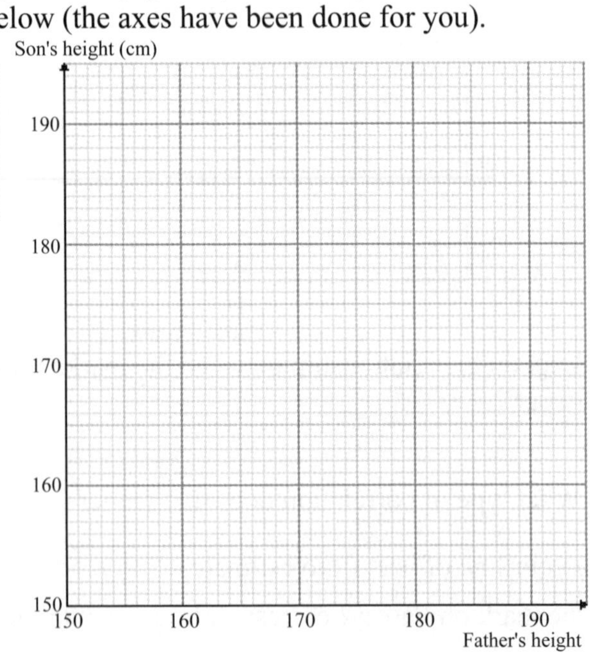


a) Explain the relationship between father's height and son's height.

b) What type of correlation does the graph show?

Draw a line of best fit on the scatter diagram.

c) Predict the height of a son whose father is 177 cm tall.

d) Would you use the graph to predict the height of a son whose father's height is 193 cm? Give a reason.

## Other straight line graphs:

Jane went on a visit from home. Here is the distance time graph for the journey.

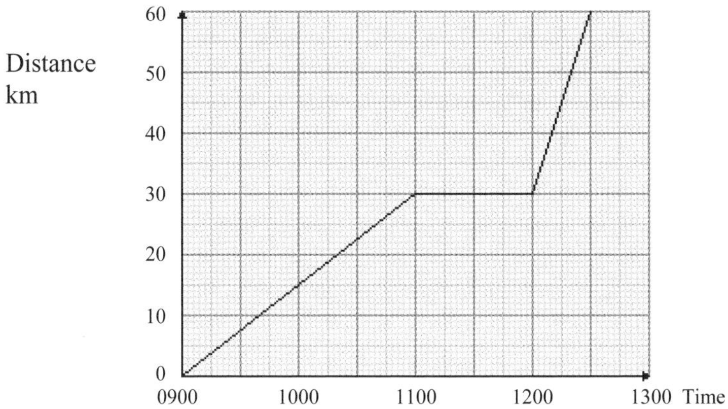


To find speed.

Draw in a right angled triangle.
(The bigger the better)
Work out

$speed = \frac{distance}{time}$

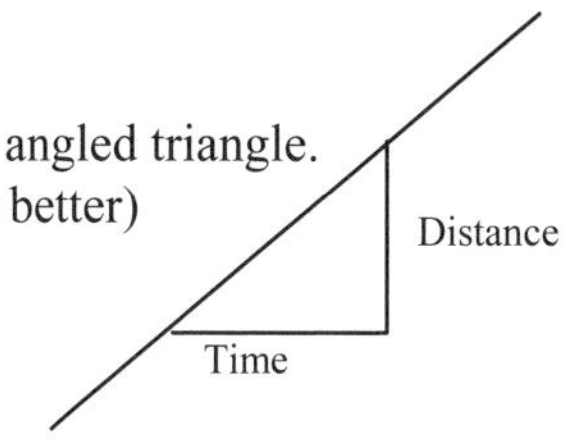


Describe the journey.

Include:
Start time

| First part of journey | Second part of journey | Third part of journey |
|---|---|---|
| time travelled | time | time travelled |
| speed | speed | speed |
| distance covered | distance covered | distance covered |

Jane's brother John set off from home at 9.30 a.m. and travelled for ½ hour at 40km/h. He stopped for 1 hour and then travelled another 40km in the next 1½ hours. Show his journey on the graph above.

1. Use the following graph to convert between miles and kilometres (read the values as accurately as you can)

Convert:

a) 80 miles to kilometres

b) 40 kilometres to miles

c) 66 miles to kilometres

d) 90 kilometres to miles

e) 31 miles to kilometres

f) 146 kilometres to miles

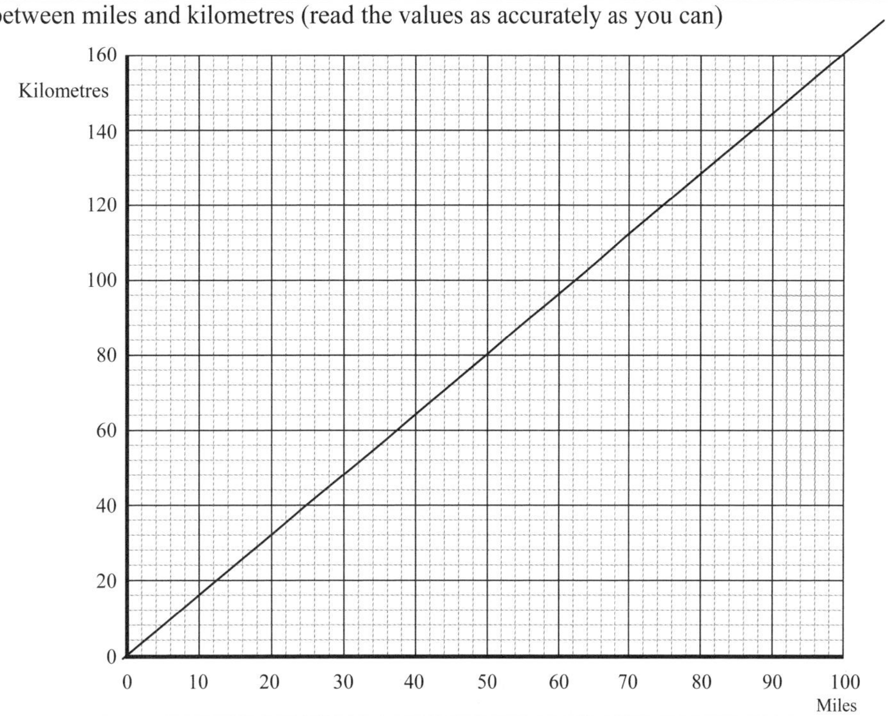


2. The cost of using water (on a metered supply) in a particular year is shown by the graph.

a) How much would it cost for a year where the following amounts of water were used:
   i) 60 $m^3$

   ii) 70 $m^3$

   iii) 84 $m^3$

b) How much water was used if the cost was

   i) £60

   ii) £106

   iii) £130

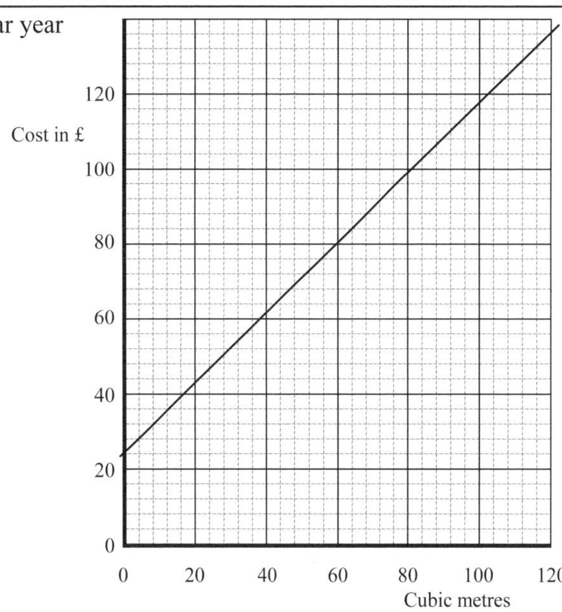

## Probability:

**Theoretical** - using equally likely outcomes - e.g for a 'fair' die you are equally likely to obtain a 1 or a 2 or a 3 or a 4 or a 5 or a 6

$$\textit{The probability of an event happening} = \frac{\textit{The number of possible outcomes that include the event}}{\textit{Total number of possible outcomes}}$$

**Experimental**

If you are unable to find the probability from equally likely outcomes (because you have made a die and it is likely to be 'biased' or the object you are using is not symmetrical) then you would have to do an experiment to find an estimate for the possible outcomes.

$$\textit{Estimate of the probability that an event happens} = \frac{\textit{The number of trial outcomes that include the event}}{\textit{Total number of trials}}$$

This is also called the **relative frequency**

If you threw a drawing pin 100 times and it landed 'point up' 57 times then you could estimate the probability as

Estimate of the probability that the drawing pin lands 'point up' = P(point up ) = $\frac{57}{100}$ or 0.57

The more trials (e.g. throws of a drawing pin) the more confident you can be of your estimate. If you were throwing a biased die labelled 1 to 6, you would not get a good estimate of the probability of throwing a six if you only had 20 trials (throws). You would be more confident of your estimate if you threw the die 100 times or even better 1000 times. The more trials you have the more confident you can be.

## Probabilities:

If an event will never occur, the probability of that event happening is 0
If an event will definitely occur, the probability of that event happening is 1
All other probabilities lie between 0 and 1. Write them as a fraction or a decimal (or a percentage).

A The probability that a cow will jump over the moon is 0

B The probability that you will read the next number is 1

A fair die is thrown

C The probability of getting a six is written P(six) or P(6) and so P(6) = $\frac{1}{6}$

A card is drawn at random from a pack of 52 playing cards

D The probability of getting a black card P(black) = $\frac{26}{52} = \frac{1}{2}$

E The probability of getting a diamond card P(diamond) = $\frac{13}{52} = \frac{1}{4}$

Using a probability scale: You may be required to label probabilities on a scale like this

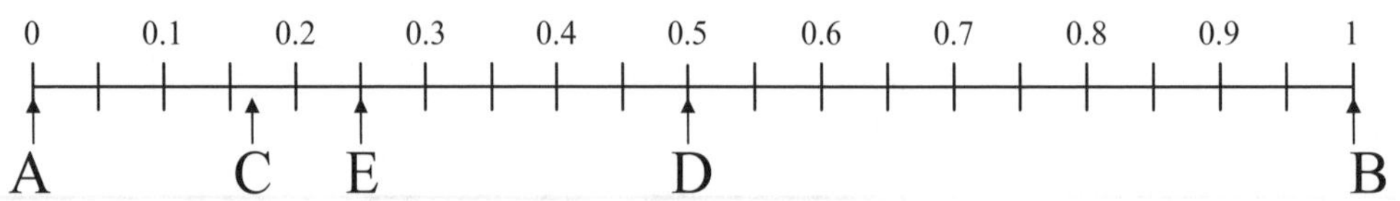


1. There are two red cards, three blue cards and five green cards in a bag. One card is chosen without looking. On the number line, mark with a cross X, the probability that the card chosen is
a) a red card (label A) b) a green card (label B) c) a blue or green card (label C) d) a yellow card (label D)

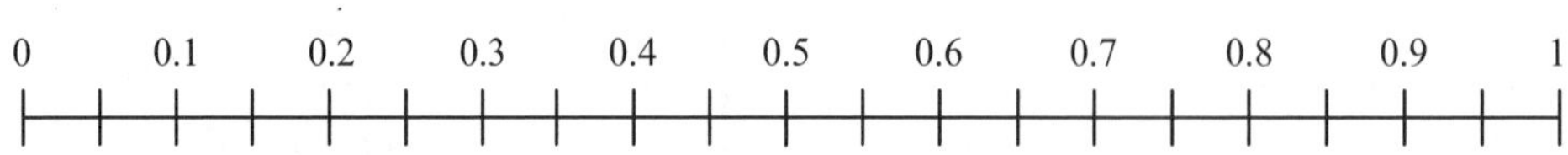


## The probability of an event NOT happening

P(an event will not happen) = 1 - P(an event will happen) Similarly P(an event will not happen) = 1 - P(an event will happen)

Example: A fair die is thrown P(6) = $\frac{1}{6}$ P(not a 6) = 1 - $\frac{1}{6} = \frac{5}{6}$

## Mutually exclusive events - The addition law:

If two events are mutually exclusive, that is they both cannot happen at the same time,

then $$P(A \text{ or } B) = P(A) + P(B)$$

Example: There are 5 red counters, 4 blue counters, 9 green counters and 2 white counters in a bag. One is taken at random. What is the probability of picking a red counter or a white counter?

P(Red or White) = P(Red) + P(White) = $\frac{5}{20} + \frac{2}{20} = \frac{7}{20}$ OR There are 7 red + white counters so P(Red or White) = $\frac{7}{20}$

## Expected number of outcomes

The expected number of outcomes of an event = probability of the outcome × the total number of trials

Example: A fair die is thrown 120 times

Expected number of sixes = $\frac{1}{6} \times 120 = 20$

1. Work out the following

   a) 1 - ½ = (b) 1 - ¾ = (c) 1 - ⅓ = (d) 1 - ⅜ = (e) 1 - $\frac{2}{5}$ =

   f) 1 - 0.7 = (g) 1 - 0.1 = (h) 1 - 0.35 = (i) 1 - 0.71 = (j) 1 - 0.27 =

   k) 1 - (0.2 + 0.4) = (l) 1 - (0.3 + 0.45) = (m) 1 - (⅛ + ¼) =

2. If the probability of a person choosing a fiction book from a library is 0.68 what is the probability that they will not choose a fiction book?

   *1 - P(fiction)*

3. The probability that Mark does not go to badminton club on Tuesday nights is 0.03 What is the probability that he does go?

   *1 - P(not go)*

4. The probability that Jay is late arriving at the bus stop is $\frac{1}{5}$. Find the probability that Jay is not late arriving at the bus stop.

   *1 - P(late)*

5. There are red, blue and green sweets in a bag. If the probability of randomly picking a red sweet is 0.7 and the probability of randomly picking a blue sweet is 0.2 What is the probability of

   a) randomly picking a green sweet?

   b) randomly picking a blue or green sweet?

   c) randomly picking a sweet that is not red?

   *If you pick a sweet it **must** be either red or blue or green so the probabilities must add to give 1*

6. A card is picked at random from a pack of 52 playing cards.

   Find a) P(red) =

   b) P(heart) =

   c) P(king) =

   d) P(king or ace) =

   After the card is looked at it is replaced and the cards shuffled. Another card is then picked.

   e) If this is repeated 60 times in total, how many times would you expect a heart to turn up?

   *a) Probability of picking a red card. 26 reds out of 52 cards and simplify the fraction.*

   *b) Probability of picking a heart.*

   *c) Probability of picking a king.*

   *d) Probability of picking a king or an ace.*

   *Expected number of hearts, so P(heart) × 60*

7. A home made spinner numbered 1, 2, 3, 4, 5 is spun 50 times. If it landed 15 times on a 5 give an estimate of the probabilty of obtaining a 5 on any spin.

   *Use the second definition above for the estimate of probability and simplify the fraction.*

## Listing outcomes:

One way of solving some probability questions is to list equally likely outcomes.

Example: A 10p coin and a 2p coin are thrown together and the Head or Tail result noted.

Possible outcomes HH , HT , TH , TT ( Note: HT is different from TH i.e. a head on the 10p and a tail on the 2p is different from a tail on the 10p and a head on the 2p)

4 possible outcomes, all equally likely.

Complete these probabilities. P(2 heads) = P(1 head) = (two outcomes give one head)

P(at least one head) = (Note: at least one head is one head or more than one head. Can be found by 1 - P(no heads))

8. A coin and a die are thrown. Complete this list of possible outcomes.

H1, H2,

a) What is the probability of obtaining a tail and a 3?

b) What is the probability of obtaining a head and a number greater than 2?

*H1 is a head on the coin and a 1 on the die. (Die is the singular of dice. 2 dice, 1 die)*
*You should obtain 12 outcomes.*
*(a) How many outcomes give this result? Write as a fraction out of the total number of possible outcomes.*
*(b) How many outcomes give this result? Write as a fraction out of the total number of possible outcomes.*

9. A 10p coin, a 50p coin and a £2 coin are thrown. List all the possible outcomes of heads and tails.

Find a) P(3 heads)

b) P(At least one tail)

c) P(Exactly 2 heads)

*You should get 8*

*a)How many outcomes give this result? Write as a fraction out of the total number of possible outcomes.*
*b) Can be found by 1 - P(no tails) OR by counting outcomes as before.*
*c) How many outcomes give this result? Write as a fraction out of the total number of possible outcomes.*

**Possibility diagrams for two events:**
A diagram may help when solving problems where there are two events to consider.
Example: Two dice are thrown and the numbers showing are multiplied to give a score.
This diagram shows the possible outcomes.

2nd die

| | × | 1 | 2 | 3 | 4 | 5 | 6 |
|---|---|---|---|---|---|---|---|
| 1st die | 1 | 1 | 2 | 3 | 4 | 5 | 6 |
| | 2 | 2 | 4 | 6 | 8 | 10 | 12 |
| | 3 | 3 | 6 | 9 | 12 | 15 | 18 |
| | 4 | 4 | 8 | 12 | 16 | 20 | 24 |
| | 5 | 5 | 10 | 15 | 20 | 25 | 30 |
| | 6 | 6 | 12 | 18 | 24 | 30 | 36 |

10. a) What is the total number of possible outcomes?

b) Find P(score 24) =

c) Find P(score 6) =

d) Find P(score is odd) =

11. A coin is thrown and a four sided spinner labelled 1, 2, 3 and 4 is spun. Complete this table to show the possible outcomes.

Spinner

| | | 1 | 2 | 3 | 4 |
|---|---|---|---|---|---|
| Coin | H | H1 | H2 | | |
| | T | T1 | | | |

Find a) P(H and 2)

b) P(head and even)

*Only the shaded part gives you the outcomes.*

12. Eight discs numbered 1, 2, 3, 4, 5, 6, 7 and 8 are in bag A. Five discs numbered 1, 2, 3, 4, and 5 are in bag B. One disc is chosen at random from each bag and the numbers added.
Complete this table to show the possible outcomes.

| + | 1 | 2 | 3 | 4 | 5 | 6 | 7 | 8 |
|---|---|---|---|---|---|---|---|---|
| 1 | | | 4 | | | | | |
| 2 | 3 | | | | | | | |
| 3 | | | | | | | | |
| 4 | | | | | | | | |
| 5 | | | | | | | | |

a) What is the total number of possible outcomes?

b) Find P(score 2) =

c) Find P(score 6) =

d) Find P(score is even) =

**Two way tables:**
This is just a table where the numbers in the middle tell you how many people or households or …. have the two variables being looked at and listed at the side and the top.

1. Example: This two-way table shows the results of a survey of households in a town.

Number of TV sets (columns); Number of computers (rows)

| Number of computers | 0 | 1 | 2 | 3 | Total |
|---|---|---|---|---|---|
| 0 | 6 | 8 | 4 | 0 | |
| 1 | 2 | 7 | 15 | 3 | |
| 2 | 0 | 1 | 1 | 3 | |
| Total | | | | | |

*i.e. 8 households have no computers and 1 TV set.*
*7 households have 1 computer and 1 TV set.*

*Total the rows. Only add the numbers in the shaded boxes. e.g. 6+8+4+0*
*Total the columns. Only add the numbers in the shaded boxes.*
*Add the totals in the column.*
*Add the totals in the row.*
*These both give the same answer which you should put in the bottom right hand box.*

Complete the totals.

a) How many households were in the survey?

*The shaded numbers added up.*

b) How many households have no computers?

*The numbers in the 0 computers row.*

c) How many households have at least one computer?

*The households that have 1 or 2 computers.*

d) If a household is chosen at random from the households surveyed, what is the probability it has two or more TV sets?

*The number that have 2 or more TV sets out of the total number of households.*

e) If there are 1200 households in the town estimate how many have 2 or more TV sets.

*The expected number, so multiply the probability by the number of households.*

2. In a survey people were asked if they had visited a newly opened shopping centre. Part of the results are shown in the two-way table below. Fill in the missing numbers to complete the table.

| | Had visited the shopping centre | Had NOT visited the shopping centre | Totals |
|---|---|---|---|
| Female | 65 | | 96 |
| Male | | 55 | |
| Totals | 102 | | |

a) How many people were in the survey?

b) How many had visited the shopping centre?

c) If a person is chosen at random, what is the probability that the person chosen had visited the shopping centre?

*Write down the fraction: the total number of people who had visited the centre over the total number of people in the survey.*

d) If a person is chosen at random, what is the probability that the person chosen was male and had visited the shopping centre?

*Write down the fraction: the number of males that had visited the centre over the total number of people in the survey.*

# Test Yourself:

Try these questions. If you are unable to do a question go back and revise the relevant section.

**Mean median mode and range**

1. Find the mean, median, mode and range for the following set of data.
   3, 5, 5, 9, 6, 3, 4, 9, 7, 5, 4, 6
   Make it clear which is which.

**Frequency tables**

2. This table opposite shows the scores obtained when a five sided spinner was spun a number of times.
   Find the mean, median and modal score.
   Make it clear which is which.

| *Score* | *Frequency* | |
|---|---|---|
| *1* | *8* | |
| *2* | *5* | |
| *3* | *12* | |
| *4* | *10* | |
| *5* | *15* | |

**Pie charts**

3. The following table shows the goals scored by teams in a particular league on a Saturday.

| Goals | no. of teams |
|---|---|
| 0 | 4 |
| 1 | 8 |
| 2 | 6 |
| 3 | 4 |
| 4 | 2 |

Draw a pie chart to represent this information.

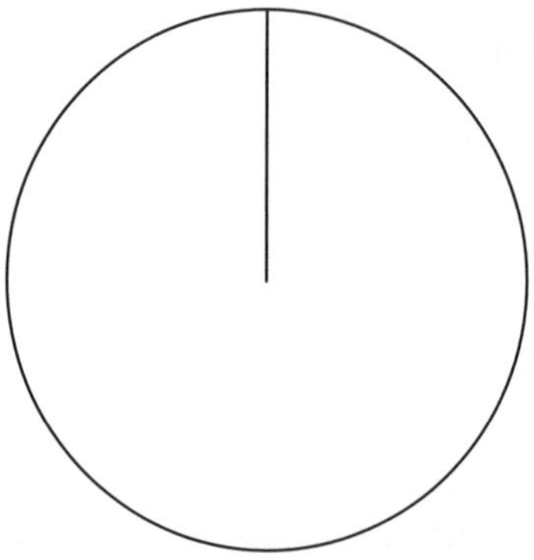

Pie charts

4. The following table shows the colour of cars passing a particular street corner on a Wednesday lunchtime.

| Colour | no. of cars |
|---|---|
| Red | 6 |
| Black | 14 |
| Silver | 10 |
| White | 8 |
| Blue | 2 |

Draw a pie chart to represent this information.

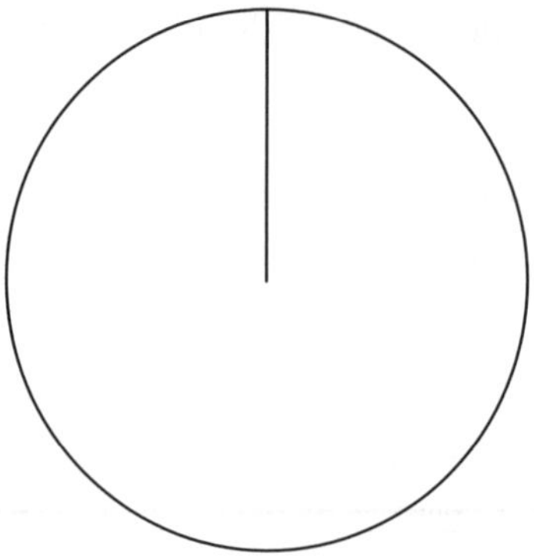

**Bar graphs**

5. Draw a bar graph to show the following information.

| Type of drink sold | Week 1 | Week 2 | Week 3 |
|---|---|---|---|
| Hot | 160 | 100 | 120 |

a. What was the weekly average sales of hot drinks?
b. What was the range of weekly sales of hot drinks?
c. If 140 hot drinks were sold in week 4 add a bar showing this on your bar graph.

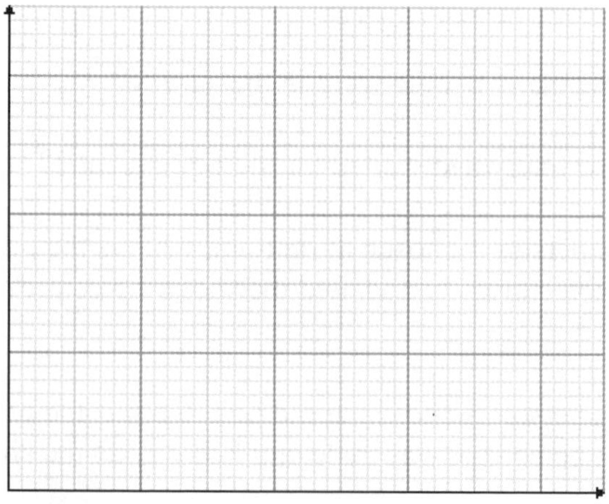

**Two-way tables**

6. In a survey, a class of children were asked how many brothers and sisters they had. The results are shown in the two-way table below. Complete the totals row and column.

| | | Brothers | | | | |
|---|---|---|---|---|---|---|
| | | 0 | 1 | 2 | 3 | totals |
| Sisters | 0 | 7 | 3 | 2 | 0 | |
| | 1 | 4 | 5 | 1 | 1 | |
| | 2 | 2 | 0 | 1 | 1 | |
| | 3 | 1 | 1 | 0 | 0 | |
| | totals | | | | | |

a) How many children were in the class?

b) How many children have 1 sister?

c) How many children have more than 2 brothers or sisters?

d) What percentage of children have 1 brother (answer to the nearerst integer)?

**Scatter diagrams**

7. Draw the scatter diagram and the line of best fit for the following set of measures of $x$ and $y$.

| $x$ | $y$ |
|---|---|
| 10 | 11 |
| 15 | 19 |
| 19 | 22 |
| 23 | 17 |
| 26 | 24 |
| 30 | 28 |
| 36 | 28 |
| 41 | 38 |
| 44 | 33 |
| 44 | 36 |

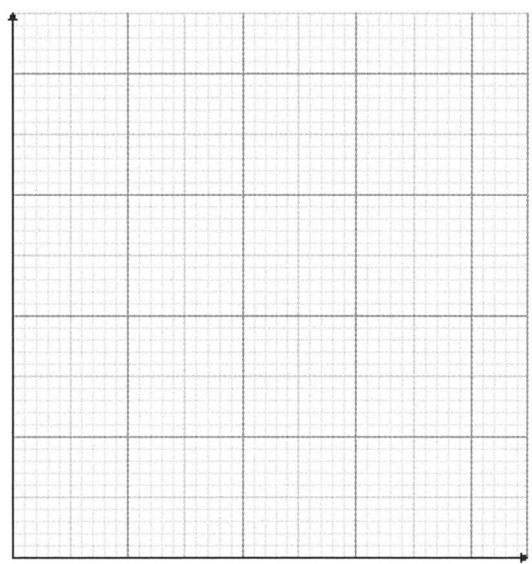

a) What type of correlation does this diagram show?

b) Use your line of best fit to estimate $y$ when $x$ is 20.

c) Explain the relationship between $x$ and $y$.

**Probability**

8. The probability of a drawing pin landing point up is 0.46. (a) What is the probability of the pin landing point down? (b) If the pin is thrown 50 times, how many times would you expect it to land point up?

9. Two dice are thrown. List the possible outcomes. What is the probability of obtaining a score of 7?

10. Draw a sample space diagram for the possible outcomes when two spinners labelled 1, 2, 3, 4 (all numbers being equally likely to occur) are spun and the numbers on the spinners are added. What is the probability of obtaining a score of 5?

# SHAPE, SPACE and MEASURES

**Angles:**

Angles less than $90^\circ$ are called **acute angles**

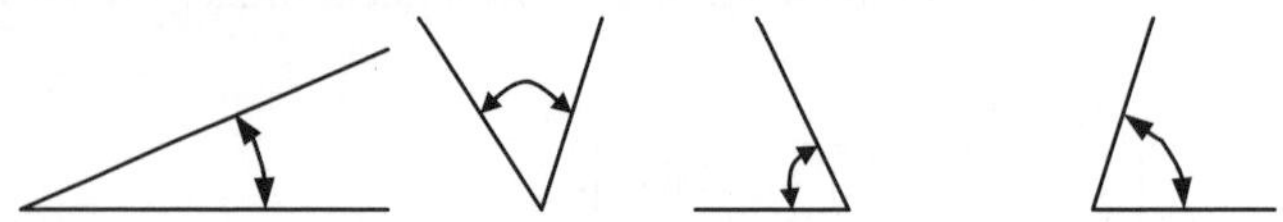

Angles equal to $90^\circ$ are called **right angles**
Lines that are at right angles are called **'perpendicular lines'**

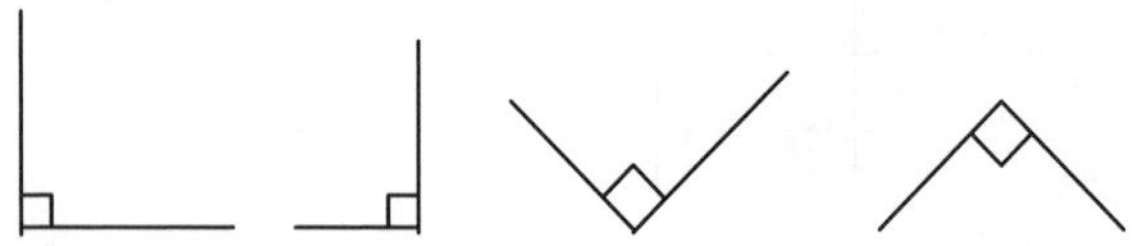

Angles greater than $90^\circ$ but less than $180^\circ$ are called **obtuse angles**

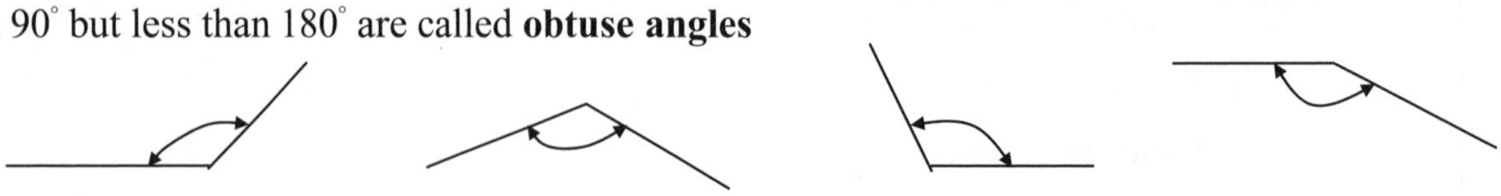

Angles greater than $180^\circ$ are called **reflex angles**

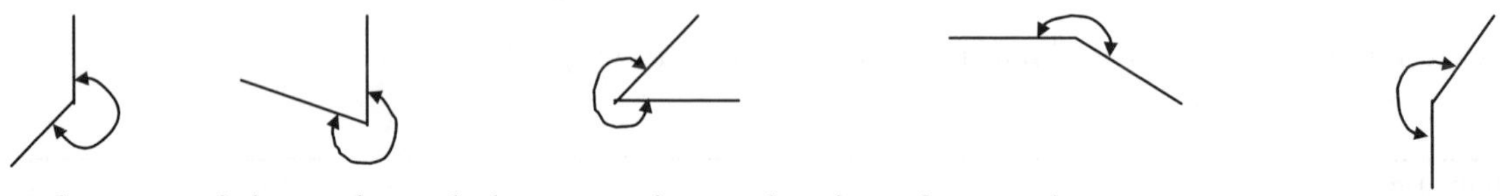

Estimating angles - use right angles to help you estimate the size of an angle
e.g. estimate the size of angle $a$

First draw in right angles from one line

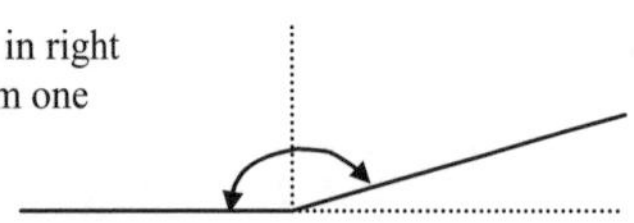

So you can see that the angle is between one right angle $90^\circ$ and two right angles $180^\circ$

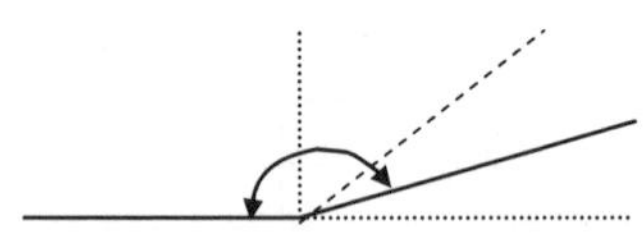

Now you can halve this right angle and make your estimate.
Either 90 + 45 plus just over half of 45 say about 25 to give $160^\circ$
OR just less than half of 45 say about 20 away from 180 to give $160^\circ$

If two or more lines never cross, even if you extend them as far as you like, then they are called parallel lines. Parallel lines are indicated in a diagram with arrowheads. A different set of parallel lines on the same diagram is indicated with two arrowheads and so on.

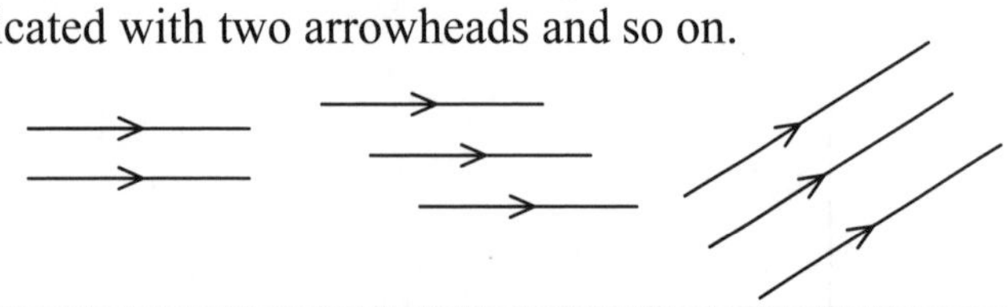

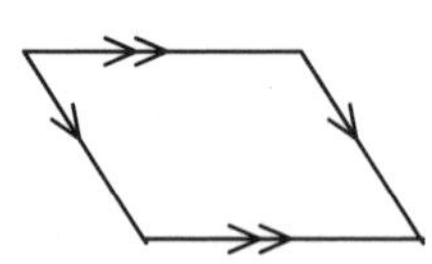

A parallelogram has opposite sides parallel

1. Estimate the size of each of these angles and say whether they are acute, obtuse or reflex:

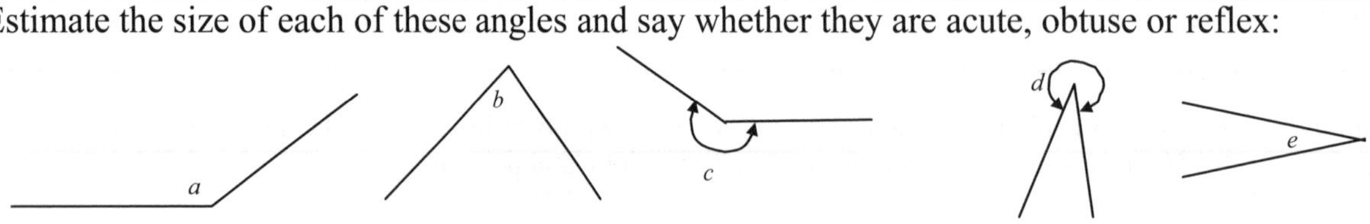


The angles on one side of a straight line add up to $180^\circ$

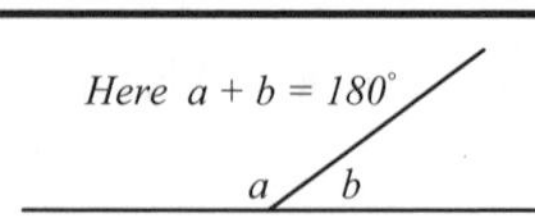


*Here* $a + b = 180^\circ$

*So if* $a = 145^\circ$ *then* $b = 180^\circ - 145^\circ = 35^\circ$

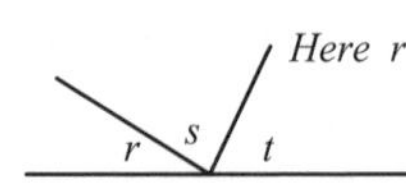


*Here* $r + s + t = 180^\circ$

*So if* $r = 45^\circ$ *and* $s = 80^\circ$ *then* $t = 180^\circ - (45^\circ + 80^\circ) = 180^\circ - 125^\circ = 55^\circ$

The angles round a point add up to $360^\circ$

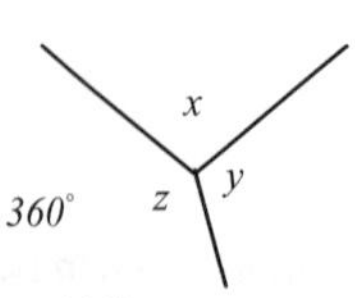


*Here* $x + y + z = 360^\circ$

*So if* $x = 95^\circ$ *and* $y = 110^\circ$ *then* $z = 360^\circ - (95^\circ + 110^\circ) = 360^\circ - 205^\circ = 155^\circ$

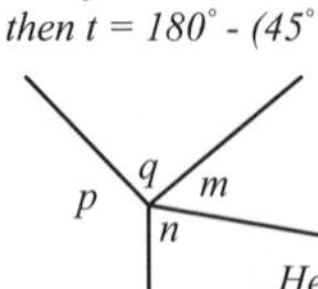


*Here* $p + q + m + n = 360^\circ$

*So if* $p = 135^\circ$ $q = 95^\circ$ *and* $m = 60^\circ$ *then* $n = 360^\circ - (135^\circ + 95^\circ + 60^\circ) = 360^\circ - 290^\circ = 70^\circ$

Opposite angles are equal

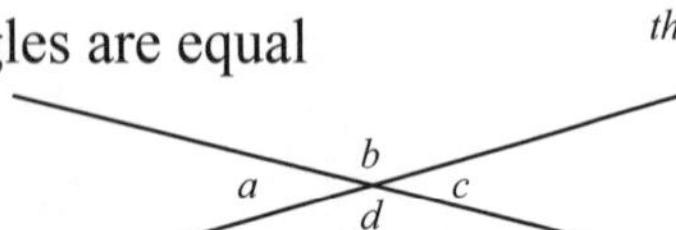


*Here* $a = c$ *and* $b = d$

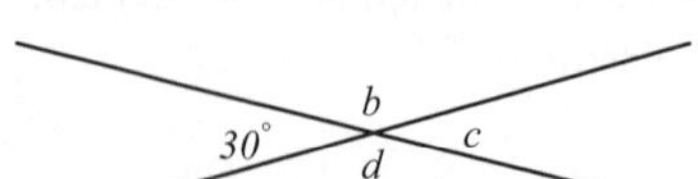


*So if* $a = 30^\circ$ *then* $c = 30^\circ$
*Also* $30^\circ$ *and b are on a straight line and so they add to give* $180^\circ$
*Then* $b = 180^\circ - 30^\circ = 150^\circ$ *and also* $d = 150^\circ$

Angles between parallel lines

Z (alternate) angles are equal

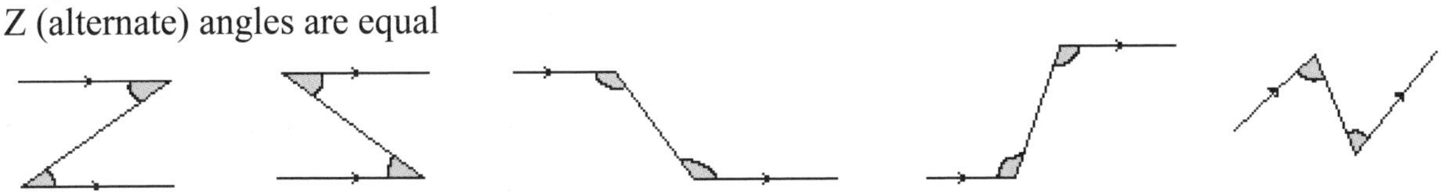

F (corresponding) angles are equal

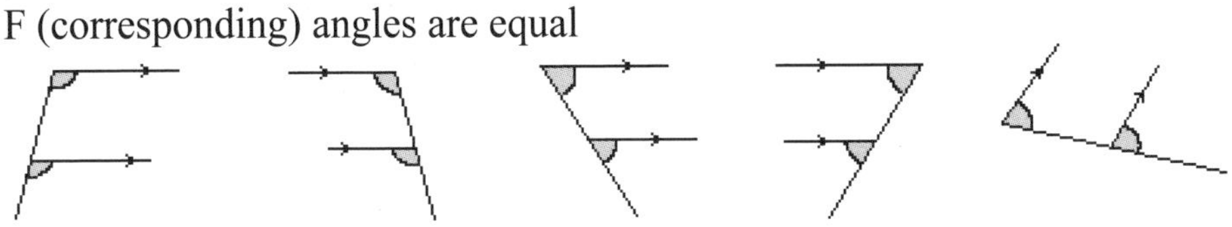

not drawn accurately

The following diagrams are not drawn accurately - they are sketches. Do not measure the angles.

2. Find the angles marked with a letter.

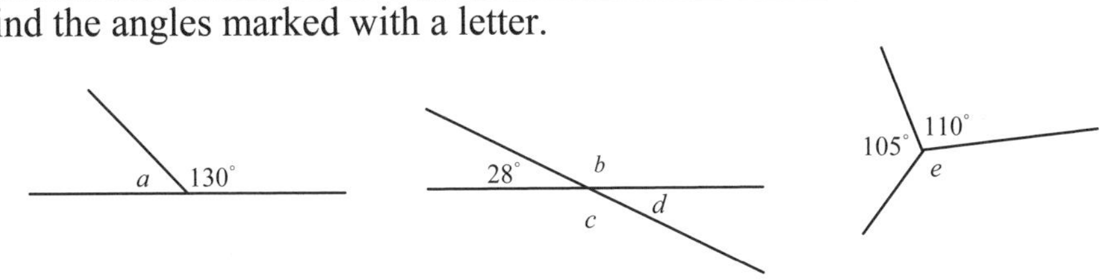


*a - angles on a straight line*
*b - angles on a straight line*
*c - opposite angles (or angles on a straight line)*
*d - opposite angles (or angles on a straight line)*
*e - angles round a point*

3. Find the angles marked with a letter.

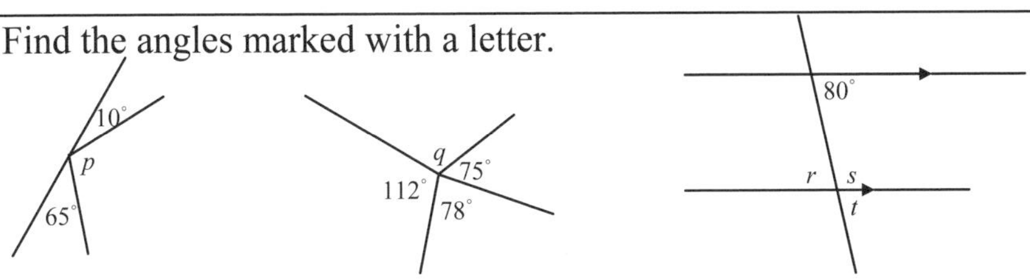


*p - angles on a straight line*
*q - angles round a point*
*r - alternate(Z) angles*
*s - angles on a straight line*
*t - opposite angles (or corresponding(F) angles or angles on a straight line)*

4. Find the angles marked with a letter.

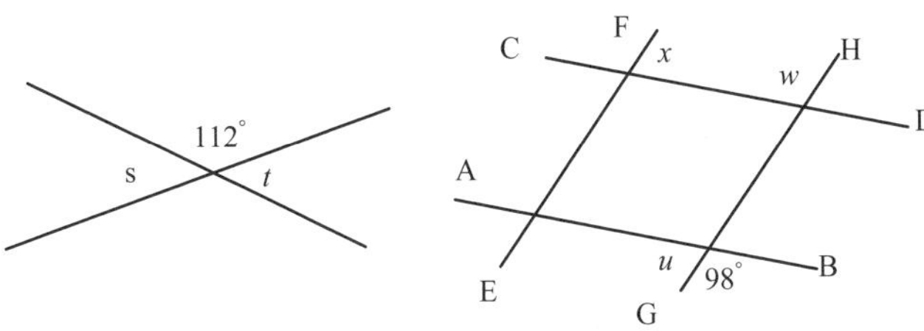


AB and CD are parallel.
EF and GH are parallel.

*s - angles on a straight line*
*t - opposite angles (or angles on a straight line)*

*For more complicated shapes try and find all the angles that you can. For the second one you should be able to label all the angles.*

*u - angles on a straight line opposite angle to 98°*
*w - corresponding(F) angles*
*x - alternate(Z) angles*

5. Find the angles marked with a letter.

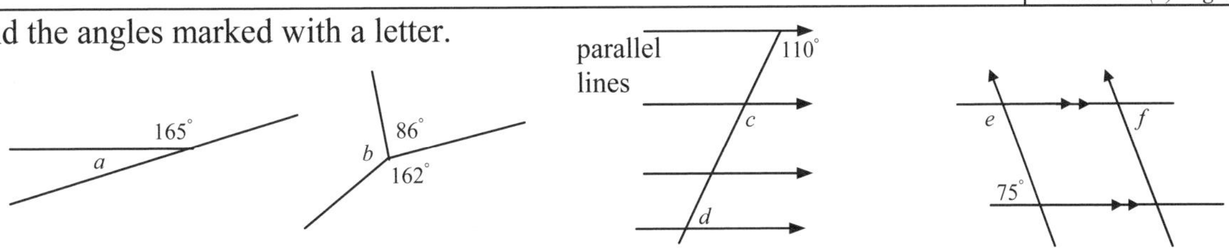


6. Find $x$, $y$ and $z$ for each of these:

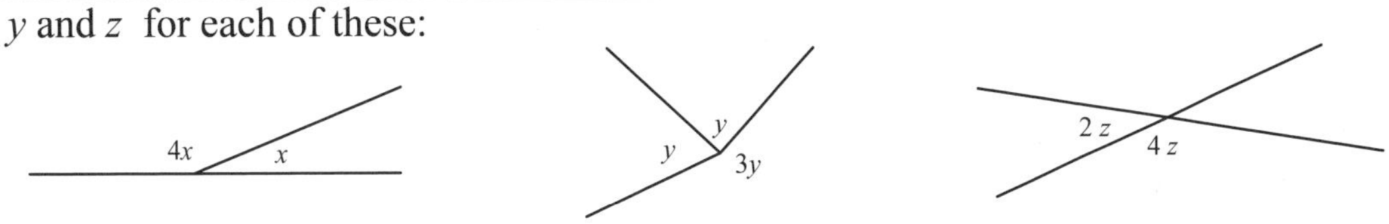


**Shapes:**

You should know the names of these shapes and their properties.

Draw the lines of symmetry for each shape if they exist.

**Triangles**

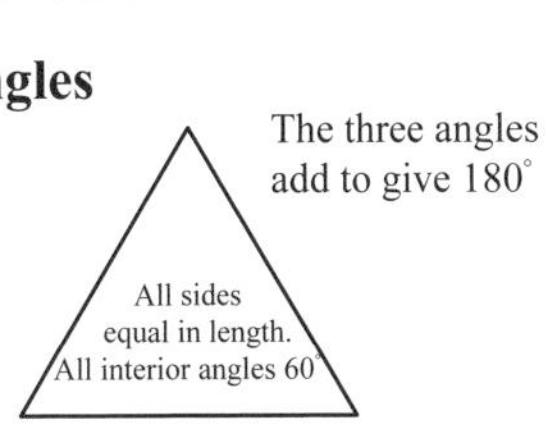


Equilateral triangle
Three lines of symmetry
Rotational symmetry of order 3

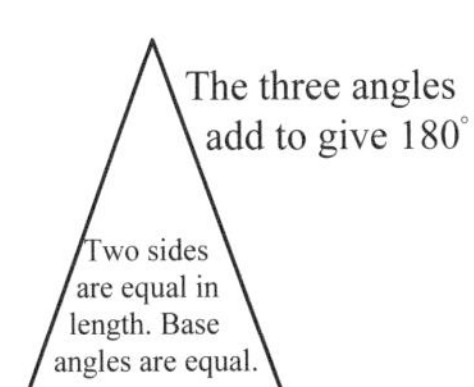


Isosceles triangle
One line of symmetry
Rotational symmetry of order 1

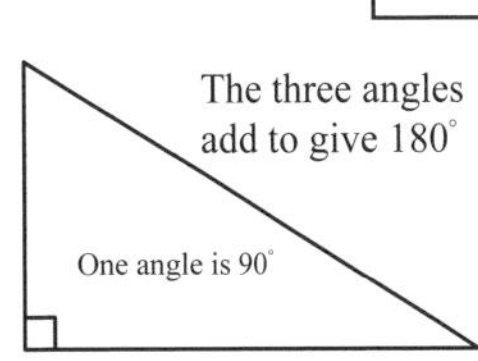


Right-angled triangle

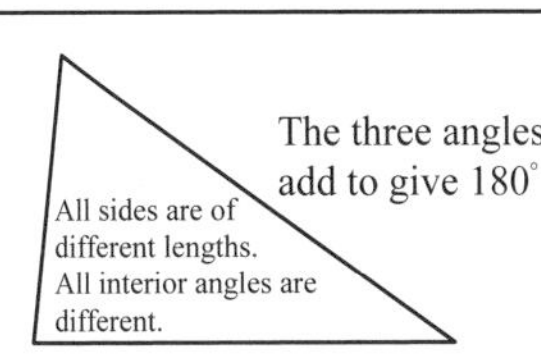


Scalene Triangle

1.Find the angles marked with a letter.

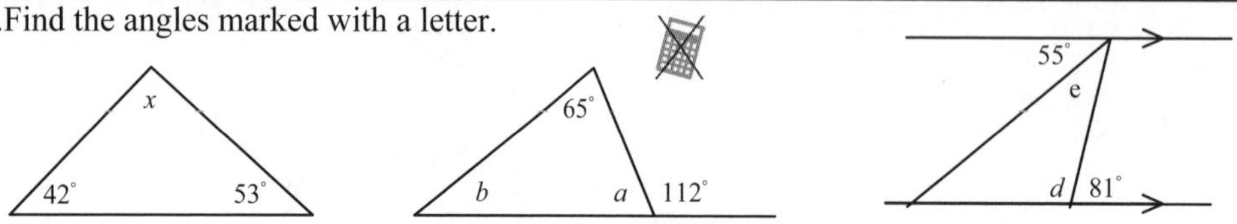


*x - the angles add to give 180°*

*a - angles on a straight line*
*b - angles in a triangle*

*d - angles on a straight line*
*Angle in bottom left of triangle is an alternate (Z) angle*
*e - angles in a triangle*

2. Find the angles marked with a letter.

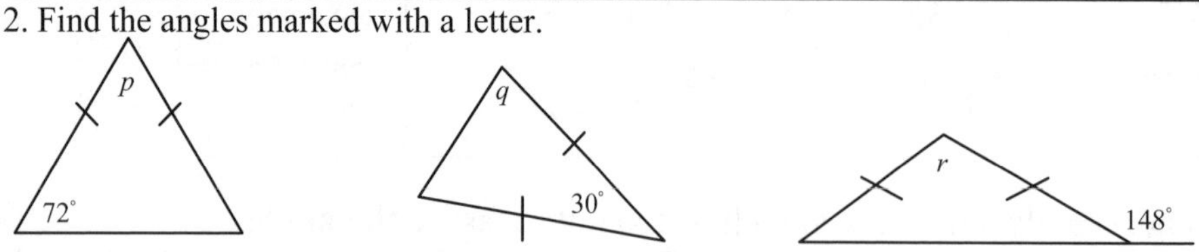


*Isosceles triangles - the equal sides are marked*

*The other angle is 72° - base angles are equal. p - angles in a triangle*

*q and the other angle are equal*
*180 - 30 then ÷ 2*

*Angles on a straight line to give one base angle and hence the other*
*r - angles in a triangle*

3. Find the angles marked with a letter.

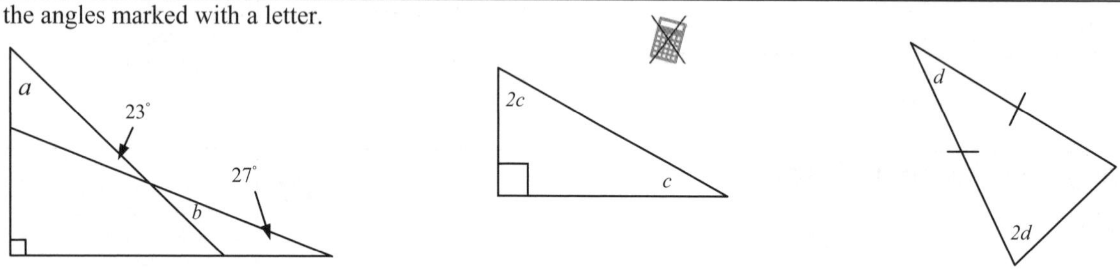


4. Find the angles marked with a letter.

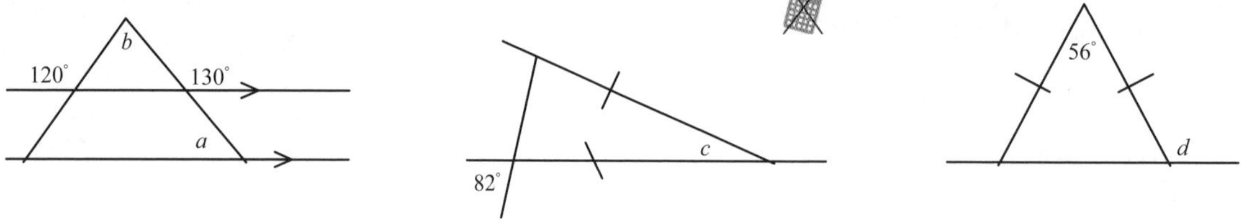


## Quadrilaterals

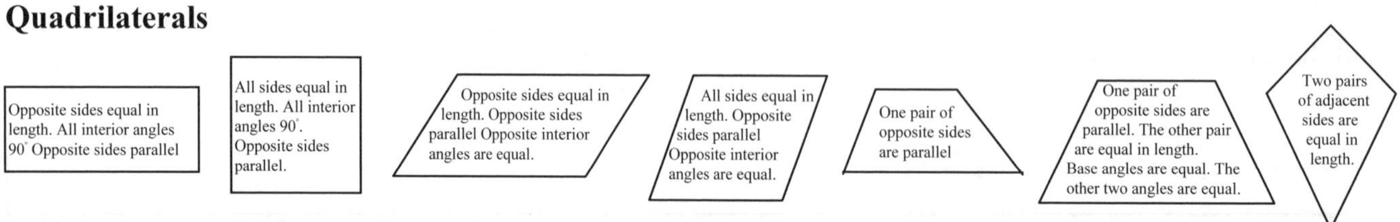


| Rectangle | Square | Parallelogram | Rhombus | Trapezium | Isosceles trapezium | Kite |
|---|---|---|---|---|---|---|
| 2 lines of symmetry symmetry | 4 lines of symmetry | NO lines of symmetry | 2 lines of symmetry | NO lines of symmetry | 1 line of symmetry | 1 line of symmetry |
| Rotational symmetry of order 2 | Rotational symmetry of order 4 | Rotational symmetry of order 2 | Rotational symmetry of order 2 | Rotational symmetry of order 1 | Rotational symmetry of order 1 | Rotational symmetry of order 1 |

The angles in a quadrilateral add up to 360°. You can show this by drawing a diagonal. You then have two triangles whose angles together make up the angles of the quadrilateral. So $2 \times 180° = 360°$

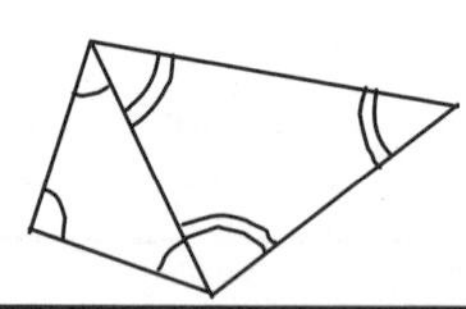

5. Find *p*, *q*, *r* and *x*

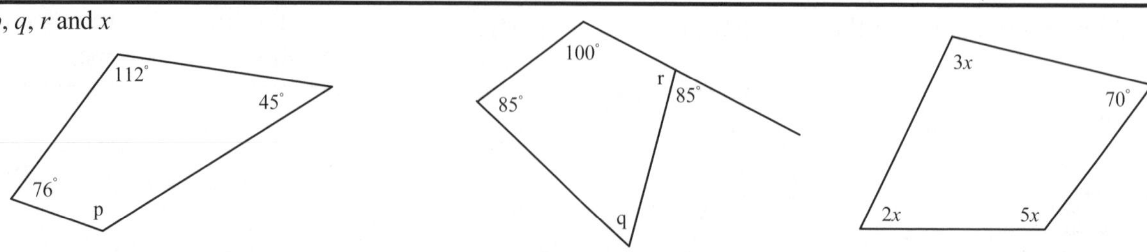

## Other Polygons

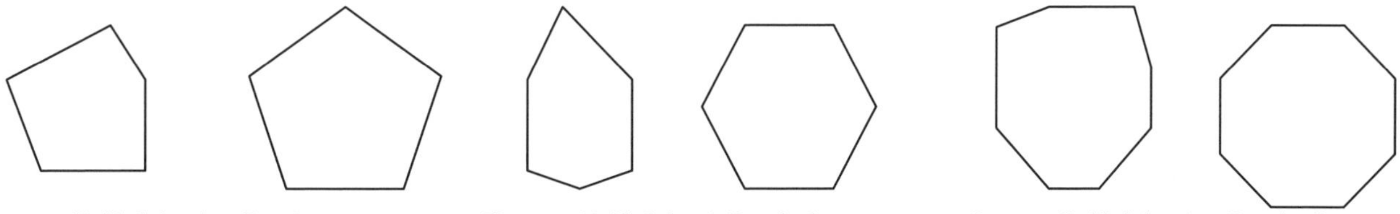

**Pentagon** (5 sided shape) Regular pentagon 5 lines of symmetry Rotational symmetry of order 5

**Hexagon** (6 sided shape) Regular hexagon 6 lines of symmetry Rotational symmetry of order 6

**Octagon** (8 sided shape) Regular Octagon 8 lines of symmetry Rotational symmetry of order 8

Other shapes Heptagon (7 sides) Nonagon (9 sides) Decagon (10 sides)

If not sure about lines of symmetry just think ' if I fold along the line do the two folded parts fit exactly on top of each other?' - if it does it is a line of symmetry. Be careful with rectangle and parallelogram.
Shapes that ***tessellate*** fit together on a surface without leaving any gaps.
***Regular polygons*** have equal sides, equal angles and the same number of lines of symmetry as sides.

### Angle Sum for Polygons

The angle sum of any polygon can be found by splitting it into triangles.
For example a pentagon splits into 3 triangles so the angle sum is $3 \times 180^\circ = 540^\circ$.
In general the number of triangles is always <u>2 less than the number of sides</u>.

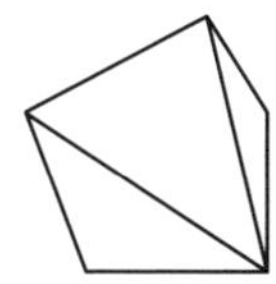

1. Find $p$, $q$ and $x$

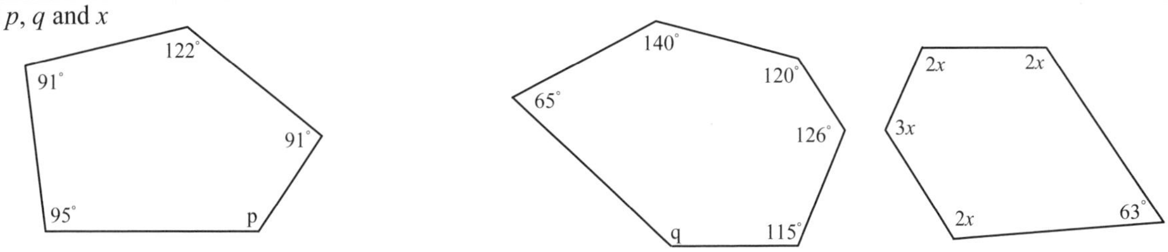


**Regular polygons:**
Side lengths are equal.

Exterior angles are equal.

Interior angles are equal.

e.g. for a regular pentagon

Exterior angles are marked in grey

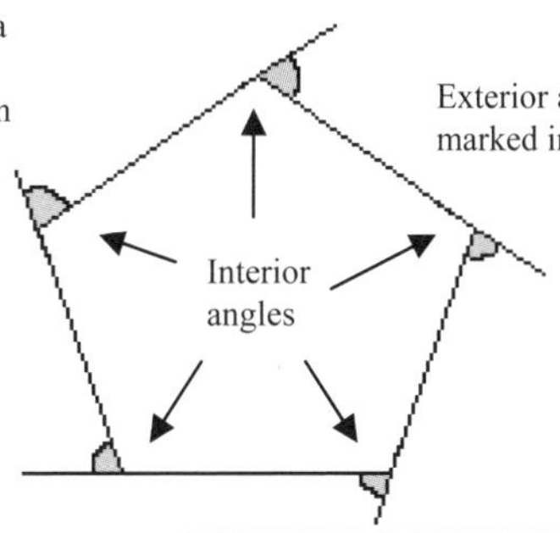


The sum of the exterior angles is 360°

Exterior angle + interior angle = 180°

**The angle at the centre of a regular polygon** is $360^\circ \div$ number of sides
(This is NOT the interior angle)

e.g. for regular pentagon angle at the centre = $360^\circ \div 5 = 72^\circ$

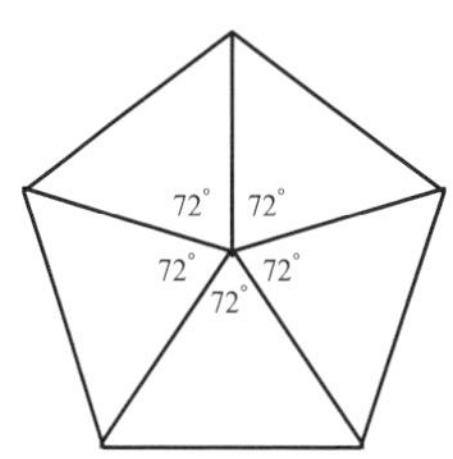


2. Name these shapes and draw in any lines of symmetry

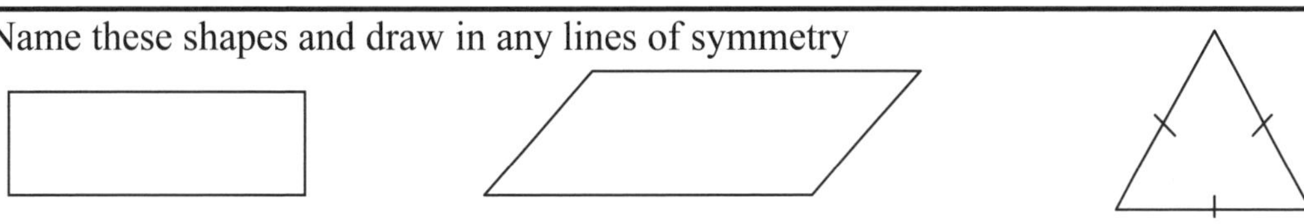

3. Shade two more squares so that this shape has exactly one line of symmetry.

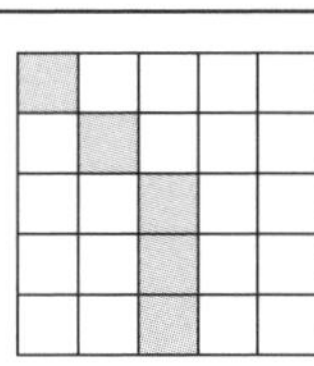

4. Shade two more squares so that this shape has rotational symmetry of order 2.

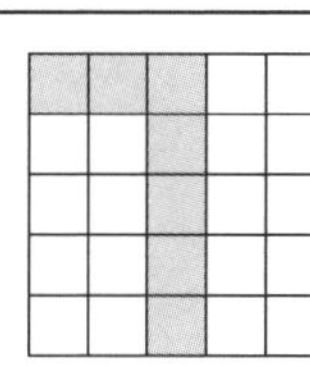

| Question | Hint |
|---|---|
| 5. Find the size of the exterior and interior angles of a regular pentagon.<br>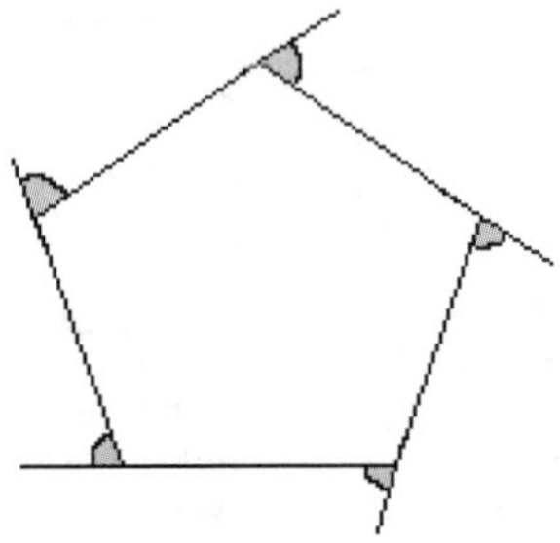<br>5 exterior angles add up to<br>Each exterior angle = ÷ 5 =<br>Each interior angle = 180° - = | *A sketch helps to see what you are trying to find and may jog the memory.*<br>*The sum of the exterior angles.*<br>*The 5 angles are the same.*<br>*Angles on a straight line.*<br>*If you need to find the interior angles only then this method is easiest.* |
| 6. Find the size of the exterior and interior angles of a regular octagon. | *Draw a sketch. Extend each side at one end.*<br>*Write down the sum of the exterior angles.*<br>*The 8 angles are the same so find one of them.*<br>*Angles on a straight line to give the interior angle.* |
| 7. Find the angle, $a$, at the centre of a regular octagon.<br>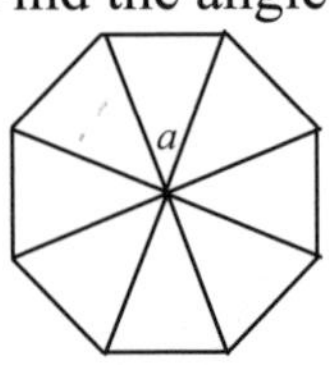 | *Just 360° ÷ number of sides.* |
| 8. Find the size of the exterior and interior angles of a regular 20 sided shape.<br>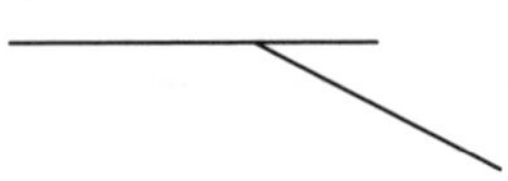<br>Exterior angles add up to<br>Each exterior angle =<br>Each interior angle = | *Hard to sketch a 20 sided shape - just draw a couple of sides and an exterior angle.* |
| 9. If a regular polygon has interior angles of size 150°, how many sides does the polygon have? | *First find the size of the exterior angle.*<br>*Then how many of these in 360°.* |
| 10. Find the size of the interior angles of a regular hexagon. | *Draw a sketch. Extend each side at one end.*<br>*Write down the sum of the exterior angles. The angles are the same so find one of them.*<br>*Angles on a straight line to give the interior angle.* |
| 11. Find the size of the exterior and interior angles of a regular 9 sided shape. | *Hard to sketch a regular 9 sided shape - just draw a couple of sides.*<br>*Write down the sum of the exterior angles. The angles are the same so find one of them.*<br>*Angles on a straight line to give the interior angle.* |

## The circle:

DIAMETER = 2 × RADIUS

The CIRCUMFERENCE is the distance around the outside edge of the circle.

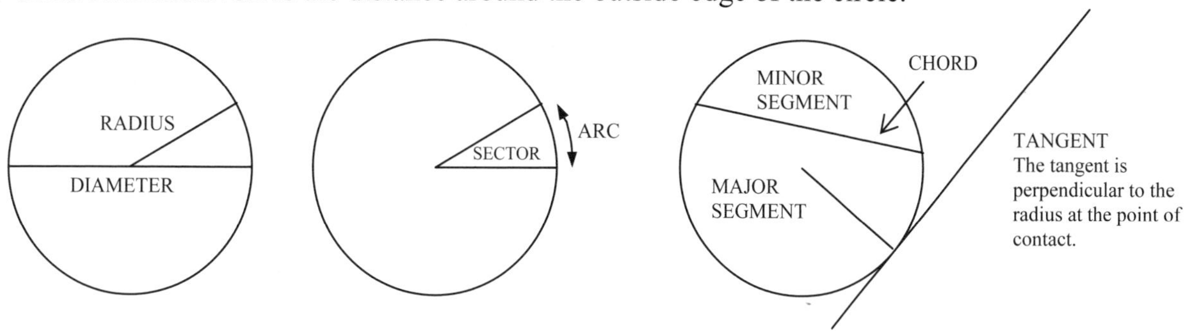


## 3-D shapes and nets:

Draw a net for each of these shapes. The net is the 2-D shape that folds to give the 3-D shape.

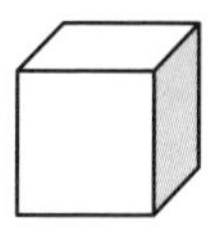

A cube of side 1cm

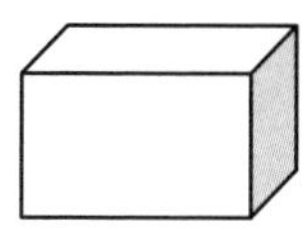

A cuboid 2cm by 1cm by 1cm

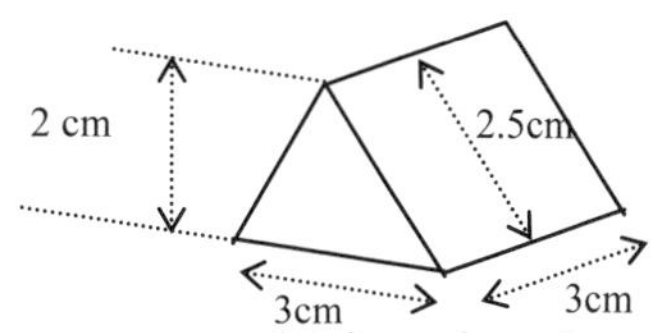


A triangular prism

(Take 1 square = 1 cm)

Other shapes

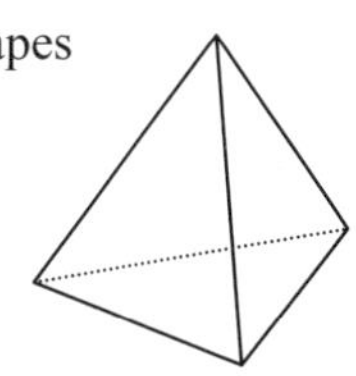

Tetrahedron
or
triangular based pyramid

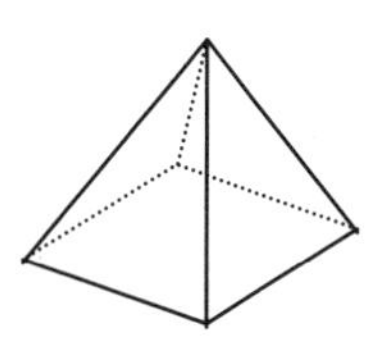

Square based pyramid

## Plans and elevations:

You need to be able to draw a plan (a view from above) or an elevation (a side view) given a 3-D figure.
Try these:

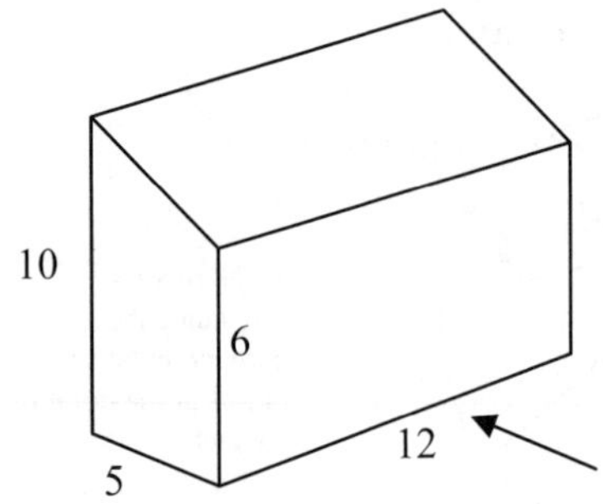


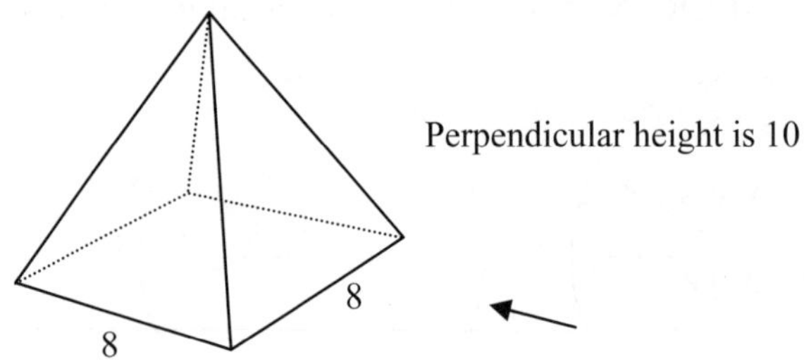


Draw a plan view and an elevation from the direction given for each of the above. (Take 1 square = 1 unit of measurement)

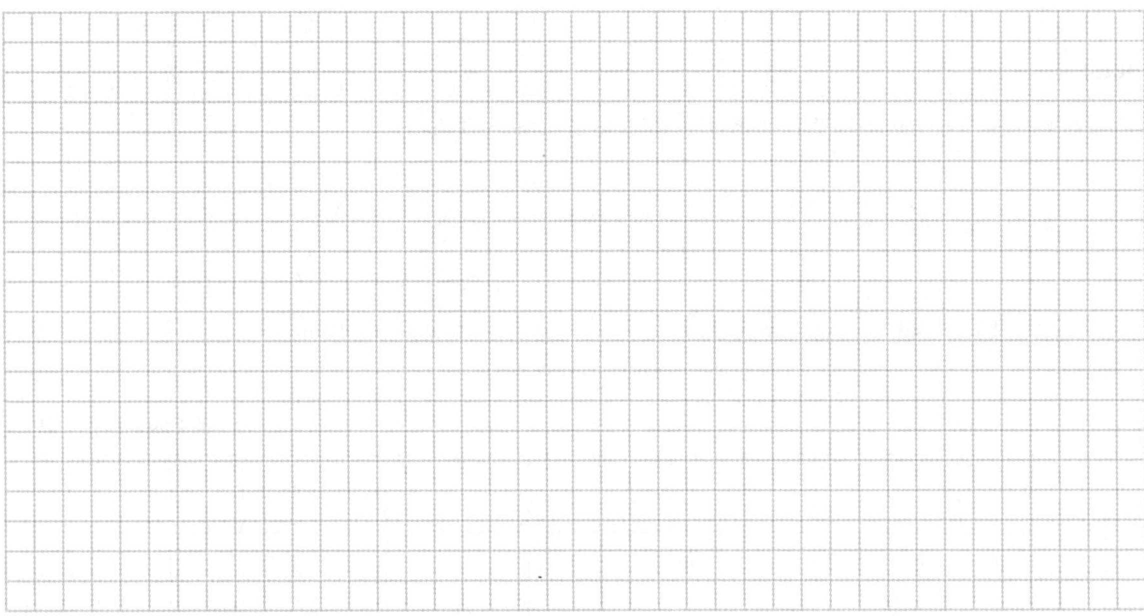

Using an isometric grid/dotty paper to draw 3D cube structures.
To draw a unit cube

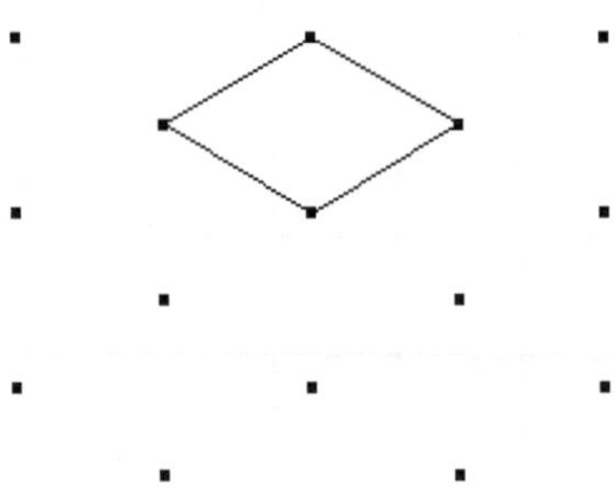

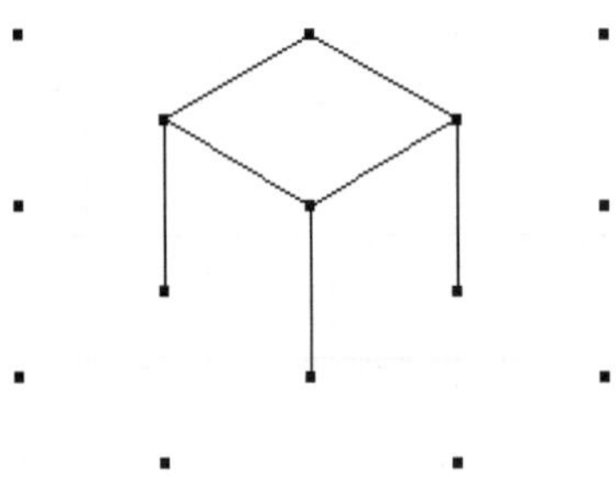

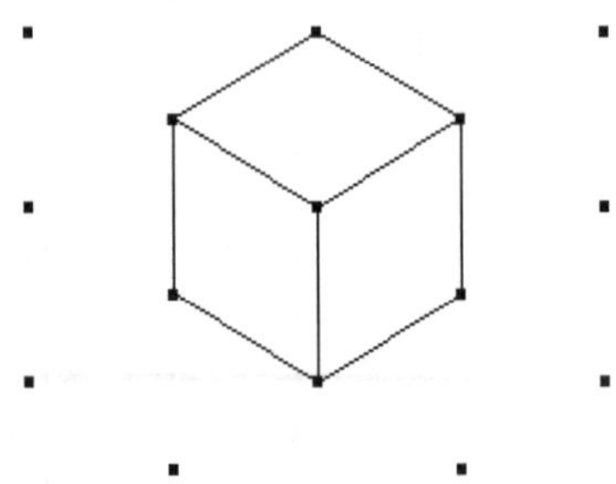

Draw a diamond

Drop down lines

Complete the cube

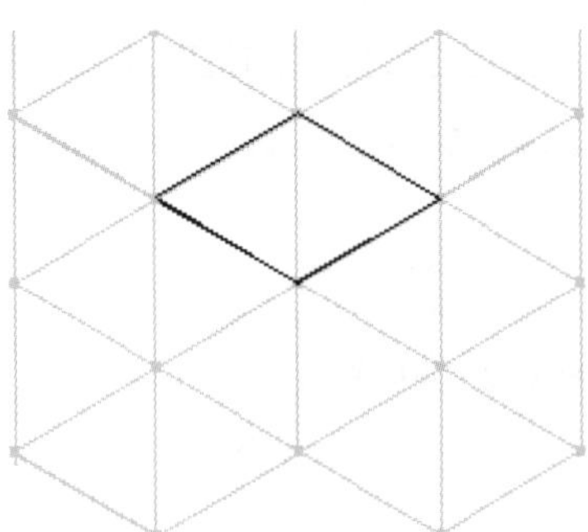

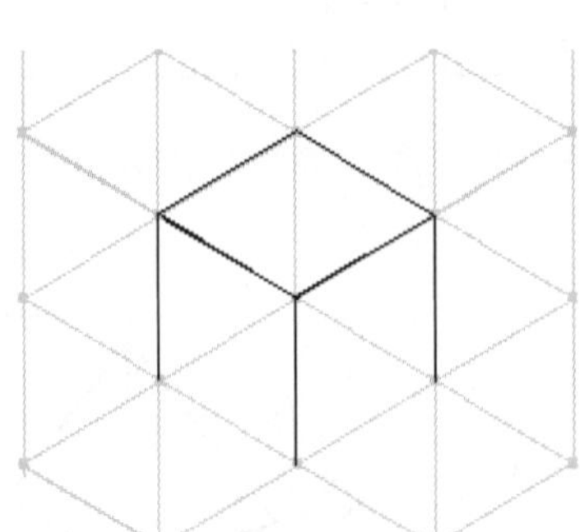

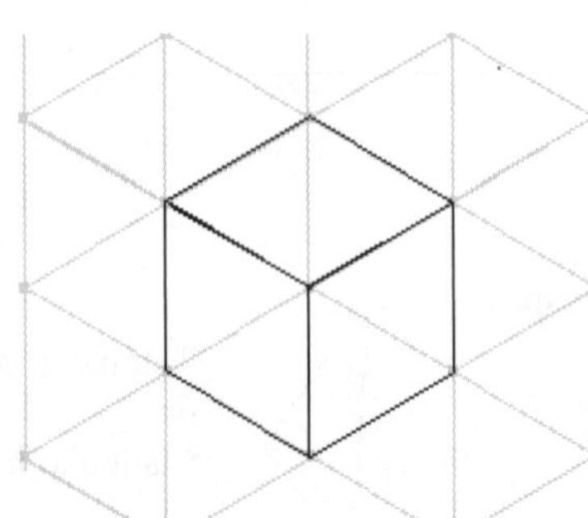

1. On the isometric grid draw a cube of side 3units.

2. On the isometric grid draw a cuboid length 3 units, width 2 units and height 1 unit.

3. Four unit cubes are stacked one on top of another. On the isometric grid draw a diagram of the cubes.

4. Five cubes are used to make some shapes. If every cube has at least one face completely against the face of another cube sketch: (a) an L shape and (b) a cuboid that can be made with the five cubes.

5. A child is playing with some cubes. She makes a shape that has this front elevation (view).

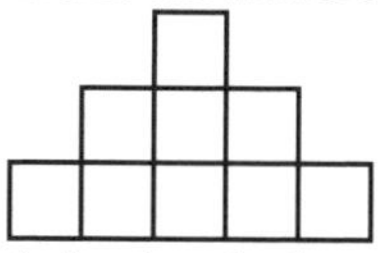

If the shape is 1 unit in depth draw the shape on the isometric grid below.

6. The following is a sketch of a shape made up from unit cubes. On the square grid below draw (a) a plan and (b) a side elevation looking from the direction of the arrow.

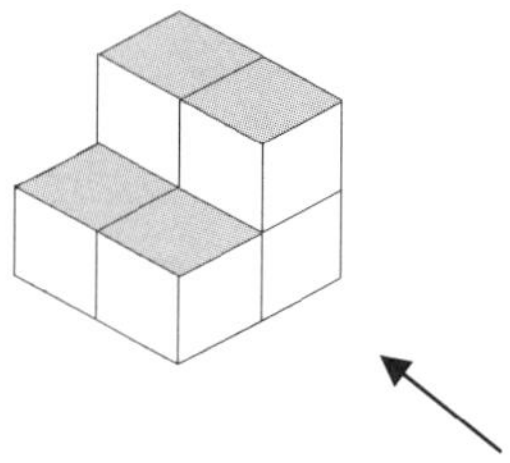

(a) (b)

**Perimeter, area and volume:**

Perimeter is the length of the boundary of the shape.

Area of a rectangle = length × width

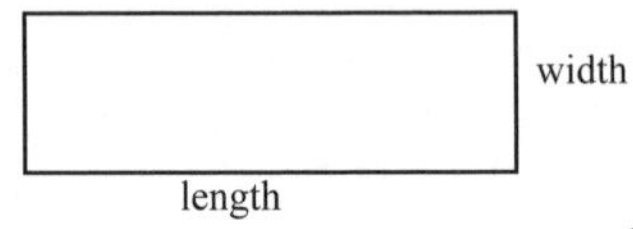


Area of a triangle = ½ × base × perpendicular height

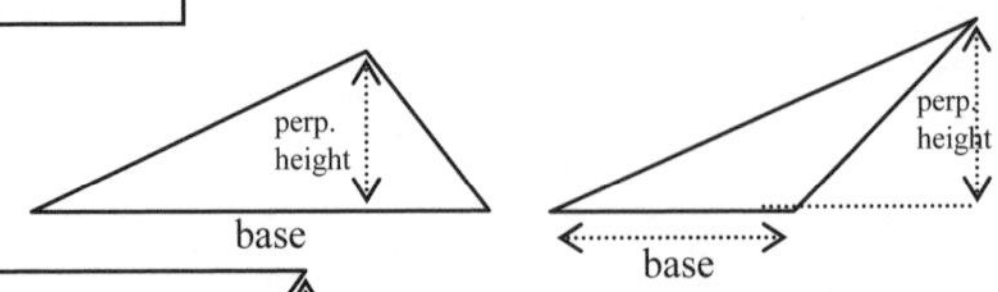


Area of a parallelogram = base × perpendicular height

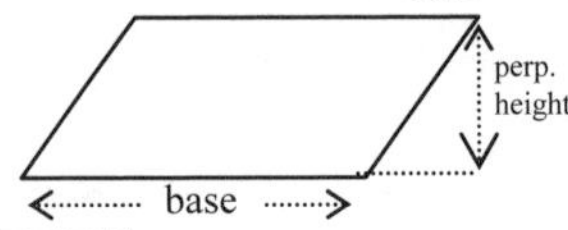


Area of a trapezium = ½ × sum of parallel sides × distance between the parallel sides

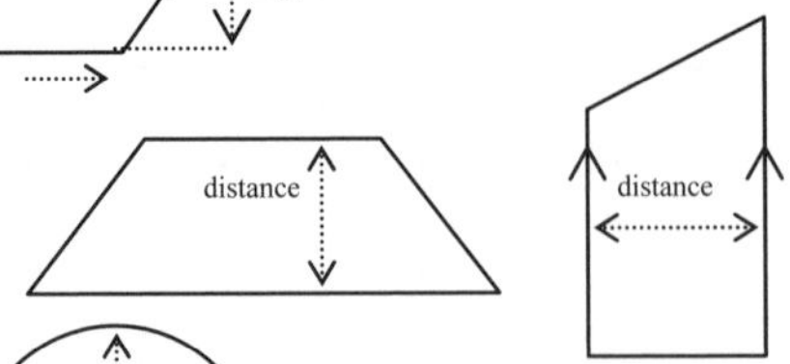


Circumference of a circle = π × diameter OR 2 π r

Area of a circle = $\pi r^2$ (π × radius × radius)

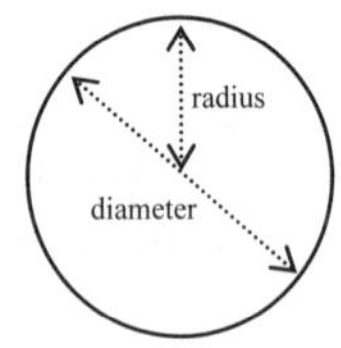


Volume of a cuboid = length × width × height

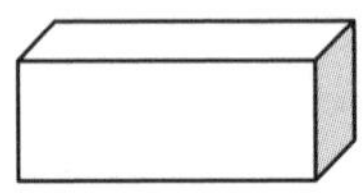

Volume of a prism = area of cross section × length

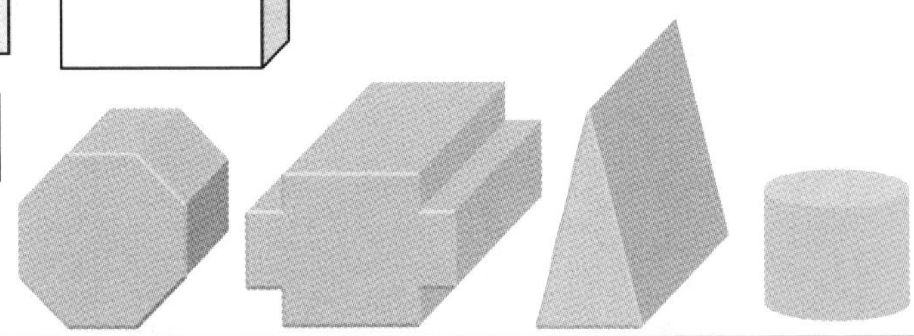

A prism is any shape with uniform cross-section (it will have the same shape at the ends)

1. Find the perimeter and area of each of these shapes drawn on a cm grid

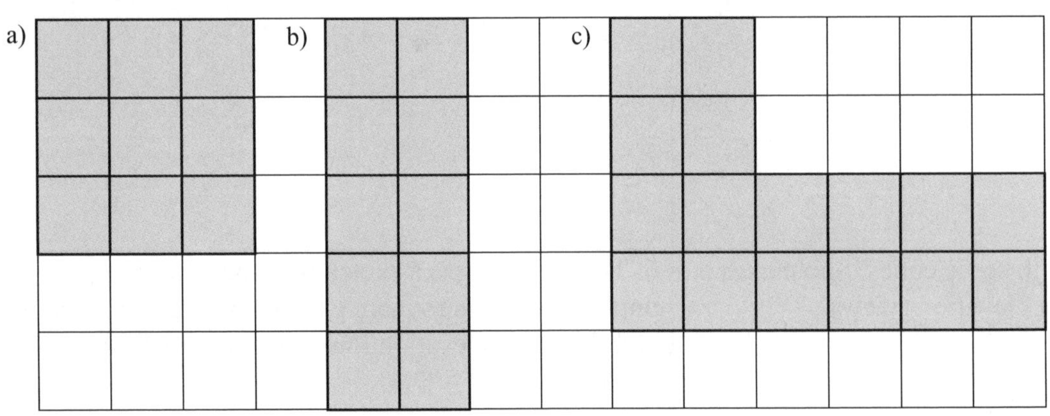


*Remember: the perimeter is the length of the boundary. Count the squares for the area.*

*Don't forget the units.*

2. Find the perimeter and area of each of these shapes (not drawn to scale). Name each shape.

a.

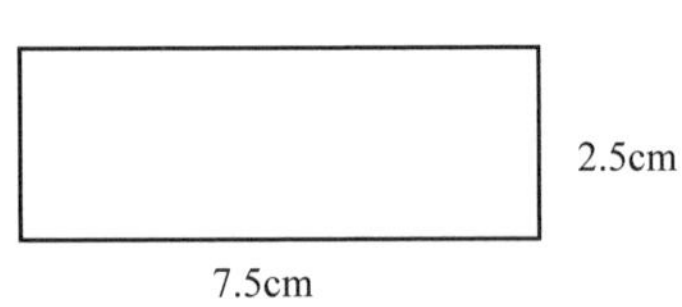


b.

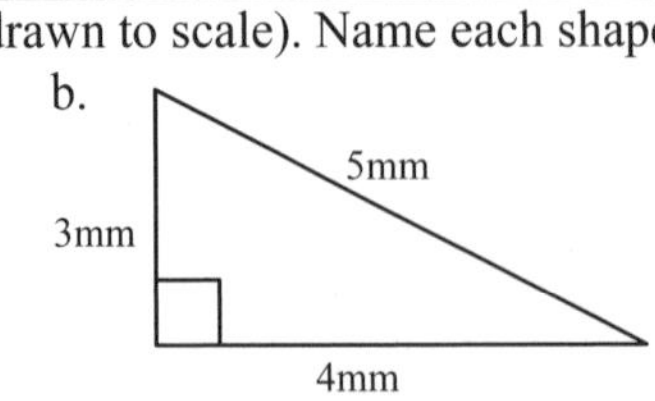


c.

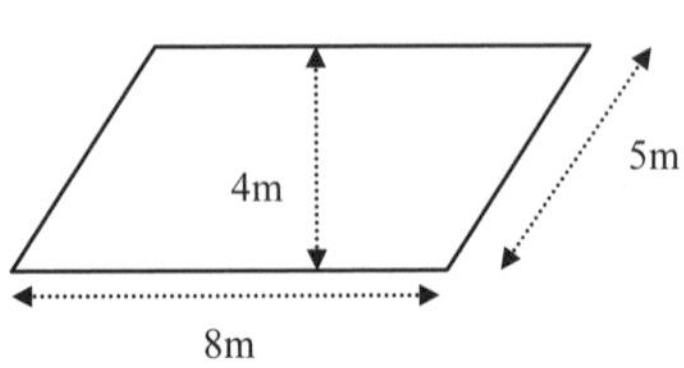


d.

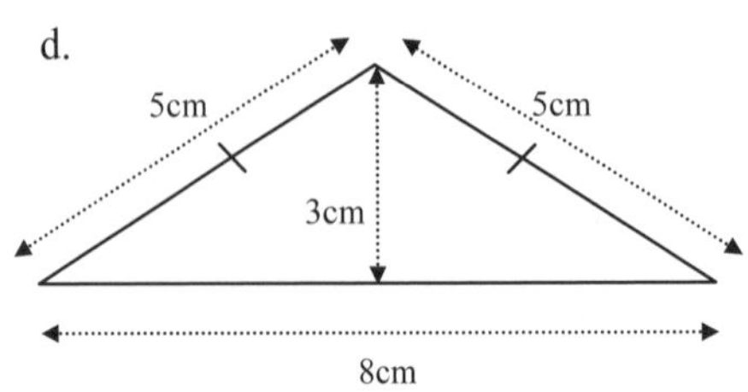


*Remember the units. Check the units are the same for any shape.*

*You must write down the units for the answers. i.e. for perimeter mm or cm or m and for area $mm^2$ or $cm^2$ or $m^2$. For some questions in the examination these will be given but for at least one you will need to write in the units to gain a mark.*

3. Find the areas of these shapes (not drawn to scale).

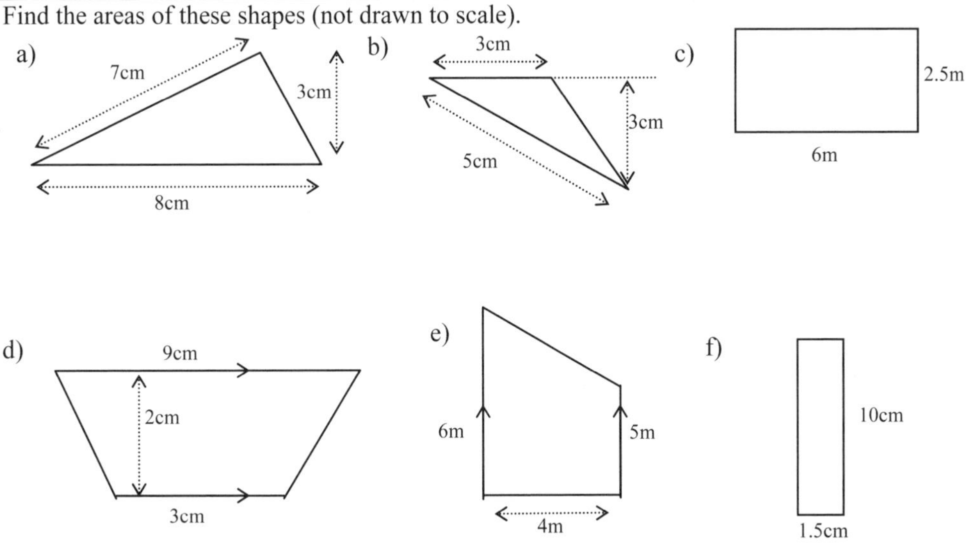


*Remember the units. Check the units are the same for any shape.*

*You must write down the units for the answers i.e. mm $^2$ or cm $^2$ or m $^2$.*

4. Find the areas of these shapes (not drawn to scale).

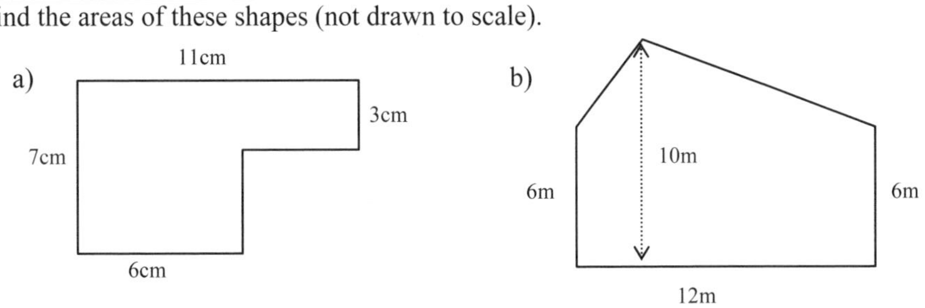


*Use a calculator - but show your working.*

*Don't forget the units.*

5. Find the volumes of these shapes (not drawn to scale).

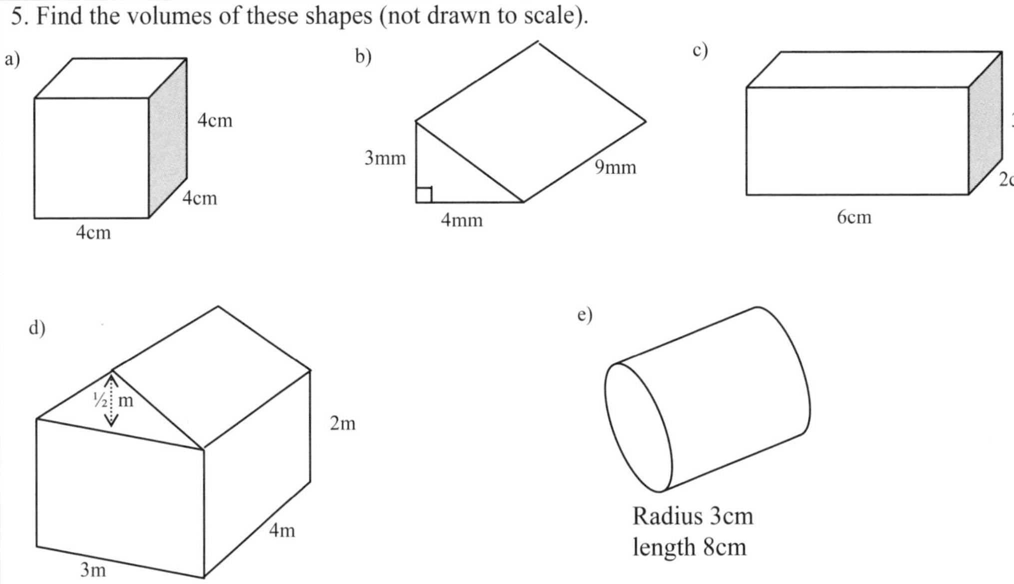


*a) volume of a cuboid.*

*b) A prism.*
*First find the area of the end. Area of a triangle.*
*Then multiply by the length to give the volume.*

*c) volume of a cuboid.*

*d) A prism.*
*First find the area of the end. Area of a triangle plus the area of the rectangle.*
*Then multiply by the length to give the volume.*

*e) The cylinder is a prism.*
*Area of cross section is the area of the circle.*
*Then × length to give volume.*
*Give answer to 3 sig.fig.*
*Don't forget the units.*

6. a) A square has a perimeter 30 m. What is the length of one side of the square?
   b) A rectangle has a perimeter of 36 cm. One length is 7 cm. What is the other length?

*The sides are all the same for a square!*
*If you are not sure, sketch the shape and put in the known lengths.*
*The sides add to give the perimeter.*

7. a) A square has an area of 64 cm $^2$. What is the length of one side of the square?
   b) A rectangle has an area of 54 cm $^2$. One length is 6 cm. What is the other length?

*Area is length × width.*
*Here you are working backwards.*

| Question | Hint |
|---|---|
| 8. a) A cube has a volume of 27 $cm^3$. What is the length of one side of the cube?<br>b) A cuboid has a volume of 96 $cm^3$. If the length of the cuboid is 4cm and the width is 2 cm, what is its height? | *Volume is*<br>*length × width × height* |
| 9. Giving your answers to 3 significant figures, find the circumference and area of<br>a) a circle of diameter 10 cm<br>b) a circle of radius 4 cm | *Use your calculator value of π.*<br>*Remember - check if you have been given the radius or the diameter and use*<br>*diameter = 2 × radius*<br>*to find the other value.* |
| 10. Giving your answers to 3 significant figures, find the circumference and area of<br>a) a circle of diameter 9 cm<br>b) a circle of radius 1.5 m | *Use your calculator value of π.*<br>*Remember - check if you have been given the radius or the diameter and use*<br>*diameter = 2 × radius*<br>*to find the other value.* |
| 11. Giving your answers to 3 significant figures, find the circumference and area of<br>a) a circle of diameter 15 cm<br>b) a circle of radius 12 mm | *Use your calculator value of π.*<br>*Remember - check if you have been given the radius or the diameter and use*<br>*diameter = 2 × radius*<br>*to find the other value.* |
| 12. Giving your answers to the nearest integer, find the circumference and area of<br>a) a circle of diameter 2.8 m<br>b) a circle of radius 4.3 cm | *Use your calculator value of π.*<br>*Remember - check if you have been given the radius or the diameter and use*<br>*diameter = 2 × radius*<br>*to find the other value.* |
| 13. Find the exact values of the circumference and area of a circle of radius 5 cm. | *For **exact** values leave π in your answers.*<br>*e.g. 100π* |
| 14. Find the perimeter of this semi-circle.<br>Give your answer to 3 significant figures.<br>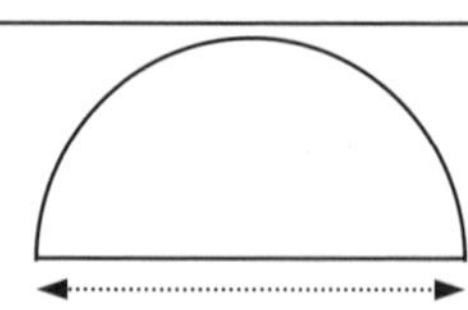<br> | *Half the circumference PLUS the diameter.* |
| 15. Find the radius of a circle whose circumference is $24\pi$ cm. | *Given the circumference. Use the formula to work out the diameter and then the radius.* |
| 16. A wheel has radius 15 cm. Work out:<br>a) how far the wheel travels in 20 rotations<br>b) how many complete rotations the wheel makes to travel a distance of 471 cm | *Work out the circumference. Use this to work out the distance travelled and the number of rotations.*<br>*a) to 3 sig. fig.* |

Note: For length: 1m = 100cm

For area $1m^2 = 100cm \times 100cm = 10000cm^2$

For volume $1m^3 = 100cm \times 100cm \times 100cm = 1\ 000\ 000cm^3$

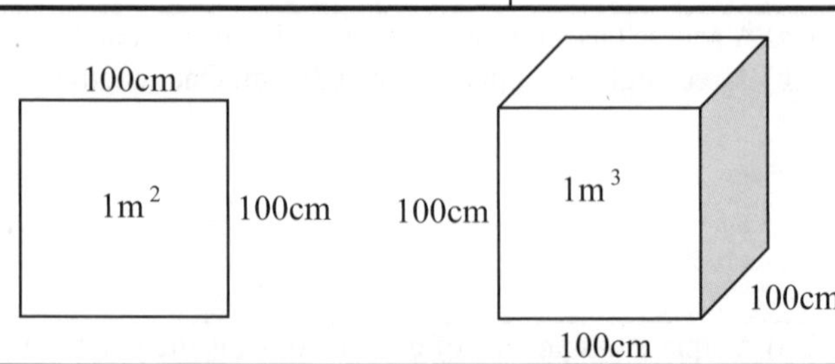


| Question | Hint |
|---|---|
| 17. Change 500 000 $cm^2$ to $m^2$ | *$100cm \times 100cm = 10\ 000cm^2 = 1m^2$*<br>*So ÷ by 10 000. (Be careful it is easy to make the mistake of dividing by 100)* |
| 18. Change 10 $m^2$ to $cm^2$ | *$100cm \times 100cm = 10\ 000cm^2 = 1m^2$*<br>*So × by 10 000* |

## Plotting points:

For a pair of coordinates

( 3 , 5 )

The $x$ coordinate.
This tells you how far to go across the grid.
+ to the right
- to the left

The $y$ coordinate.
This tells you how far to go up or down the grid.
+ to go up
- to go down

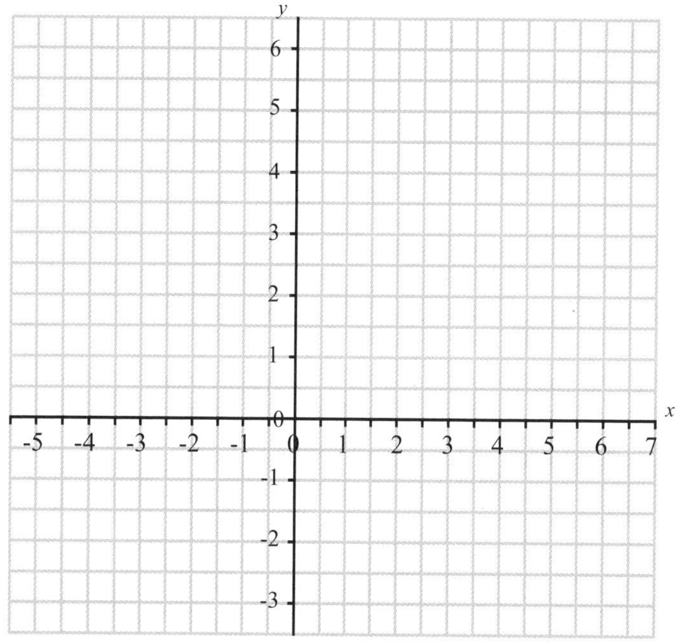

Plot the following point on this grid and label them A, B, C etc.

A (3, 5)
B (6, 1)
C (5, -3)
D (1, -2)
E (-5, 5)
F (-2, -3)
G (-2, 1)
H (-5, -3)
I (4, 0)
J (0, -1)

Use a cross like this + (as you can use the lines of the grid to help with accuracy)
Be as accurate as you can. If your crosses are not accurate you will not gain marks.

This is not accurate enough for the intersection of the grey lines.
If you are asked to mark with this type of cross make sure it crosses **exactly** at the point you want to indicate.

### Drawing straight line graphs:

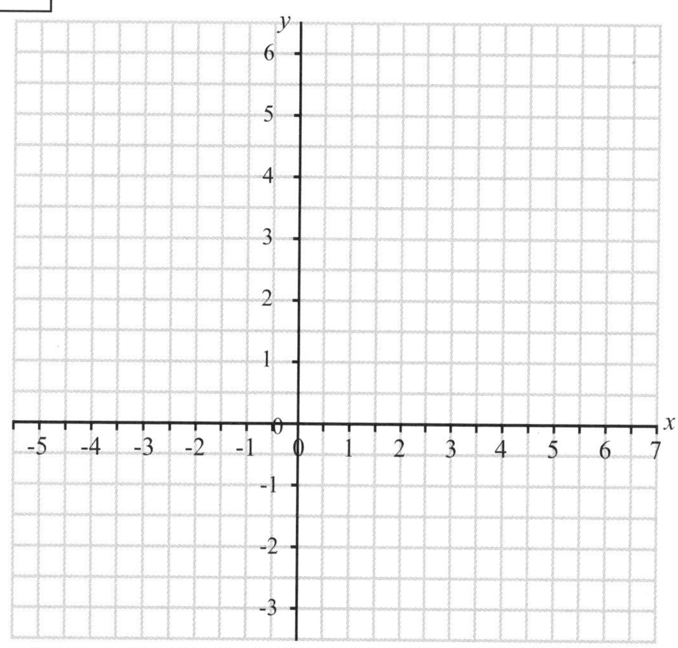

On the grid mark in the following points:
(0,4) , (1,4) , (3,4) , (5,4) , (-2,4) , (-4,4)
Join up the points.
Every point on the line has $y$ coordinate 4 so the line is called $y = 4$. Label the line.

On the grid mark in the following points:
(2,0) , (2,1) , (2,3) , (2,5) , (2,-1) , (2,-3)
Join up the points.
Every point on the line has $x$ coordinate 2 so the line is called $x = 2$. Label the line.

On the grid mark in the following points:
(0,0) , (1,1) , (2,2) , (-2,-2) , (-4,-4) , (-3,-3)
Join up the points.
Every point on the line has the same $x$ and y coordinates so the line is called $y = x$.
Label the line.

On the grid mark in the following points:
(0,0) , (1,-1) , (2,-2) , (2,-2) , (-4,4) , (3,-3)
Join up the points.
Every point on the line has the same value for $x$ and y but opposite sign.
The line is called $y = -x$. Label the line.

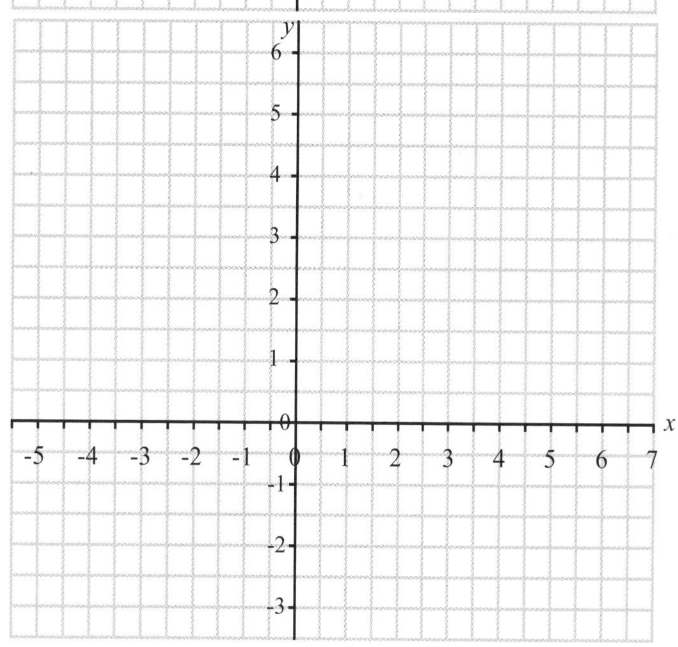

Now draw and label the following lines on the axes given.
$y = 1$, $y = 6$, $y = -2$, $x = 5$, $x = -1$, $x = -3$, $y = x$ and $y = -x$

## Transformations:

**Translations** - here the shape moves right/left and/or up/down by an amount given by a vector.

$\begin{bmatrix}2\\3\end{bmatrix}$ means 2 to the right and 3 up $\begin{bmatrix}-4\\5\end{bmatrix}$ means 4 to the left and 5 up $\begin{bmatrix}3\\-7\end{bmatrix}$ means 3 to the right and 7 down etc.

Translate triangle A by vector $\begin{bmatrix}4\\2\end{bmatrix}$ and label it B

Translate triangle A by vector $\begin{bmatrix}-7\\3\end{bmatrix}$ and label it C

Translate triangle A by vector $\begin{bmatrix}-4\\-2\end{bmatrix}$ and label it D

Translate triangle A by vector $\begin{bmatrix}2\\-5\end{bmatrix}$ and label it E

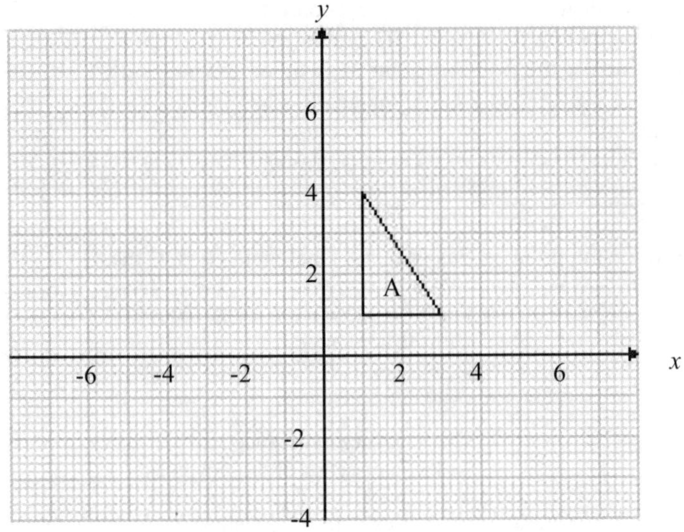


**Reflection** - here the shape and the image must fit exactly on top of each other if you fold the paper along the line of reflection. Reflect these shapes in the given lines.

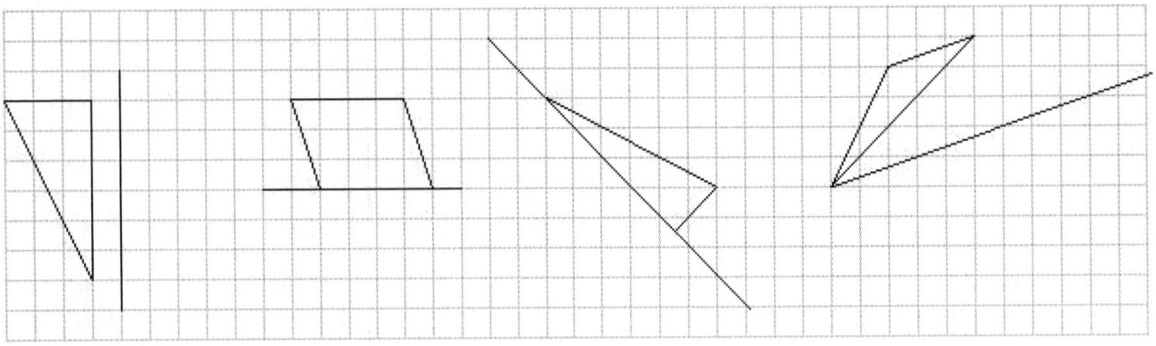

Reflect triangle A in the $x$ axis and label it B

Reflect triangle A in the $y$ axis and label it C

Reflect triangle A in the $y = x$ line and label it D
(the $y = x$ line goes through (1, 1) (2, 2) (3, 3) etc.)

Reflect triangle A in the $y = -x$ line and label it E
(the $y = -x$ line goes through (1, -1) (2, -2) (3, -3) etc.)

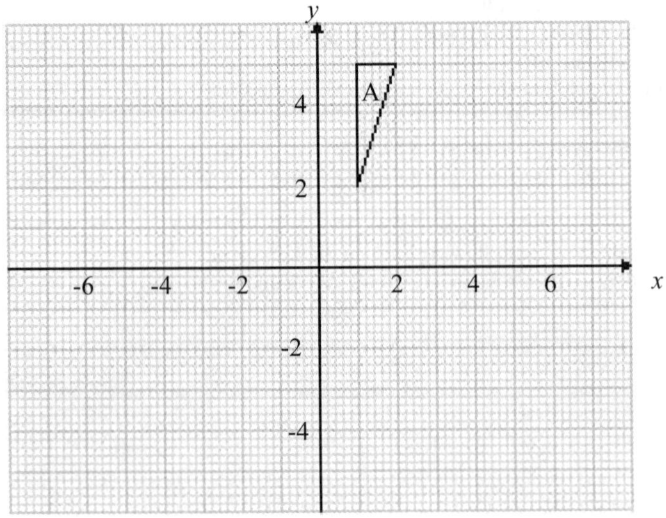

**Rotations** - here you need an angle, a direction of rotation and a point about which to rotate.

To rotate triangle A $90^\circ$ clockwise about the origin think about rotating the axes. Point X is 1 right and 2 up from the origin. Rotating the $x$ axis $90^\circ$ about the origin will make it point down, then X on the rotated triangle will be 1 down and 2 right from this line - at point X′
Complete the rotation. Label the triangle B.

Alternatively, use tracing paper. Place it so that it covers the triangle and the centre of rotation ( in this case the origin). Put x's where the corners of the triangle are. Put a pencil point on the centre of rotation to keep that point fixed and rotate the paper $90^\circ$. Note where the x's have moved to, lift off the tracing paper and draw the new triangle.

Rotate the triangle $180^\circ$ clockwise about the origin. Label the triangle C.

$+90^\circ$ means an anticlockwise rotation of $90^\circ$
$-90^\circ$ means a clockwise rotation of $90^\circ$

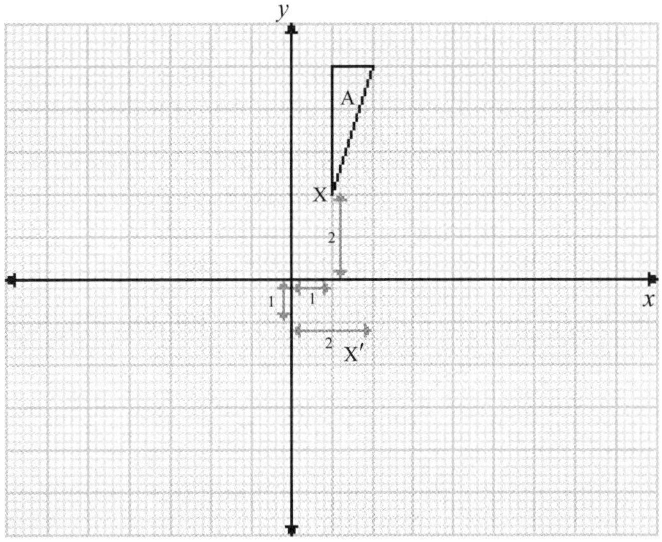


**Enlargements** - here you need a scale factor of enlargement and a centre of enlargement.

To enlarge triangle A by scale factor 2 with the origin as the centre of the enlargement first draw lines from the origin through each of the points of the triangle (the one through X has been drawn for you). X is 4 along and 2 up from the centre of enlargement. Multiply by the scale factor i.e. 8 along and 4 up. Plot X′ 8 along and 4 up from the centre of the enlargement. Complete the enlargement and label the triangle B.

**Notice the side lengths of triangle B are 2 times the lengths of triangle A.**

Enlarge triangle A by scale factor ½ using the origin as the centre of enlargement. Label the triangle C. (The triangle will be smaller - the side lengths of triangle C are half the lengths of triangle A.)

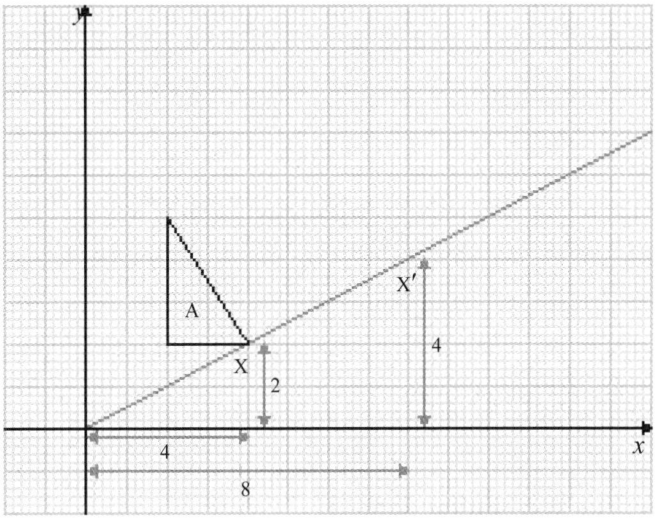


Complete:

Rotate the flag $90^\circ$ clockwise about the point (2, 2). Label P.

Enlarge the flag by scale factor 2 about the point (1, 2). Label Q.

Translate the flag by vector $\begin{bmatrix} 6 \\ -2 \end{bmatrix}$. Label R.

Reflect the flag in the line $x = 4$. Label S.

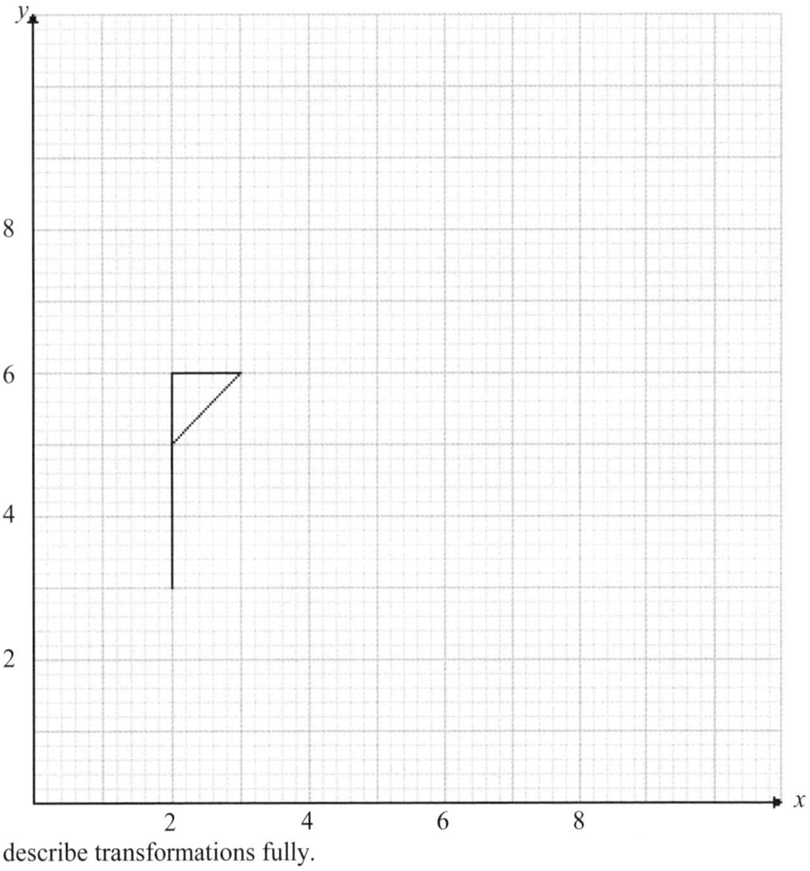


You need to be able combine transformations and describe transformations fully.

Check that you know how to:

1. Tell if one shape is a translated version of another – they will be the same shape, size and same way around.
2. Tell if one shape is a reflected version of another – one will fold over onto the other ( tracing paper will help ).
3. Tell if one shape is a rotated version of another – use tracing paper to help.
4. Find the centre of enlargement (draw lines through corresponding points and find where they intersect).

On the axes below are examples of each of these:
1. Which shape(s) is a translated version of another shape?
2. Which shape(s) is a reflected version of another shape?
3. Which shape(s) is a rotated version of another shape?
4. Which shape(s) is an enlarged version of another shape?
5. For each of questions 1 to 4 describe exactly the transformation which takes one shape onto the other.
   For example you might say to get from shape E to shape A you reflect in line $x = 1$ (which in this case is not correct)

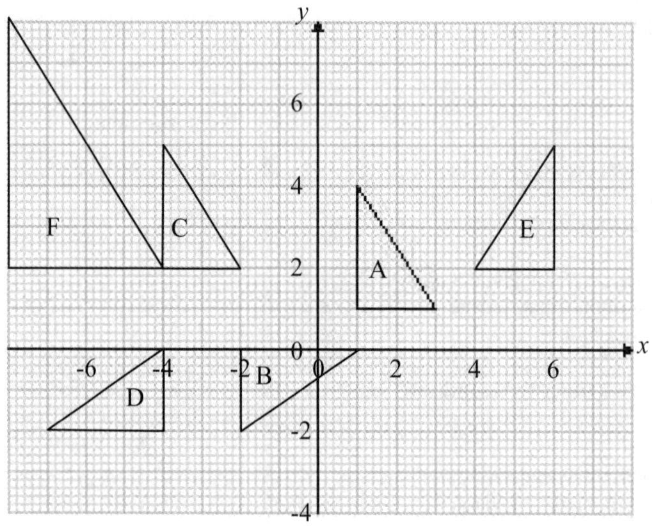


**Congruent and similar shapes:**

Congruent shapes: exactly the same SHAPE, exactly the same SIZE (may be rotated and/or reflected)

Similar shapes: exactly the same SHAPE, but <u>different</u> SIZES

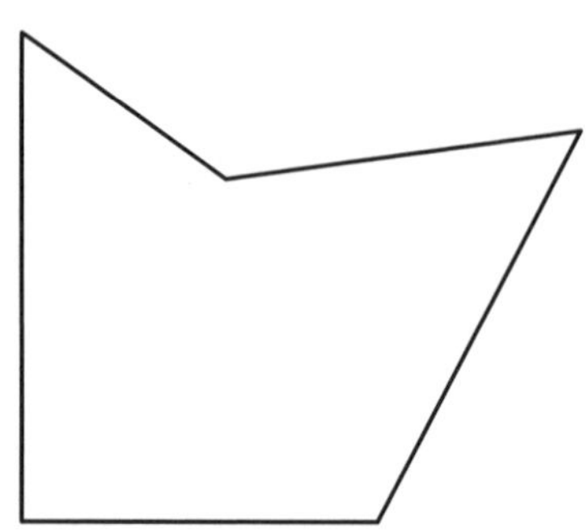

Two triangles are similar if they have the same angles.

Shapes with more than 3 sides are similar if corresponding angles are equal.

**Maps and scale drawings:**

Map scales are just ratios.

A Scale of 1 : 25 000 means 1 cm on the map is 25 000 cm in actual distance. (25 000 cm = 250 m = 0.25 km)

You may find it easier to take two zeros off and change it into m, so 1 : 25000 is the same as 1cm : 250m

Examples:

4 cm on the map is 4 × 250m = 1000m = 1 km actual distance.

10 km actual distance is 40 cm on the map since every 1cm is 250m = ¼ km, so 4cm on the map for every km.

| Question | Hint |
|---|---|
| 1. A road map has a scale of 1 : 50 000.<br>a) The distance between two towns on the map is 8 cm. What is the actual distance in km?<br><br>b) Two different towns are 9 km apart. What is the distance on the map? | *Just × or ÷ by 50 000 and convert units if necessary.*<br>*1:50 000 means 1cm on the map is 500m in actual distance. So 8 cm on the map is 8× 500m actual distance.*<br>*Change to km.*<br><br>*1cm is 500m ( or ½ km ), so you want to know how many ½ km make 9km.* |
| 2. A scale drawing of a house has a lounge 6 cm by 4.5 cm. If the scale is given as 1 : 125 what are the actual measurements of the lounge in metres? | *Just × or ÷ by 125 and convert units if necessary.* |
| 3. A scale drawing uses a scale of 1 : 500<br>a) A length on the drawing is 30 mm. What is the actual distance in m?<br><br>b) An actual length is 2.5 m. What is the distance on the scale drawing in mm? | *Remember: 10 mm = 1cm*<br>*100 cm = 1 m*<br><br>*Just × or ÷ by 500 and convert units.* |

**Bearings:**

Bearings are angles measured **clockwise from north**. Use 3 figures.

Using a scale of 1cm:1km, draw a scale drawing of the following journey: Starting at point B travel 5km on a bearing of 070° followed by 4 km on a bearing of 140°.

Note: it is useful to remember

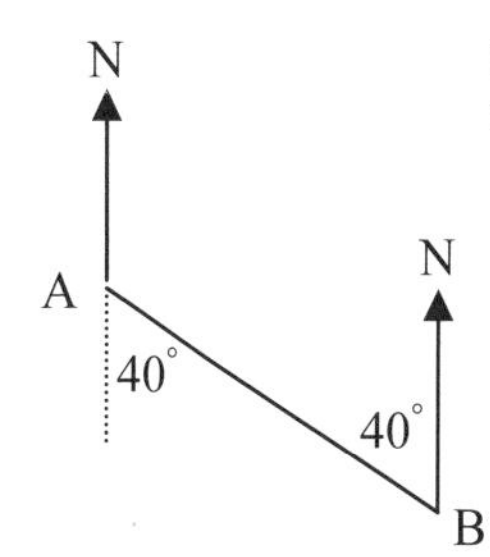


Diagram not drawn accurately.

These angles are the same (Alternate angles).

The bearing of B ***from*** **A** means that you measure at **A**. Here 140°

The bearing of A ***from*** **B** means that you measure at **B**. Here 360° - 40° = 320°

What is the bearing and distance of the start from the end?

Find and label point P which is on a bearing of 160° from A and a bearing of 205° from B. How far is it from A to P?

Scale 1: 50000

1. Write down the bearing of (i) P from O (ii) Q from O

Diagram not drawn accurately

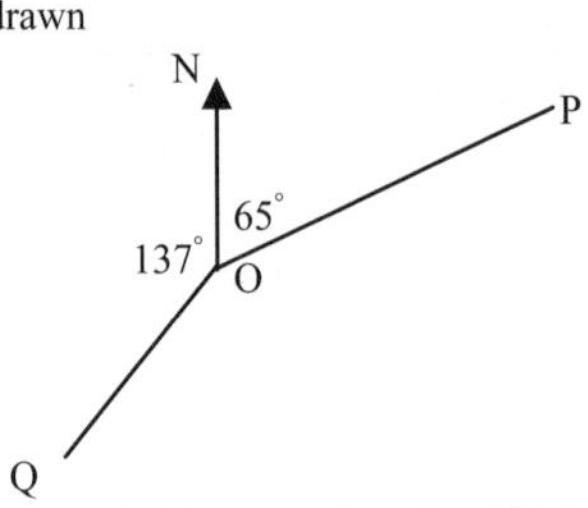


2. Write down the bearing of (i) S from R (ii) R from S

Diagram not drawn accurately

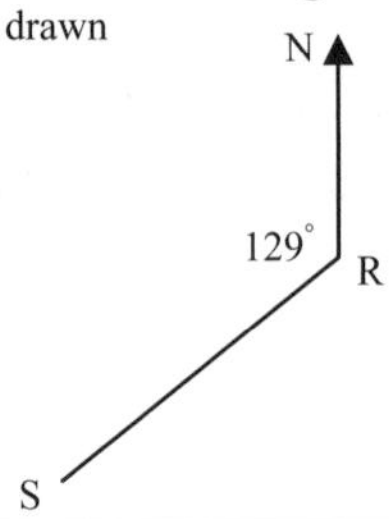


3. Brian travels from point A on course 055° for 6km and then goes on bearing 155° for 8.4km. After a rest he runs on course 260° for 5km. He then runs back to his starting point at point A. Draw his route using scale 1cm : 1km

a. On what bearing did he run on the final part of his journey?

b. How far did he run on this bearing?

4. Jim travels from point A on course 275° for 5km and then goes on bearing 205° for 6.5km. He then walks on course 085° for 8km and then jogs back to his starting point at point A. Draw his route using scale 1 : 100000

   a. On what bearing did he run on the final part of his journey?   b. How far did he go altogether?

5. John travels from point A on course 355° for 400m and then goes on bearing 275° for 720m. He then walks on course 222° for 380m and then jogs back to his starting point at point A. Draw his route using scale 1cm : 100m

   a. On what bearing did he run on the final part of his journey?   b. How far did he go altogether?

# Constructions

### Lines

A line is given by 2 letters eg. XY. Make sure that you measure accurately, correct to the nearet mm.

### Angles

An angle could be written in several ways using either one letter,eg. ∠A, or 3 letters eg. ∠ABC. If the angle has 3 letters then the angle is at the middle letter, so ∠ABC is at B. To see the angle draw it with your finger moving from A to B to C.

### Triangles

There are 3 basic types, follow the instruction to draw the examples given below:

a. Given 2 sides and the angle between them.
eg. Construct triangle ABC with AB = 4.2cm BC = 5cm ∠ABC = 50°

*Start by drawing the longest side BC 5cm long. Label B at one end and C at the other.*
*Put your protractor at B, measure 50° and put a pencil mark.*
*Draw a line from B 4.2cm long towards this mark. Label the end A.*
*Join A to C.*
*Use your ruler to measure AC and your protractor to measure ∠ACB.*
*If you have been accurate your answers should be:*
*AC =4cm and ∠ACB=55°*
*(answers ±1mm or ±1°)*

b. Given One side and 2 angles
eg. Construct triangle EFG with:
EF = 6.2cm ∠EFG = 53° ∠FEG = 45°

*Start by drawing EF 6.2cm long, label E at one end and F at the other.*
*Put your protractor at E, measure 45° and put a pencil mark.Draw a line from E through this mark.*
*Put your protractor at F, measure 53° and put a pencil mark.*
*Draw a line from F through this mark and continue it until it crosses the line you drew from E. If they don't cross extend the line you drew from E.*
*Label G the point where the lines meet. Use your ruler to join GE and GF.*
*Use your ruler to measure FG and EG.*
*If you have been accurate your answers should be:*
*FG =4.5cm and EG=5cm*
*(answers ±1mm or ±1°)*

c. Given all three sides
Eg. Construct triangle ABC with:
AB = 4.8cm BC = 5cm AC = 6.1cm

*Start by drawing the longest side AC 6.1cm long, label A at one end and C at the other.*
*Set your compasses to 5cm. Put your compass point on C and draw an arc.*
*Set your compasses to 4.8cm. Put your compass point on A and draw an arc which crosses the other arc. If they don't cross reset your compasses and extend the first arc.*
*Label B the point where the arcs meet. Join BC and BA with your ruler.*
*Use your ruler to measure ∠ABC and your protractor to measure ∠ACB.*
*If you have been accurate your answers should be:*
*∠ABC=79° and ∠ACB=53°*
*(answers ±1mm or ±1°)*

**Special Constructions and loci:**

Locus (plural loci) is the name given to a set of points that satisfy certain conditions.
Examples:

The locus of a point that is equidistant (the same distance) from a fixed point is a circle.

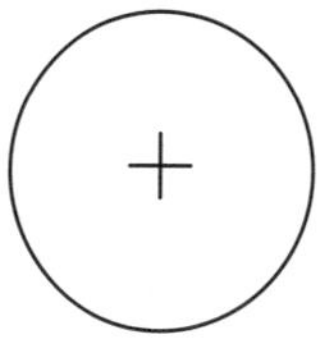

The locus of a point that is equidistant from a line of fixed length.

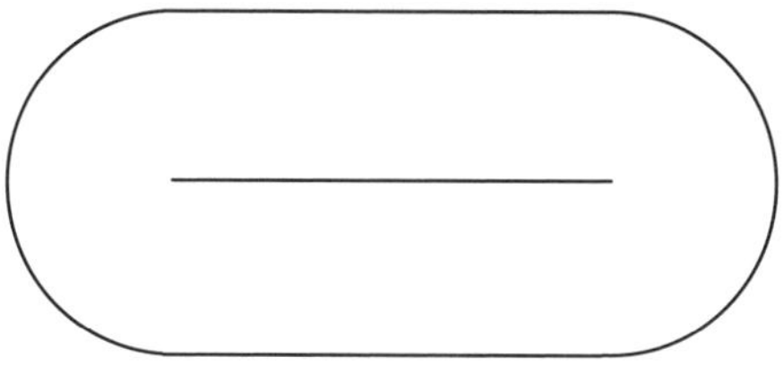

Draw the semi-circles with a pair of compasses.

Complete these:

## Angle Bisector

This is the locus of a point equidistant from two given lines

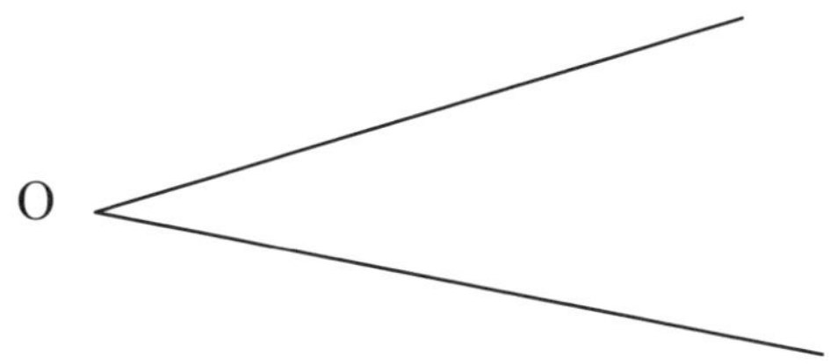


1. Set your compasses at any distance.
2. With the point of the compasses on O draw an arc that cuts both lines.
3. Put the point of the compasses where the arc cuts the top line and draw an arc so that it lies between the lines or where the lines would be if extended.
4. Repeat with the point of the compasses on the other intersection of the first arc and the bottom line. This should intersect with the second arc - if it does not then extend the arcs.
5. Join O with the point of intersection of the arcs and extend it. This is the required locus.

DO NOT RUB OUT YOUR CONSTRUCTION LINES.

## Perpendicular Bisector

This is the locus of a point that is equidistant from the two points A and B

1. Place the point of the compasses on A.
2. Open your compasses so that the distance is over half way.
3. Draw an arc above and below the line joining A and B.
4. Keep the compasses at the same distance apart. Place the point on B and draw an arc above and below the line joining A and B so that it cuts the other arcs. If it does not cut extend the arcs.
5. Join the intersections of the arcs with a straight line. This is the required locus.

DO NOT RUB OUT YOUR CONSTRUCTION LINES.

THE LOCUS IS THE *PERPENDICULAR BISECTOR* OF LINE AB.
- IT CUTS THE LINE AB IN HALF AT $90^\circ$ TO THE LINE.

Note: It also gives you the mid point of AB

## Perpendicular from a point to a line

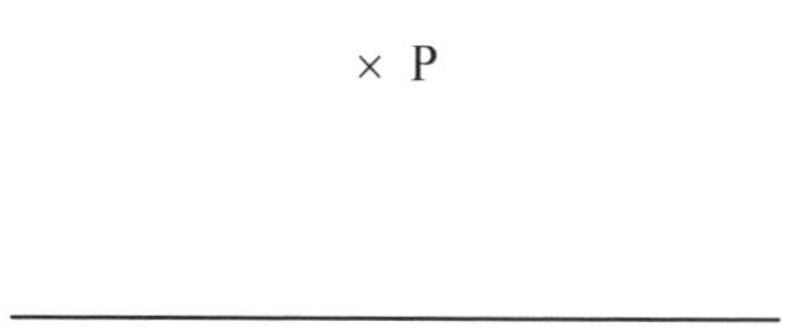


1. Place the point of the compasses on P.
2. Open your compasses so that the distance is past the line.
3. Draw an arc so that it cuts the line in two places. Label these points A and B.
4. Leaving the compasses the same distance apart place the point on A and draw an arc below the line.
5. Leaving the compasses the same distance apart place the point on B and draw an arc below the line so that it cuts the other arc. If it does not cut extend the arcs.
6. Join P to the point of intersection. This line is perpendicular to the given line.

DO NOT RUB OUT YOUR CONSTRUCTION LINES.

## Perpendicular from a point on a line

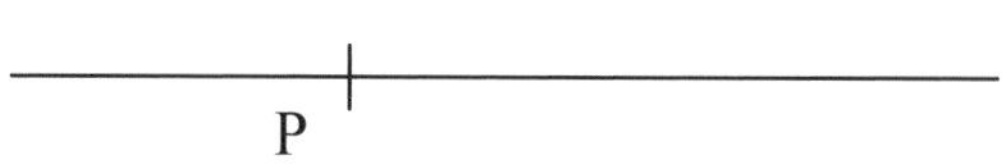


1. Place the point of the compasses on P.
2. Draw arcs that cut the given line either side of P. Label these points A and B.
3. Place the point of the compasses on A.
2. Open your compasses so that the distance is further than P.
3. Draw an arc above and below the line. (Could just do above or below).
4. Keeping the compasses at the same distance apart. Place the point on B and draw an arc above and below the line so that it cuts the other arc. If it does not cut, extend the arcs.
5. Join the intersections of the arcs with a straight line. This line through P is perpendicular to the line.

DO NOT RUB OUT YOUR CONSTRUCTION LINES.

## Mid point of a line:

Just add the $x$ coordinates together and divide by 2 and add the $y$ coordinates together and divide by 2.

e.g. for the points ( 7 , 6 ) and ( 1 , 4 ) the mid point is $\left(\frac{7+1}{2}, \frac{6+4}{2}\right)$ *i.e.* ( 4 , 5 ) (Check on graph above.)

Find the mid points of the lines joining these points and mark them on the graph.

| | |
|---|---|
| 1. ( 3 , -1 ) and ( 6 , 3 ) | 2. ( - 4 , -1 ) and ( 1 , -3) |
| 3. ( -1 , 3 ) and ( 2 , -2 ) | 4. ( -3 , 1 ) and ( -2 , 5 ) |

Now check that you can do these on your calculator

## Scales:

When reading scales look for simple counting patterns

e.g count in 1s

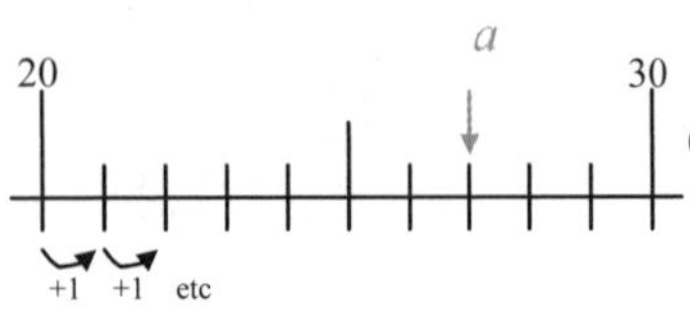


(30 - 20) ÷ 10 spaces = 1

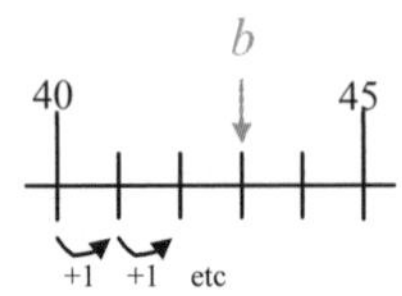


(45 - 40) ÷ 5 spaces = 1

or 2s

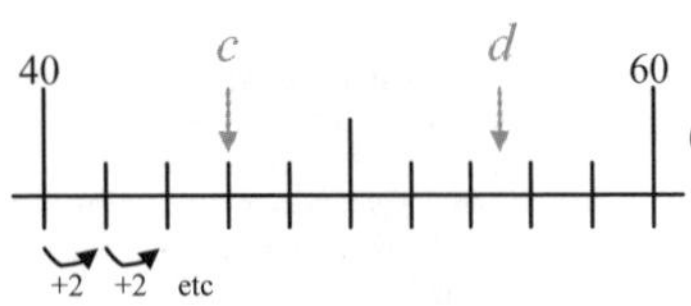


(60 - 40) ÷ 10 spaces = 2

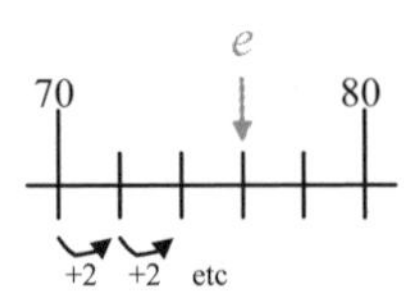


(80 - 70) ÷ 5 spaces = 2

or 5s

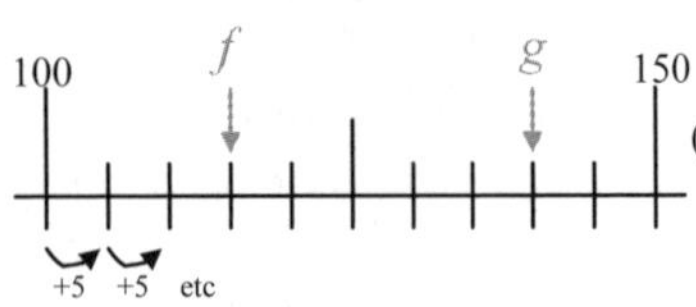


(150 - 100) ÷ 10 spaces = 5

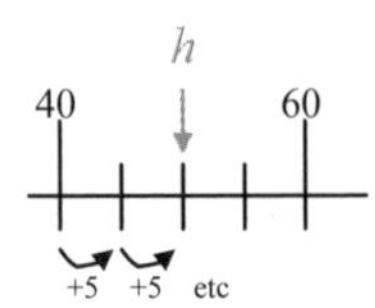


(60 - 40) ÷ 4 spaces = 5

or 10s or 20s

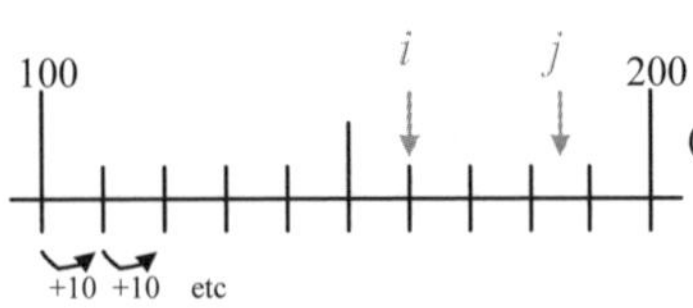


(200 - 100) ÷ 10 spaces = 10

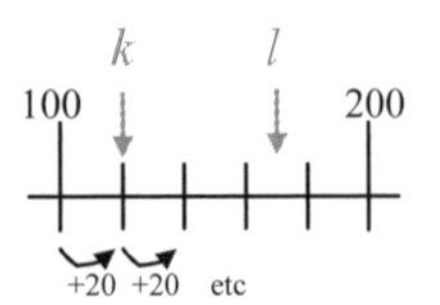


(200 - 100) ÷ 5 spaces = 20

or .1s

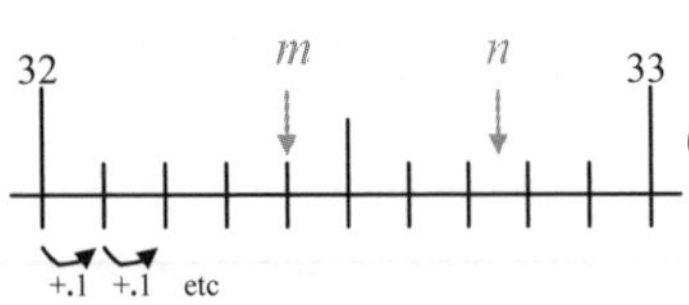


(33 - 32) ÷ 10 spaces = .1

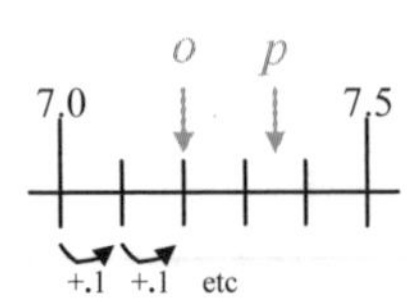


(7.5 - 7.0) ÷ 5 spaces = .1

or .2s

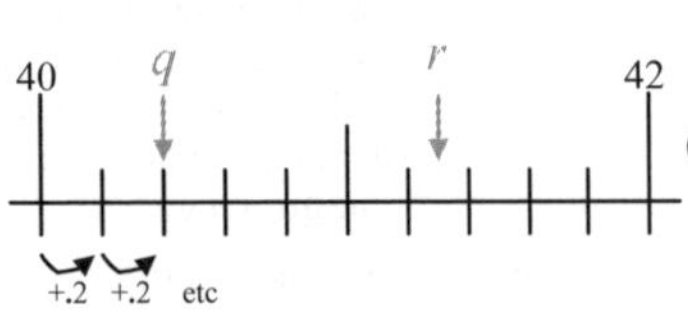


(42 - 40) ÷ 10 spaces = .2

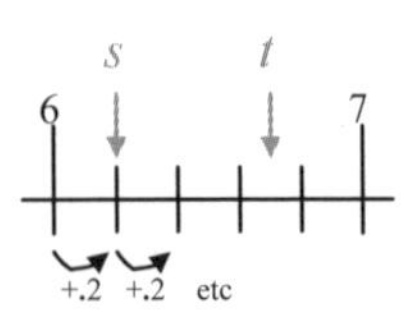


(7 - 6) ÷ 5 spaces = .2

or .5s

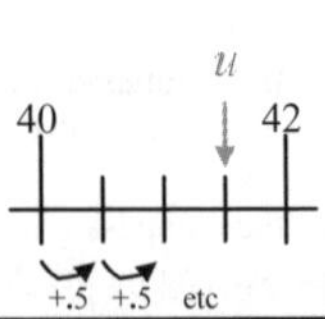


(42 - 40) ÷ 4 spaces = .5

5. Give the reading for each labelled arrow above.

| | | | | | | |
|---|---|---|---|---|---|---|
| *a.* | *b.* | *c.* | *d.* | *e.* | *f.* | *g.* |
| *h.* | *i.* | *j.* | *k.* | *l.* | *m.* | *n.* |
| *o.* | *p.* | *q.* | *r.* | *s.* | *t.* | *u.* |

6. Give the reading for each labelled arrow below.

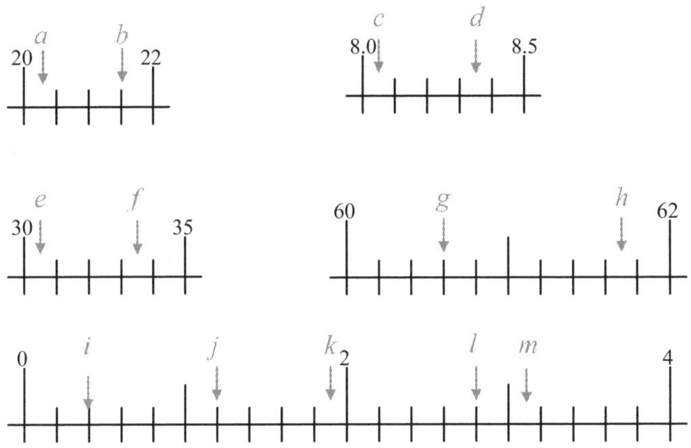


a.
b.
c.
d.
e.
f.
g.
h.
i.
j.
k.
l.
m.

*Be extra careful when the reading is in the first gap. It is easy to rush the reading and get it wrong.*
*a is **not** 20.5 it is between 20 and 20.5*
*c is **not** 8.5 it is between 8.0 and 8.1*

**Measurement:**

Metric and Imperial units: You should know these:

| | Metric | Imperial | Examples of when to use the units |
|---|---|---|---|
| LENGTH | 10 millimetres(mm) = 1 centimetre (cm)<br>100 centimetres (cm) = 1 metre (m)<br>1000 metres (m) = 1 kilometre (km) | 12 inches = 1 foot<br>3 feet = 1 yard | Km - distance between towns<br>m - length of a football pitch<br>height of a house<br>cm - length of a book<br>mm - length of a nail |
| MASS | 1000 grams (g) = 1kilogram (kg)<br>1000 kilograms (kg) = 1 tonne (t) | 16 ounces (oz) = 1 pound (lb)<br>14 pounds = 1 stone | tonne - weight of a lorry<br>Kg - weight of a bag of potatoes<br>g - weight of a bag of sweets |
| CAPACITY | 1 $cm^3$ or 1cc = 1 millilitre (ml)<br>1000 cubic centimetres (cc) = 1 litre (l)<br>1000 millilitres (ml) = 1 litre (l) | 8 pints = 1 gallon | ml - amount of liquid in a cup<br>l - amount of water in a pond |

Learn the following approximate conversions and use them to complete the questions below:

| | |
|---|---|
| 1 inch ≈ 2.5 centimetres | 2.2 lb ≈ 1 kg |
| 1 foot ≈ 30 centimetres | 1.75 pint ≈ 1 litre |
| 5 miles ≈ 8 kilometres | 1 gallon ≈ 4.5 litres |

1. Complete: a) 300 cm = m b) 6 kg = g c) 2 feet = inches

d) 5 km = m = cm e) 2000 cc = litres

f) 10 miles ≈ km g) 24 km ≈ miles h) 2 kg ≈ lb

i) 4 inches ≈ cm j) 20 oz = lb oz k) 7000 $cm^3$ = litres

2. Complete: a) 5400 cm = m b) 2.6 kg = g c) 3 feet = inches

d) 3.1 km = m = cm e) 6400 cc = litres

f) 50 miles ≈ km g) 184 km ≈ miles h) 3 kg ≈ lb

i) 8 inches ≈ cm j) 53 oz = lb oz k) 58900 $cm^3$ = litres

**Time:**

2 hours 45 minutes is **NOT** 2.45 hours ( a common error)

There are 60 minutes in an hour therefore 45 minutes is $\frac{45}{60}$ hour

So 2 hours 45 minutes is $2\frac{45}{60}$ hours = 2.75hours (as 45 ÷ 60 = 0.75)

For a calculator paper it is useful to be able to use the [DMS] or [° ' "] key

So 2h 45m would be entered [2] [° ' "] [4] [5] then press [=] to give the decimal number of hours.

7.4 hours can be changed to hours and minutes by entering

[7] [.] [4] [° ' "] [=]

> Your calculator may work differently. Check that you know how your calculator changes from decimal hours to hours and minutes and vice versa.
> OR
> minutes ÷ 60 gives decimal hours
> and decimal hours × 60 gives minutes.

Careful when finding a time difference. It is best not to take away one time from the other as you are more likely to make a mistake.

1. Complete: How long did a train journey take if the start time was 1350 and the finish time was 1623?

   1350 up to 1400 is ____ minutes (find the time up to the next whole hour)
   1400 up to 1600 is ____ hours (then the hours)
   1600 up to 1623 is ____ minutes (then the minutes)

   Journey time = ____ hours ____ minutes

2. Change these times to decimal hours:

   a) 3 hours 18 minutes b) 6 hours 51 minutes c) 12 hours 33 minutes

3. Change these decimal hours to hours and minutes

   a) 5.65 hours b) 8.7 hours c) 13.923 hours

4. Find the time it takes to travel from Brighton to Colchester if the departure time is 1842 and the arrival time is 2128.

   *Do this in stages as above.*

**Distance, Speed and Time problems:**

It is easiest to use the formula triangle to help solve problems.

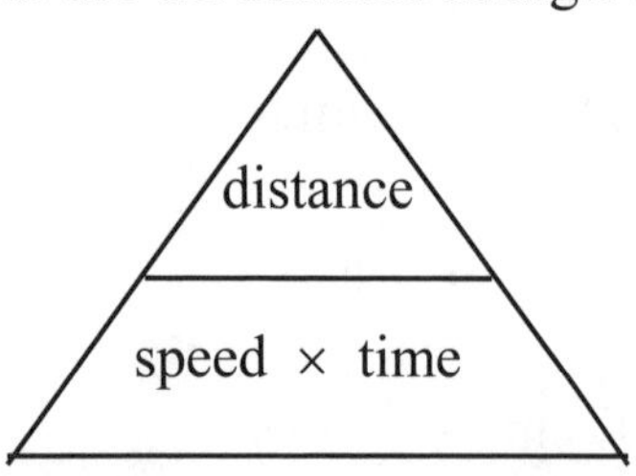


If you want to know what speed equals, cover up speed. This gives

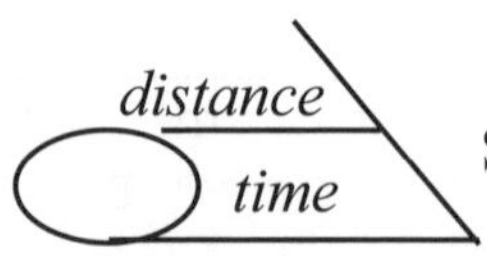


So $speed = \frac{distance}{time}$

If you want to know what distance equals, cover up distance. This gives $distance = speed \times time$ and so on.

5. A car travels at an average speed of 65 miles per hour. How far does it travel in 3 hours?

   *'how far' is a distance so use:*
   *Distance = speed × time*
   *Don't forget the units - speed was miles per hour so the distance will be miles.*

| Question | Hint |
|---|---|
| 6. It took an animal 2 hours to cover a distance of 5 km. What was the animal's average speed? | *Speed = distance / time*<br>*Remember a fraction is a division.*<br>*Top ÷ bottom* |
| 7. How long does it take for an object to travel 25 m at a speed of 4 m $s^{-1}$? | *Time required.*<br>*$ms^{-1}$ is m/s or metres per second*<br>*Time = distance / speed* |
| 8. A journey of 150 miles takes 3 hours 20 minutes. Calculate the average speed in mph. | *During the journey the speed may change - so we work out the average speed.*<br>*mph is miles per hour.*<br>*Miles on the top and time* ***<u>in hours</u>*** *on the bottom. Use fractions of an hour for the 20 minutes or write hours and minutes as decimal hours.* |
| 9. Find the time it takes, in hours and minutes, to travel a distance of 80 km at a speed of 35 km/h. | *km/h means kilometres per hour.*<br>*Use the triangle to give*<br>$time = \frac{distance}{speed}$<br>*i.e. ÷*<br>*Time will be in decimal hours.*<br>*Use your calculator to change to hours and minutes. Answer to nearest minute.* |
| 10. John cycles for 20 minutes at 36 km/h. How far does he travel? | *km/h means kilometres per hour.*<br>*Be careful with units! Since the speed is in kilometres per hour you must put the time into hours before using the triangle.*<br>*Use fractions.* |
| 11. If an object travels at 4 m/s for 18 seconds, find the distance travelled. Do not use a calculator. Show all working. | *Use the triangle to give distance.*<br>*A simple case of ×.* |
| 12. Chris runs 100 m in 15 seconds. What is his speed in km/h? | *Rememeber km/h is how far he will go in one hour.*<br>*Find how far he goes in 1 minute( ×4).*<br>*Then ×60 to find how far he goes in 1 hour.*<br>*Change m in km and now you have how many km he travels in 1 hour i.e. his speed in km/h.* |
| 13. A car travels at 40 km/h. How many seconds does it take to go 150 m ? | *Be careful with units. The distance is given in metres but the speed is in km/h, so change 150m into km and use the formula.*<br>$time = \frac{distance}{speed}$<br>*Your answer will be in hours. ×60 ×60 to change it firstly into minutes then into seconds.* |
| 14. James cycles for 2 hours at 30 km/h and then goes another 20 km at 40 km/h. What was his average speed? | *You cannot simply average the two speeds. To find the average speed you have to:*<br>*1. Find the total distance James travelled.*<br>*2. Find the total time he took.*<br>*3. Use the triangle with those amounts.*<br>*Speed = Distance/Time* |

# Test Yourself:

Try these questions. If you are unable to do a question go back and revise the relevant section.

1. Sketch the following shapes showing any lines of symmetry a) parallelogram b) rhombus c) trapezium d) regular pentagon

2. How many lines of symmetry does a circle have?

3. Find the angles marked with a letter. Diagrams not drawn accurately.

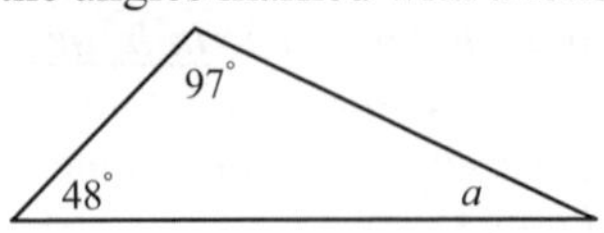


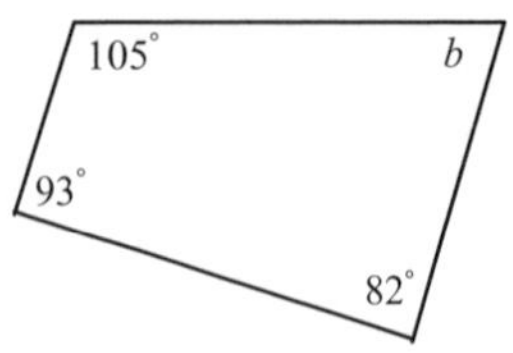


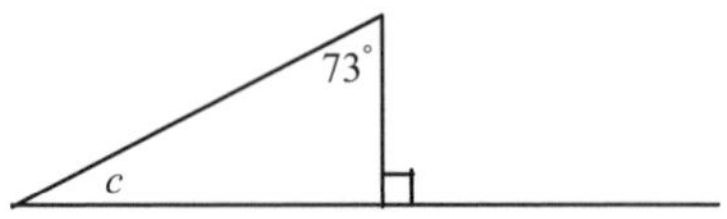


4. Find the angles marked with a letter. Diagrams not drawn accurately.

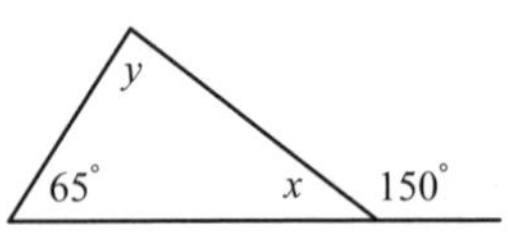


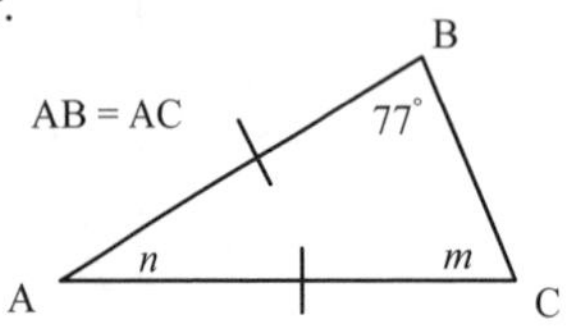


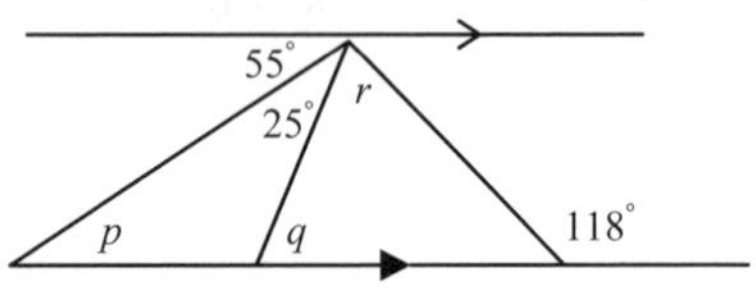


5. What is size of the interior angle of a regular decagon (10 sides)?

6. Draw the net of this square based pyramid with base side 3 units perpendicular height 2 units and the perpendicular height of each triangular face 2.5 units

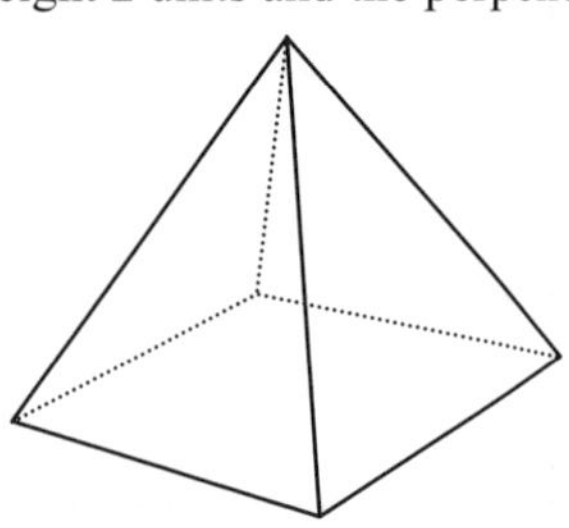

Net

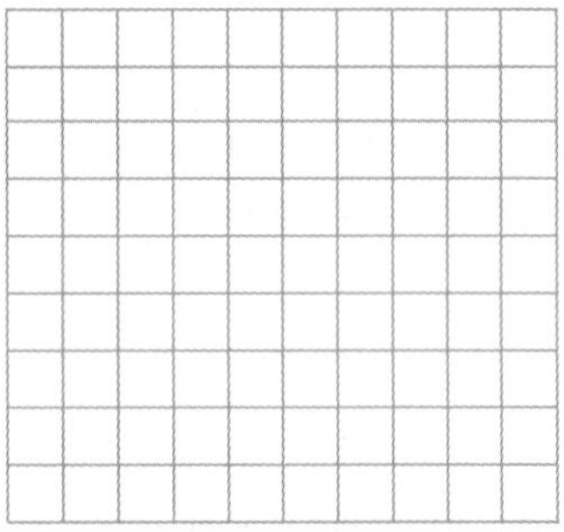

7. a) Find the perimeter and area of these shapes

i)

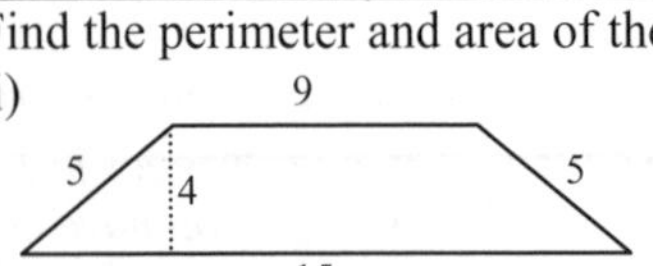


The lengths are in cm

(ii)

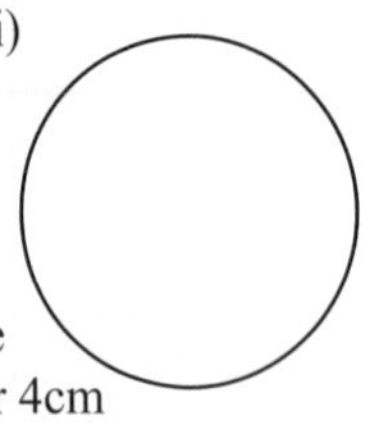

circle
diameter 4cm

b) If a)(i) is the end view of a container of length 20 cm, find the volume of the container.

8. a) Reflect triangle T in the line $y = x$. Label it R.
   b) Rotate triangle T through $90^\circ$ anticlockwise about the origin. Label it S.
   c) Reflect triangle T in the line $y = 0$ ($x$-axis) and then in the line $x = 0$ ($y$-axis). Label it P. Describe fully the single transformation that is equivalent to these two transformations combined.

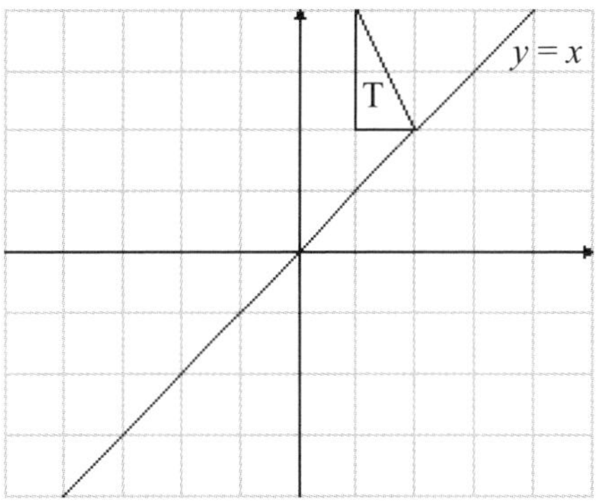


9. In the scale drawing a village church is at C and a Tudor house at T. The scale is 1cm to 100 m.
   What is the distance between the church and the house?
   A car park is on a bearing of $115^\circ$ from the church and $320^\circ$ from the house. Find the position of the car park and label it P.

C ×

× T

10. Find the mid-point of the line joining (5, 4) and (1, -2).

11. On the isometric grid draw a cuboid length 4 units, width 3 units and height 2 units.
    What is the surface area of the cuboid?
    What is volume of the cuboid?

12. On the isometric grid draw a cuboid with length 3 units, width 1 unit and height 2 units.
    Find:
    a. The surface area of the shape.

    b. The volume of the shape.

13. ABC is a scale drawing of a plot of land. A mast is to be erected on the plot. The mast is to be equidistant from AB and AC and equidistant from A and C. By using constructions, find and label the position of the mast, M, on the drawing.

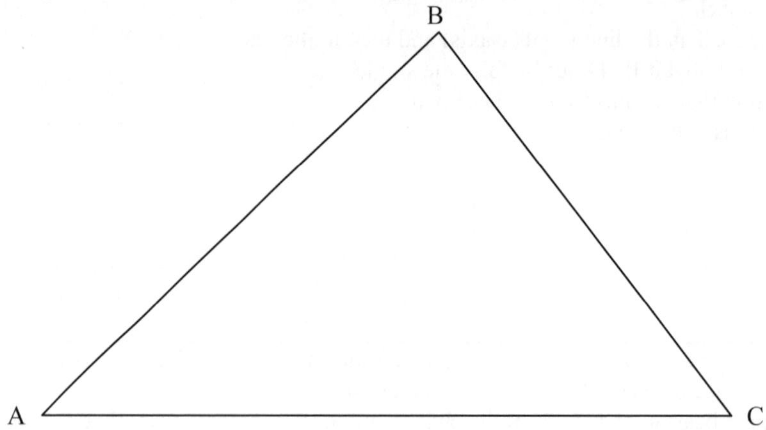


14. Construct an equilateral triangle of side length 5 cm.

15. Change a) 3568 m to km (b) 32.7 kg to g (c) 3.5 kg to lb. (d) 65 miles to km

16. Find the time difference between 0917 h and 1429 h.

17. A car travels 80 km at a speed of 64 km/h. How long does the journey take?

18. Jason cycles for 2 hours 20 minutes at a speed of 48 km/h. How far does he cycle?

# ALGEBRA and NUMBER

**Simplifying**

**i. Multiplying and Dividing – Rules of Indices:**

Index (plural : indices) means power $7^3$ means 7 raised to the power 3 or $7 \times 7 \times 7$

| | | | Examples |
|---|---|---|---|
| *Multiplying* | *ADD THE POWERS*<br>If the base number is the same. | $a^m \times a^n = a^{m+n}$ | $3^2 \times 3^3 = 3 \times 3 \times 3 \times 3 \times 3 = 3^5$<br>$z^3 \times z^7 = z^{10}$ |
| *Dividing* | *SUBTRACT THE POWERS*<br>If the base number is the same. | $\frac{a^m}{a^n} = a^m \div a^n = a^{m-n}$ | $7^6 \div 7^2 = \frac{7\times7\times7\times7\times7\times7}{7\times7} = 7^4$ |

Note $\frac{a^7}{a^7} = 1$ and $a^7 \div a^7 = a^{7-7} = a^0$ so $a^0 = 1$ for any $a$ *(a not zero)* — $6^0 = 1$, $x^0 = 1$

Any number to the power 1 is itself……. .so $a^1 = a$ for any $a$ — $7^1 = 7$, $x^1 = x$

And … 1 to any power is still 1 — $1^5 = 1$

1. Complete: Simplify the following

i. $x^4 \times x^5 =$ ii. $y^2 \times y^2 =$ iii. $x^3 \times x =$

*Just use the rules of indices.*

iv. $p^{10} \div p^2 =$ v. $\frac{x^8}{x^3} =$ vi. $\frac{x^2}{x} =$

*x on its own is the same as $x^1$*

vii. $\frac{x^7}{x^4} =$ viii. $z^2 \times z^5 \div z^3 =$

ix. $2x^3 \times 4x^2 = 2 \times x^3 \times 4 \times x^2 = 2 \times 4 \times x^3 \times x^2 =$

x. $5x^2 \times 3x =$

*Deal with the numbers and letters separately.*

xi. $3k^2 \times 4k^3 =$

xii. $6q^5 \div 2q^3 =$

*Work out $6 \div 2$ and $q^5 \div q^3$ separately.*

xiii. $12q^3t^4 \div 3qt^2 =$

*Work out $12 \div 3$, $q^3 \div q$ and $t^4 \div t^2$ separately.*

xiv. $\frac{12h^2y^4}{8hy^4} =$

*Remember a fraction is the same as a division.*

xv. $\frac{16p^3r^4}{8pr^5} =$

xvi. $\frac{12h^2y^7}{18h^5y^4} =$

**ii. Addition and Subtraction – Collecting Like Terms:**

A term is a collection of numbers, letters, functions and brackets all multiplied together.

e.g. $3x^2y$ and $5\sqrt{x}$ and $x^2$ are three different terms.

"Like terms" have exactly the same combination of letters - e.g. $x$ terms or $x^2y$ terms

Like terms can be added or subtracted. The sign in front of the term goes with the term. If there is no sign at the beginning of the expression then it is a +

| | |
|---|---|
| 1. Simplify the following by collecting like terms.<br>Complete:<br>(i) $3x + 7y - 5x + 2y = 3x - 5x +$     $=$     $+$<br>$=$<br>(ii) $x^2 - 3x + 5x^2 - 4x - 3x^2 = x^2 + 5x^2 - 3x^2 -$<br>$=$ | *Collect similar terms together and then combine them.*<br>*9y-2x is slightly neater than -2x+9y* |
| 2. Simplify (i) $y + y + y =$    (ii) $3x + 2x =$    (iii) $8m - 2m =$<br>(iv) $2 \times p =$    (v) $r \times r =$    (vi) $p \times 2 \times q =$ | |
| 3. Simplify<br>(i) $x + 6 + 2x - 2 =$    (ii) $3x - 2 - 5x + 8 =$<br>(iii) $2 + 8x - 9 - 2x + 4 =$<br>(iv) $x^2 - 3x + 5x - 6$    (v) $m^2 - 6m + 10m + 8$ | *Add or subtract the xs and add or subtract the numbers. Remember the sign in front of the term goes with the term.*<br>*(iv) $x^2$s cannot be added or subtracted from xs*<br>*(v) Just ms instead of xs* |

**Substitution and Formulae:**

Don't be tempted to just write down an answer - you need to practise first to gain understanding and confidence.

REMEMBER: $2x^2$ means 2 lots of $x$ squared so if $x = 5$, $2x^2 = 2$ lots of $25 = 50$,

BUT $(2x)^2$ means the term $2x$ is squared, so if $x = 5$, $(2x)^2 = (2 \times 5)$ all squared $= 10^2 = 100$

Work out brackets and powers first then do multiplications and divisions before addition and subtraction.

| | |
|---|---|
| 1. Complete: Using the values a = 4 b = 5 c = -2, evaluate<br>i) 3a + c = (3 ×    ) + (   ) =<br>ii) 2ab - c = (2 ×    ×    ) - (   ) = | *Put the -2 in brackets.*<br>*Work out times and divide before add and subtract*<br>*-(-2) = +2*<br>*Work out times and divide before add and subtract* |
| 2. Using the values a = 4 b = 5 c = -2, evaluate<br>i) 3ab + 3c = (3×4×5) + 3×(-2) =<br>ii) 2b + $c^2$ = (2×5) + $(-2)^2$ =<br>iii) a - $c^2$ =<br>iv) a(c - b) = 4×( [-2] - [5] ) = 4×(   ) =<br>v) a(b - c) = 4×( [5] - [-2] ) = 4×(   ) = | *Work out times and divide before add and subtract*<br>*$(-2)^2 = 4$*<br>*Work out times and divide before add and subtract*<br>*Work out the power first then do the subtraction*<br>*Work out the bracket first then do the multiplication.*<br>*-2 -5 = -7*<br>*5 - -2 = 5 + 2 = 7* |

| | |
|---|---|
| 3. If $x = -4$, $y = 3$ and $z = 2$, evaluate the following | *Work out brackets and powers first then do multiplications and divisions before addition and subtraction.* |
| a) $10 - x^2$ | *Put the -4 in brackets* |
| b) $(2x)^2 - 3y^2$ | *Work out 2×(-4) then square. Work out $y^2$ then times by three. Then subtract.* |
| c) $xy^2$ | |
| d) $-7 - 2x$ | *Put the -4 in brackets* |
| e) $4xyz - \frac{xy}{3z}$ | *Put the -4 in brackets* |
| f) $\frac{(4y - z^2)}{(4y - z)^2}$ | *Work out the brackets first.* |
| 4. Express the perimeter, P, of the given rectangle in terms of $x$ and $y$. | *This means write P = .............* *With xs and ys on the right hand side.* |
| 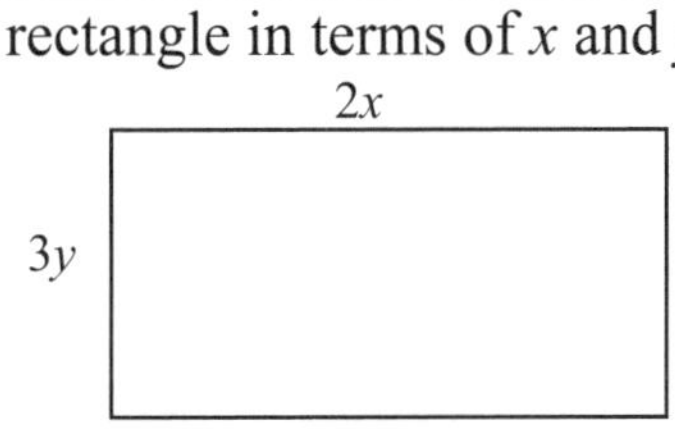 | |
| a) Find P if $x = 7$ and $y = 2$ | *Substitute for x and y to find P.* |
| b) Find $x$ if P = 56 and $y = 4$ | *Substitute for P and y and rearrange to find x.* |
| 5. Express the perimeter, P, of the given triangle in terms of $x$ and $y$. | *This means write P = .............* *with xs and ys on the right hand side.* |
| 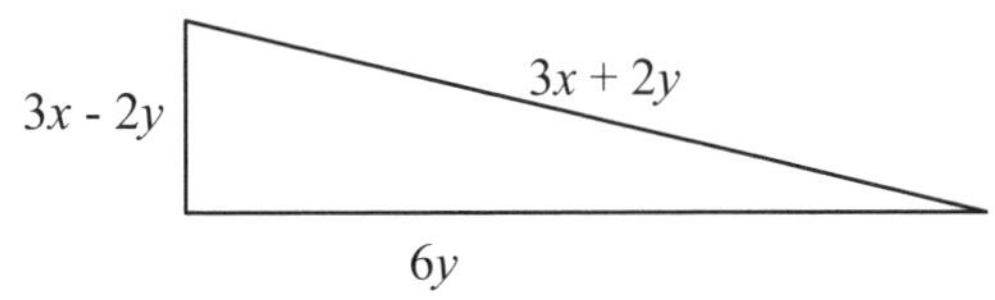 | |
| Find P if $x = 3$ and $y = 2$ | *Substitute for x and y to find P.* |
| 6. If $q = pr$ (a) find $q$ when $p = 7$ and $r = 8$ (b) find $r$ when $q = 36$ and $p = 4$ | |
| 7. The volume of a box is given by $V = x(x - 1)(x - 4)$. Find the volume if $x = 7$ cm. | *Do not multiply the brackets out! Just substitute for x and find the product.* *The answer will be in cm³.* |
| 8. If $C = \frac{5}{9}(F - 32)$ is the formula which changes Fahrenheit into Celsius, find the Celsius equivalent of $86^\circ$F . | *Just write down the formula with the numbers substituted in and then work out the answer.* |
| 9. When $x = -2$ find the value of the following | |
| (a) $x^2 + 5x$ | *Put the -2 in brackets.* |
| (b) $x^2 - 3x - 2$ | |

**Brackets:**

A term outside a bracket multiplies each of the terms inside the bracket.

| | |
|---|---|
| 1. Remove the brackets and collect like terms.<br>Complete:<br>i) $2(y + 1) = \ 2 \times y + 2 \times 1 =$ (ii) $5(m - 2) =$<br>iii) $4(x + 3) =$ (iv) $x(x - 2) =$<br>v) $2(p - 5q) =$ vi) $-(5p - 6) =$<br>vii) $-2p(6p + pq - 2) = -2\times6\times p\times p + -2\times$ $+ -2\times$<br>$=$ | *-(5p - 6) = -1×(5p - 6)*<br>*– sign outside the brackets changes each of the signs inside the brackets when you multiply it out.* |
| 2. Remove the brackets and simplify in the following<br>Complete:<br>a) $8(3c - 10) =$<br>b) $-(7 - 3d) =$<br>c) $4f - 2(3f + 7) =$<br>d) $g(2g - 4) - (3g - 5) =$<br>e) $3j(4j + 5hj - 2) =$ | *8 times 3c and 8 times -10*<br>*Remember - (......) means -1 × (......)*<br>*(-2)× 3f = -6f and (-2)× (+7) = -14*<br>*Collect together like terms.*<br>*Remove the brackets and then simplify* $g\times 2g = 2g^2$<br>*Remember - (......) means -1 × (......)*<br>*3j times each term.* |

**Factorising:**

This is putting the brackets back in.

Look at each term and see what factors (letters or numbers) are common to each term.

Write down these factors and then brackets. Inside the brackets write down the terms that when multiplied by the factor/s outside give the equivalent expression.

| | |
|---|---|
| Example Factorise a) $2a + 12$ b) $9p^2 - 3p$<br>c) $12m^2n^3 + 20mn^2$<br>a) $2a + 12 = 2 \times a + 2 \times 2\times 3 = 2(a + 6)$<br>b) $9p^2 - 3p = 3 \times 3 \times p \times p - 3 \times p = 3p(3p - 1)$<br>c) $12m^2n^3 + 20mn^2 = 2\times2\times3\times m\times m\times n\times n\times n + 2\times2\times5\times m\times n\times n$<br>$= 2\times2\times m\times n\times n(3\times m\times n + 5)$<br>$= 4mn^2(3mn + 5)$ | *a) 2a as a product of factors can be written 2 × a*<br>*12 as a product of prime factors 2 × 2 × 3*<br>*2 is common to both. Write this down. Write what is left in brackets.*<br>*b) 9p² as a product of factors can be written 3 × 3 × p × p*<br>*3p as a product of factors can be written 3 × p*<br>*3×p is common to both. Write this down. Write what is left in brackets. Here the 3p term has all been used. So you must write down -1. This is so that when the bracket is multiplied out you get 3p × -1 which gives the -3p*<br>*c) 12m²n³ as a product of factors can be written 2×2×3×m×m×n×n×n*<br>*20 m n² as a product of factors can be written 2×2×5×m×n×n*<br>*2×2×m×n×n is common to both. Write this down. Write what is left in brackets.* |

3. Factorise

a) $10x + 5$ b) $8x - 12$

c) $x^2 - 2x$ d) $x^2 + 5x$

e) $2x^2 + 10x$ f) $3x^2 + 9x$

g) $x^2 - 3x$ h) $6x + 4$

4. Factorise

a) $15xy + 5x$ b) $6x - 12$

c) $30a^2b - 12ab^2$ d) $5xy^2 + 20xy$

e) $4abc + 6bcd$ f) $9xy - 27x$

g) $8p^2q - 6pq^3$ h) $y^2 - y$

**Writing algebra - Expressions:**

Examples:

John has £3 more than Jane. If Jane has £$x$ how much does John have?

Think about numbers — If Jane had £5 John has £5 + £3
If Jane had £6 John has £6 + £3
If Jane had £$x$ John has £$x$ + £3 or £$(x + 3)$

Pens cost 12 pence and pencils cost 9 pence. How much do $x$ pens and $y$ pencils cost?

2 pens cost $2 \times 12$ — 2 pencils cost $2 \times 9$
3 pens cost $3 \times 12$ — 3 pencils cost $3 \times 9$
$x$ pens cost $x \times 12 = 12x$ — $y$ pencils cost $y \times 9 = 9y$
$x$ pens and $y$ pencils cost $12x + 9y$

If I spend 117pence on pens and pencils, write an equation to show this.

$$12x + 9y = 117$$

1. a) J has $x$ cards. He gives 5 cards away. Write down, in terms of $x$, how many cards J has left.

   b) S has $y$ computer games. each game cost £9. Write down, in terms of $y$, the total cost of S's games.

2. P has £$x$ . Q has £20 more than P. R has three times as much as P. Write down, in terms of $x$,

   a) how much Q has — b) how much R has

   c) If P, Q and R have £100 in total write down and simplify an equation in $x$.

3. A college buys $x$ chairs at £45 each and $y$ tables at £78 each.

   a) How much do the chairs cost?

   b) How much do the chairs and tables cost?

   c) If the college spends £1680 on chairs and tables write down an equation in $x$ and $y$.

4. Ice cream cones cost £ $x$ and ice lollies cost £ $y$

   If 2 ice cream cones and 4 ice lollies cost £8 write down an equation in $x$ and $y$.

   If 3 ice cream cones and 3 ice lollies cost £9 write down a second equation in $x$ and $y$.

   Find $x$ and $y$ by drawing graphs of these equations on the grid.

**Linear Equations:**

Equations are algebraic statements containing an equals sign.
Linear equations contain only numbers and usually one variable such as $x$, with no powers involved.
Here are some examples:
$3x - 2 = 10$, $5x + 1 = 2x + 7$

When you solve a linear equation, you find the value of $x$ (or $y$ or $p$ or....) that makes the equation work:
for that value of $x$ the left hand side (LHS) of the equation equals the right hand side (RHS).
To solve a linear equation you want to end up with $x =$ the solution.
To do this remember

- the equation remains true as long as you do the same thing to both sides
- collect all the $x$ terms on one side of the equation and the numbers on the other
- if there is a fraction in the equation, multiply every term by the denominator to simplify the equation

Solve the following equations:

| | | | |
|---|---|---|---|
| 1. $x + 8 = 11$ | *Subtract 8 from both sides.* | 2. $5x = 35$ | *Divide both sides by 5.* |
| 3. $2t + 2t = 32$ | *First add the ts Then divide both sides by 4.* | 4. $3p - 8 = 7$ | *Add 8 to both sides. Then divide by 3.* |
| 5. $6y = 24$ | *Divide both sides by 6.* | 6. $8 - x = 2$ | *Add x to both sides. Subtract 2 from both sides.* |

| | |
|---|---|
| 7. $3x - 2 = 10$<br>$3x =$<br>$x =$ | *Add 2 to both sides.*<br>*Divide all terms by 3.* |
| 8. $5 - 2x = 11$ | *Take 5 from both sides (or move the 5 across the equals sign and it becomes -5).*<br>*Divide all terms by -2.* |
| 9. $5x + 1 = 2x + 7$ | *Take 1 from both sides.*<br>*Take 2x from both sides.*<br>*Divide all terms by 3.* |
| 10. $4(q + 1) = 2q + 11$ | *Simplify the expression first, by removing the brackets.*<br>*Then collect x terms together and numbers together.*<br>*Take 2q from both sides, then take 4 from both sides.*<br>*Then divide both sides by 2.* |
| 11. $4x - 2(x + 1) = 5(x + 3) + 5$ | *Simplify the expression first, by removing the brackets.*<br>*Then collect x terms together and numbers together. ( Take 2x from both sides, then take 20 from both sides. )*<br>*Divide all terms by 3. Leave as a fraction. Answer can be negative.* |

Remember: if there is a fraction in the equation, multiply every term by the denominator to simplify the equation.

| | |
|---|---|
| 12. Complete: Solve this equations<br>$10 = \frac{x}{6}$<br>$10 \times \quad =$<br>$=$ | *Normally it is sensible to remove fractions as a first step to solving equations.*<br>*Multiply both sides of the equation by 6. On the RHS the 6 terms cancel.* |

| | |
|---|---|
| 13. Solve the equation $12 = 2x - 8$ | *Best to leave the x term on the RHS So add 8 to both sides. Then divide by 2. finally write x = ....* |
| 14. Find the value of $x$ for which $7 - 3x = 5 - 2x$ | *In this question collect xs on the right and you get -2x+3x = x but try to collect them on the left and you get -3x+2x = -x which you may want to avoid as it is negative.* |
| 15. Find $x$ if $\frac{x}{4} = \frac{3}{5}$ | *The denominators 4 and 5 are both factors of 20. Multiply all terms by 20 and the fractions will disappear. (or multiply by 4 and then by 5)* |
| 16. Find $x$ if $3 = \frac{12}{x}$ | *Multiply both sides by x.* <br> *Divide both sides by 3.* |

Writing down and solving equations

| | |
|---|---|
| 17. For each of the following write down an equation and then solve it to find the number.<br>a) Three times a number is 39<br>b) Eight added to a number is 25<br>c) A number minus fourteen equals 39<br>d) Four added to three times a number is 31 | *Call the number x.* |
| 18. The length of a rectangle is four times its width. If the perimeter is 60 cm write down an equation showing this information. Solve this equation to find the length of the rectangle. | *Call the width x. The length is four times this. The perimeter is the length of the boundary.* |
| 19. The length of a rectangle is twice its width. If the area is 98 cm$^2$ write down an equation showing this information. Solve this equation to find the length of the rectangle. | *Call the width x. The length is two times this. The area is the length times the width.* |
| 20. The angles at a point are $x$, $x + 10^\circ$, $x + 20^\circ$, $x + 30^\circ$ and $x + 40^\circ$. Find $x$. 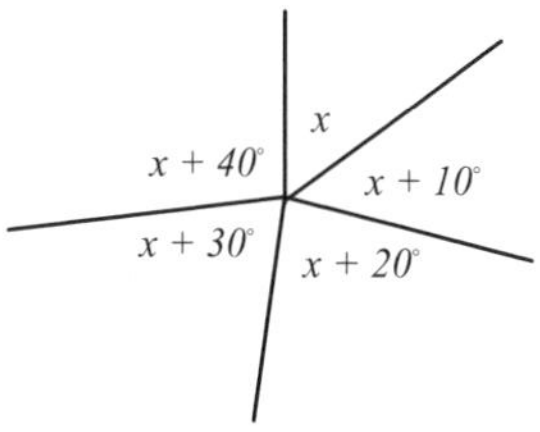 | *Remember: the angles at a point add to give..........* |

| | |
|---|---|
| 21. Find the angle $y$ in a triangle that has angles $y$, $2y$ and $90^\circ$ | *Remember: the angles in a triangle add to give ......* |
| 22. From 3am to 10am the temperature in a particular village rises by eight degrees Celsius to reach a temperature of $3\ ^\circ C$. If the starting temperature is $x\ ^\circ C$ write down an equation showing this information. Solve this equation to find the temperature at 3am. | |

**Writing Formulae:**

| | |
|---|---|
| 1. Write down in words how to find the area of a circle. | *You should know the formula. Just write it in words.* |
| 2. Write down in words how to find the perimeter and area of this triangle. 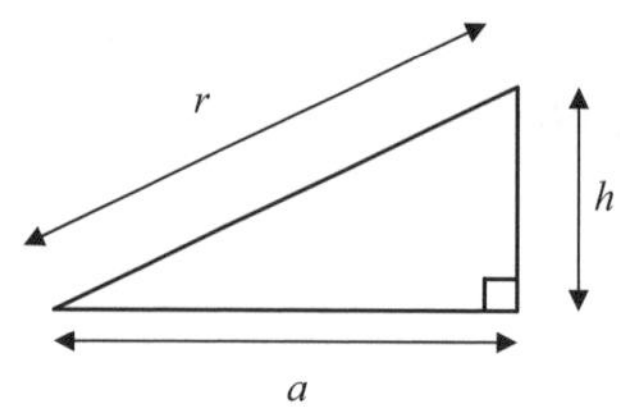  | *Perimeter is the length of the boundary and you should know the formula for the area.* |
| 3. To hire a particular tool from a tool hire company it costs £25 plus £8 per day. Write down a formula for the total cost, $C$, of hiring this tool for $d$ days | *Write C = ..........* |
| 4. The average speed of a car, s, is found by the total distance travelled, d, divided by the total time taken, t. Write down a formula connecting s, d and t. | *Write s = ...........* |

**Inequalities:**

> means 'is greater than'

< means 'is less than'

≥ or ⩾ means 'is greater than or equal to'

≤ or ⩽ means 'is less than or equal to'

Inequalities give a range of solutions (a solution set).

When solving inequalities treat them like equations ***but when you multiply or divide by a negative number you reverse the inequality sign***.

Solve these inequalities

Examples: $x + 8 < 11$ (subtract 8) $x < 3$

$3x > 18$ (divide by 3) $x > 6$

$5 - 2x \geq 13$ (subtract 5) $-2x \geq 8$ (Divide by -2) $x \leq -4$

*$8 \div -2 = -4$ Reverse the sign.*

Representing these solutions on a number line

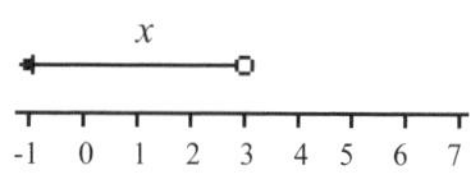


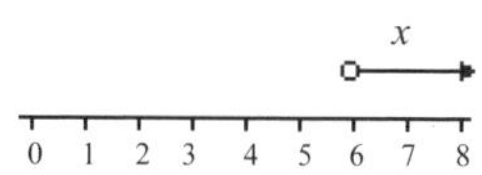


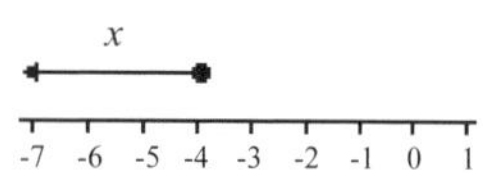


*● includes the value ≤ or ≥*

*o does not include the value < or >*

If $x^2 = 25$ then $x = 5$ or $-5$

So if $x^2 > 25$ then $x > 5$ or $x < -5$ ( try some values $x = -6$, $x^2 = 36$ etc.)

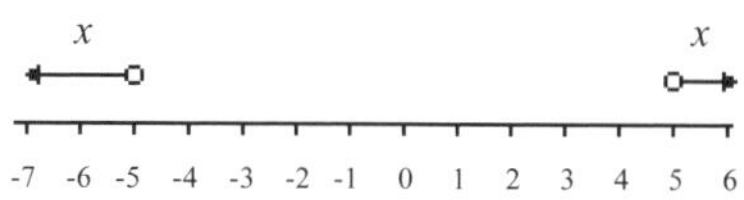


1. Solve these inequalities and represent the solutions on a number line.

a) $6x > 24$ b) $2x + 6 \leq 14$ c) $3 > 5x - 12$ d) $2x - 3 > 4x + 7$

*c) Leave the x on the right hand side. When you get the solution 3 > x you can switch it round to x < 3 (3 is greater than x is the same as x is less than 3)*

Representing intervals on a number line

$-2 < x < 3$ means $x$ is greater than -2 and less than 3

So on a number line this would be drawn

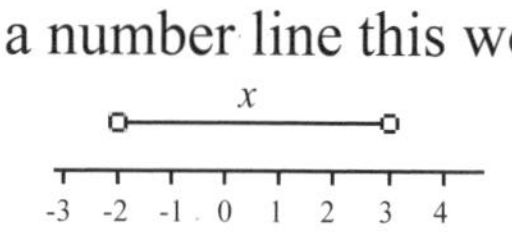


and $-2 \leq x \leq 3$ would be drawn

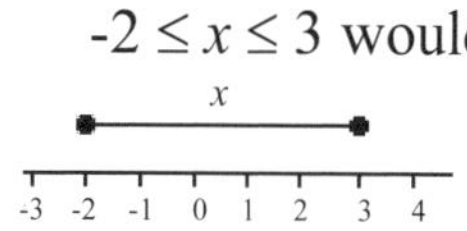


2. Represent these intervals on a number line

a) $-4 \leq x \leq 2$ (b) $1 < x < 5$ (c) $-1 \leq x < 7$ (d) $-6 \leq x \leq -2$

3. Write down the integral values of $x$ which satisfy the inequality $-2 < x \leq 3$

*Integer means positive or negative whole number, so the integral values are the whole numbered values and zero.*

**Graphs of straight lines:**

Straight line graphs are of the form

$y = \mathrm{m}x + \mathrm{c}$

e.g. $y = 3x + 2$

Gradient is 3; $y$-axis intercept is 2

Where:
m is the GRADIENT
c is the INTERCEPT with the $y$ axis
ie. where the line crosses the $y$ axis

Equations of straight lines are called <u>linear equations</u>.

The equation gives us the connection between the $x$ and $y$ co-ordinates of every point on the line.

It is usually helpful to rearrange an equation into the standard form $y = \mathrm{m}x + \mathrm{c}$

$y = 2x - 3$ (*y coordinate equals 2 times the x coordinate minus 3*)

Notice: Gradient 2 i.e. positive (uphill from left to right)

$y$ Intercept -3

Find some points on the line

$x = 1$ $y = 2\times1 - 3 = -1$
$x = 3$ $y = 2\times3 - 3 = 3$
$x = 4$ $y = 2$

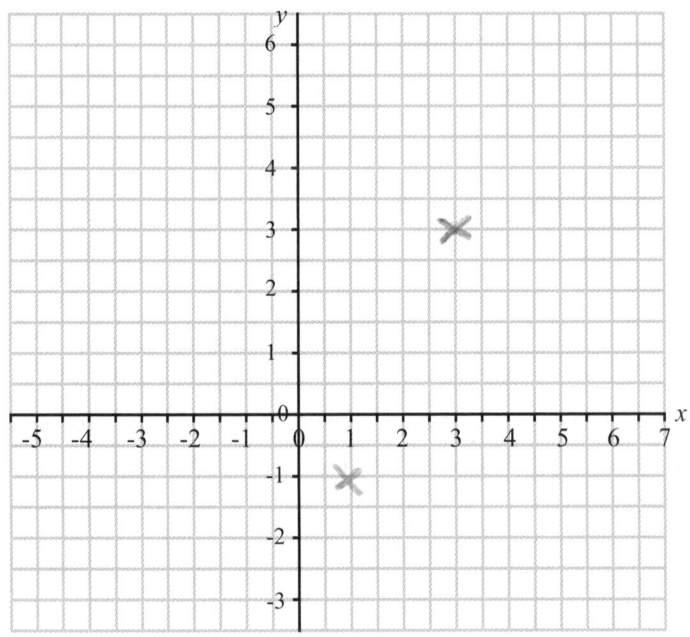

Plot the points and join them up.
Extend the line to cover the area of the grid.
Label the line.

On the same grid draw and label the lines

$y = x + 2$

$x = 1$ $y = 3$
$x = 3$ $y = 5$
$x = 4$ $y = 6$

$y = 3x - 5$

Using a table of values

| $x$ | $y$ |
|---|---|
| 1 | -2 |
| 2 | 1 |
| 3 | 4 |

$y = 2 - x$

$x = 0$ $y = 2$
$x = 2$ $y = 0$
$x = 5$ $y = -3$

$y = 8 - 2x$

Using a table of values

| $x$ | 1 | 2 | 3 | 5 |
|---|---|---|---|---|
| $y$ | 6 | 4 | 2 | -2 |

For straight line equations written $x + y = 8$ , $2x + 3y = 12$ you can use the quick method as shown:

On the grid draw the straight line given by the equation
$x + y = 6$
$x = 0$ gives $y = 6$
$y = 0$ gives $x = 6$
Label the line.

This only gives two points to plot so you may want to check they are correct by finding another point.
$x = 2$ gives $y = 4$

On the grid draw the straight line given by the equation
$2x + 3y = 12$
$x = 0$ gives $3y = 12$ so $y = 4$
$y = 0$ gives $2x = 12$ so $x = 6$
Check: $x = 3$ gives $6 + 3y = 12$
so $y = 2$
Draw and label this line.
When you draw your lines extend them in both directions as this is a line NOT a line segment.
On the same grid draw the line given by the equation $x + 2y = 5$

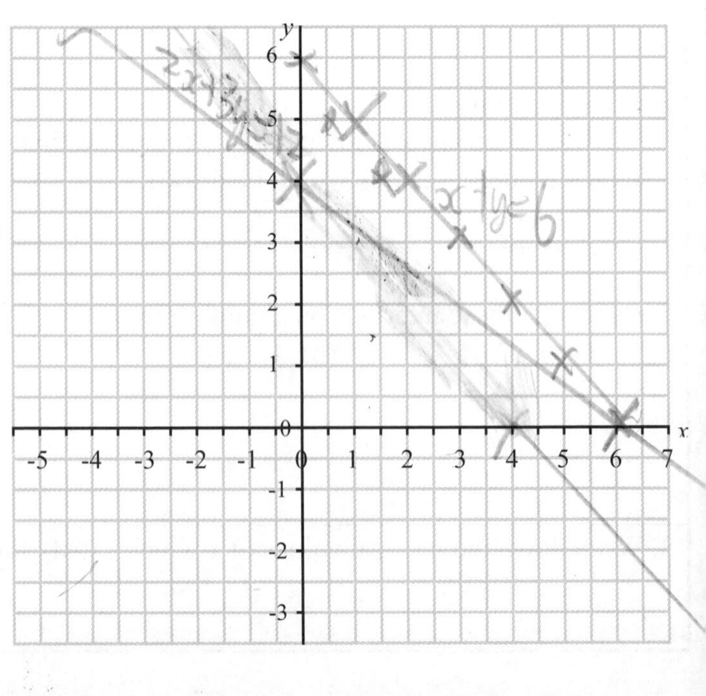

**Simple equations involving $x^2$ - quadratic equations:**

This type of equation contains numbers and usually one variable squared such as $x^2$. They are called quadratic equations have **two solutions**.

Here are some examples: $x^2 = 25$, $x^2 - 9 = 0$, $2x^2 = 32$, $5x^2 - 20 = 0$

Remember $5 \times 5 = 25$ and $(-5) \times (-5) = 25$

So if you are asked to solve

$x^2 = 25$ ← This means find a number $x$ that when it is multiplied by itself it equals 25

The answer is $x = \pm\sqrt{25}$ ← This means $+\sqrt{25}$ or $-\sqrt{25}$

$= 5$ or $-5$ There are two answers for $x$, $x = 5$ or $x = -5$

| | |
|---|---|
| 1. Solve $x^2 = 49$ | 2. Solve $x^2 = 169$ |
| 3. Solve $2x^2 = 8$ (First divide both sides by 2) | 4. Solve $5x^2 = 80$ |
| 5. Solve $x^2 - 81 = 0$ (First add 81 to both sides) | 6. Solve $3x^2 - 27 = 0$ (First add 27 to both sides and divide by 3) |
| 7. Solve $2x^2 - 128 = 0$ | 8. Solve $x^2 - 88 = 0$ giving your answers to 2 dec. pl. |

9. For each of the following write down an equation and then solve it

a) If the area of a square is 16 cm², what is its side length? — *Call the side length x.*

b) If the volume of a cube is 125 cm³, what is its side length? — *Call the side length x. Here you get an equation involving $x^3$*

*Note that for this question the answers can only be positive.*

**Sequences:**

The easy sequences to find terms for are the ones that go up in 1s or 2s or 3s etc but you also need to be able to recognise sequences of squares, cubes, powers of 2, powers of 10, triangle numbers, Fibonacci numbers and simple patterns of numbers.

The **square numbers** 1, 4, 9, 16, 25, 36, 49, 64, 81, 100, 121, 144, 169, 196, 225 The $n^{th}$ term for this sequence is $n^2$.

**Triangle numbers** - these are 1, 1 + 2 = 3, 1 + 2 + 3 = 6, 1 + 2 + 3 + 4 = 10, 1 + 2 + 3 + 4 + 5 = 15, … i.e. 1, 3, 6, 10, 15, 21,

Work out the next two numbers in the sequence.

The $n^{th}$ triangle number is $\frac{1}{2}n(n + 1)$ i.e. check with the $4^{th}$ triangle number $\frac{1}{2} \times 4 \times 5 = 10$

Write down the $20^{th}$ triangle number.

**Fibonacci sequences** - Here the previous two terms are added to give the next term i.e. 1, 1, 2, 3, 5, 8, 13, …..

Work out the next two numbers in the sequence. (1 + 1 = 2) (1 + 2 = 3)

**Powers of 2** - These come from $2^1, 2^2, 2^3, 2^4, 2^5, 2^6$, …..i.e. 2, 4, 8, 16, 32, 64, …..

The $n^{th}$ term is $2^n$. Add the next two numbers to the sequence.

**Powers of 10** - These come from $10^1, 10^2, 10^3, 10^4, 10^5, 10^6$, …..i.e. 10, 100, 1000, 10000, 100000, …….

Try these

1. Find the next three terms in the following sequences

| | |
|---|---|
| a) 2, 5, 8, 11, | (b) 5, 9, 13, 17, |
| c) 22, 17, 12, 7, | (d) -20, -13, -6, |
| e) 1, 4, 9, 16, | (f) 1, 3, 4, 7, 11, |
| g) 14, 11, 8, 5, | (h) -14, -11, -8, -5, |
| i) 1, ½, ⅓, ¼, | (j) 2, 4, 8, 16, |

## Sequences and the n$^{th}$ term:

Linear sequences - these sequences have a common difference between each term of the sequence.

Example: 6, 8, 10, 12, 14, …..

When trying to find the n$^{th}$ term it is easier to set out the sequence as below:

| | | | | | | | |
|---|---|---|---|---|---|---|---|
| *Position of term* | *1* | *2* | *3* | *4* | *5* | *6* | n |
| Sequence | 7 | 9 | 11 | 13 | 15 | 17 | |
| *Difference* | *2* | *2* | *2* | *2* | *2* | | |
| Position × 2 | 2 | 4 | 6 | 8 | 10 | 12 | 2n |
| ADD 5 | 7 | 9 | 11 | 13 | 15 | 17 | 2n + 5 |

This suggests that the sequence is something to do with the 2 times table. Try 2n (2 × position).

Now - what do you add to or subtract from 2n to get the numbers in the sequence.

**The n$^{th}$ term is 2n + 5**

1. Complete these. Find the n$^{th}$ term for the following :

a) 1, 4, 7, 10, 13, 16, …..

| | | | | | | | |
|---|---|---|---|---|---|---|---|
| *Position of term* | *1* | *2* | *3* | *4* | *5* | *6* | n |
| Sequence | 1 | 4 | 7 | 10 | 13 | 16 | |
| *Difference* | | | | | | | |
| Position × | | | | | | | |

**The n$^{th}$ term is**

*Find the difference between terms. Here it is the same value of 3. This suggests that the sequence is something to do with the 3 times table. Try 3n ( 3 × position).*

*Now - what do you add to or subtract from 3n to get the numbers in the sequence.*

b) -3, 2, 7, 12, 17, …

| | | | | | | |
|---|---|---|---|---|---|---|
| *Position of term* | *1* | *2* | *3* | *4* | *5* | n |
| Sequence | | | | | | |
| *Difference* | | | | | | |
| Position × | | | | | | |

**The n$^{th}$ term is**

*Find the difference between terms. Here it is the same value. What times table does this suggest? Position × this value.*

*Now - what do you add or subtract to obtain the numbers in the sequence.*

c) 5, 7, 9, 11, 13, ….

| | | | | | | |
|---|---|---|---|---|---|---|
| *Position of term* | *1* | *2* | *3* | *4* | *5* | n |
| Sequence | | | | | | |
| *Difference* | | | | | | |
| Position × | | | | | | |

**The n$^{th}$ term is**

*Find the difference between terms. Here it is the same value. What times table does this suggest?. Position × this value.*

*Now - what do you add or subtract to obtain the numbers in the sequence.*

**d) 13, 11, 9, 7, 5, 3, …**

| | | | | | | |
|---|---|---|---|---|---|---|
| *Position of term* | *1* | *2* | *3* | *4* | *5* | n |
| Sequence | | | | | | |
| *Difference* | | | | | | |
| Position × | | | | | | |

**The n$^{th}$ term is**

*This time the difference is -2 so the n$^{th}$ term will have -2n in it.*

**e) 38, 33, 28, 23, 18, 13, …**

| | | | | | | |
|---|---|---|---|---|---|---|
| *Position of term* | *1* | *2* | *3* | *4* | *5* | n |
| Sequence | | | | | | |
| *Difference* | | | | | | |
| Position × | | | | | | |

**The n$^{th}$ term is**

2. If the n$^{th}$ term of a sequence is 4n - 1, write down the first 4 terms and the 20$^{th}$ term.

*For the first term put n = 1 into 4n - 1. For the second term put n = 2 into 4n - 1 etc*

3. The nth term of a sequence is $n^2 - 4$. Write down the first 5 terms of the sequence.

*For the first term put n = 1 into $n^2$ - 4. For the second term put n = 2 into $n^2$ - 4 etc.*

4. The nth term of a sequence is $3n^2 + 2$. Write down the first 5 terms of the sequence.

*Remember $3n^2$ means $3 \times n^2$ so for each value of n ( 1 to 5 ) find $n^2$ and multiply it by 3.*

## Problems

Here is a tiling pattern

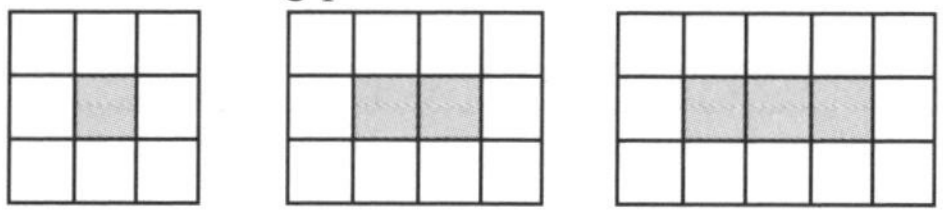

Complete:
How many white tiles are needed for 4 grey tiles?

How many white tiles are needed for 10 grey tiles?
Complete:

| Grey tiles | 1 | 2 | 3 | 4 | …. | 10 | …. | n |
|---|---|---|---|---|---|---|---|---|
| White tiles | | | | | | | | |

How many white tiles are needed for n grey tiles?

> To find the number of white tiles for n grey tiles use the method for the $n^{th}$ term.
> *Find the difference between the numbers in the white tiles row. Here it is the same value.*
> *What times table does this suggest?. Grey tiles × this value.*
> *Now - what do you add or subtract to obtain the number of white tiles?.*

1. Fence sections 1 2 3

2 posts 2 rails 3 posts 4 rails 4 posts 6 rails

Complete this table showing the number of posts and rails required for sections of fence.

| Sections | 1 | 2 | 3 | 4 | 5 | ….. | n |
|---|---|---|---|---|---|---|---|
| Posts | 2 | 3 | 4 | | | | |
| Rails | 2 | 4 | 6 | | | | |

*Draw the next one if you are not sure.*

*You should be able to 'see' what you do to the section number to obtain the post number and the rails number.*

2.

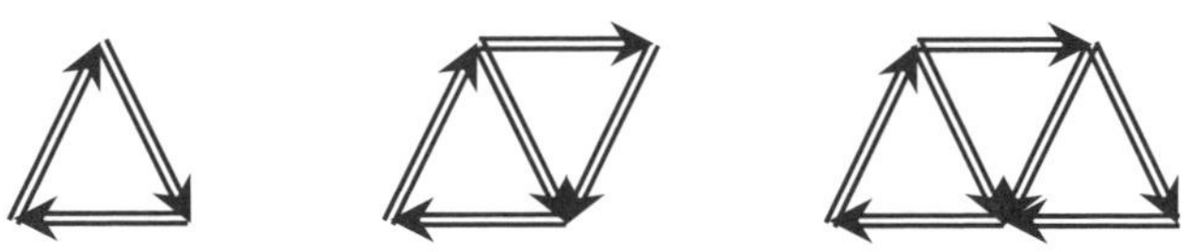

Complete this table

| Triangles | 1 | 2 | 3 | 4 | 5 | ….. | t |
|---|---|---|---|---|---|---|---|
| Arrows | 3 | 5 | | | | | |

Explain, by refering to the diagrams, how the formula for the $t^{th}$ term is built up.

*Draw the next one if you are not sure.*
*Use the method for the $n^{th}$ term.*
*Find the difference.*

*Just t instead of n.*

3. Some sticks are used to make a pattern

pattern 1 pattern 2 pattern 3

a) Draw pattern 4

b) How many sticks in pattern 5?

c) How many sticks in pattern 10?

d) How many sticks in pattern *n*?

# Test Yourself:

Try these questions. If you are unable to do a question go back and revise the relevant section.

1.Simplify a) $x^3 \times x^4$ b) $y^8 \div y^2$ c) $\dfrac{10z^8}{2z^2 \times z^3}$

2. Draw the graphs of the following equations (a) $y = x - 1$ (b) $2x - y = 4$

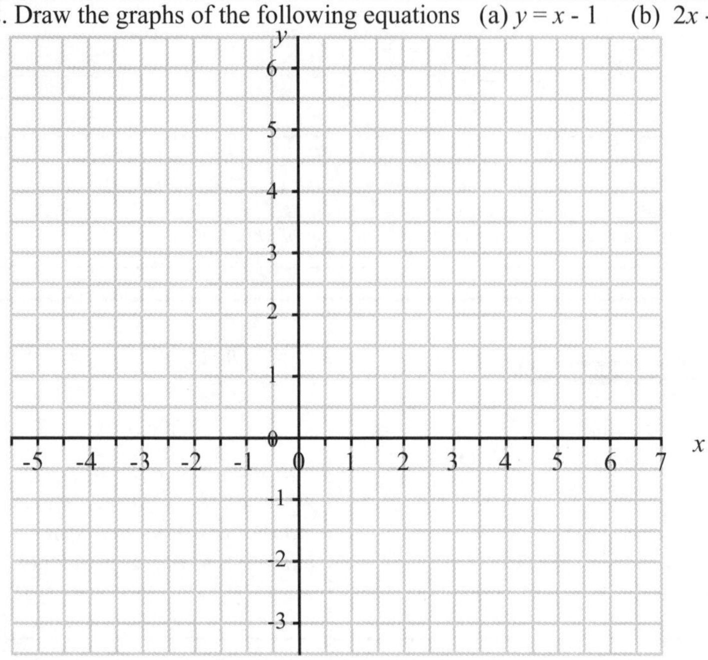


c) What are the co-ordinates of the point of intersection of the lines?

3. Draw and label the lines

(a) $x = 3$ , $y = -4$, $y = -x$

(b) $y = ½ x - 2$, $2x + 3y = 6$

(a)

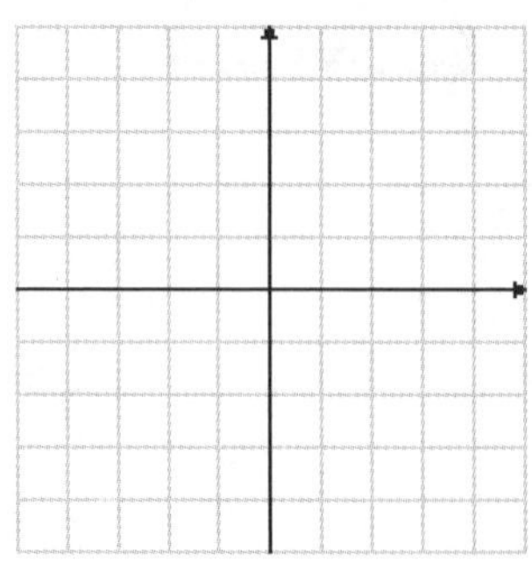

(b)

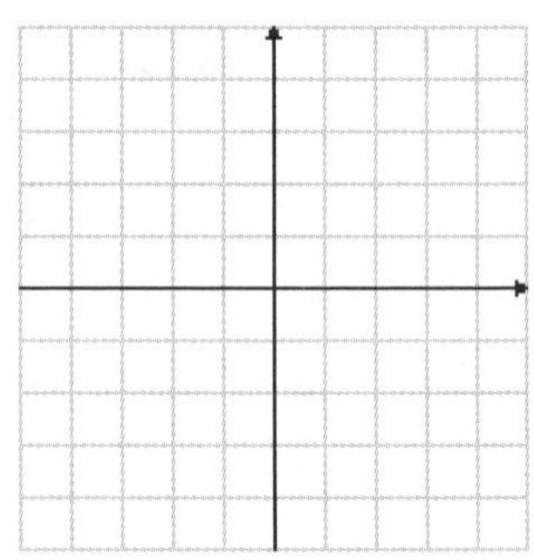

4. If $r = 4$, $s = 8$ and $t = -2$ evaluate (a) $r - t$ (b) $5r + st$ (c) $\dfrac{r-s}{t}$ (d) $\sqrt{\dfrac{2s}{r}}$ (e) $2t^2$

5. Multiply out the brackets and simplify

a) $5x - ( x + 2 )$

b) $4( p - q ) + 3( p + 2q )$

c) [illegible] $x( x - 3 )$

[illegible]kets and simplify

7. Factorise
(a) $6x - 9$

(b) $6ab^2 + 2ab$

(c) $15pqr - 3pr^2$

8. Solve the following equations

(i) $3x - 7 = 17$ (ii) $3x + 2(x - 5) = 40$

(iii) $5(x + 1) = 4 - (x - 2)$ (iv) $5x - 45 = 3(x + 2)$

(v) $\frac{x}{3} = 17$ (vi) $\frac{x}{2} + 5 = 23$

(vii) $\frac{5x}{4} + 1 = 21$ (viii) $x - 4 = \frac{3x}{2} + 2$

9. Write down the perimeter of this rectangle.

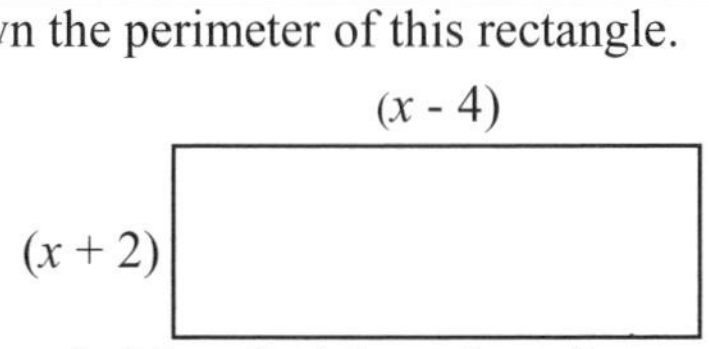


If the perimeter is 16cm find the value of $x$.

10. Here are the first five terms of a sequence
1, 5, 9, 13, 17, ….
Write down the $n^{th}$ term.

11. Write the first 4 terms, the $10^{th}$ term and the $100^{th}$ term of the sequence with $n^{th}$ term $5n + 3$

12. Solve $4n - 13 < 11$
Represent the solution on a number line.

13. Solve $2n - 7 < 11 - n$

a. Represent the solution on a number line.

b. List the prime numbers which satisfy the inequality.

# Level 3 Topics

## Solving right angled triangles - Pythagoras' theorem:

To find a side of a **right-angled triangle**, given two other sides, use **Pythagoras' theorem.**

## Pythagoras' theorem:

Two types **Type I** to find the longest side This is always the side opposite the right-angle. It is called the hypotenuse.

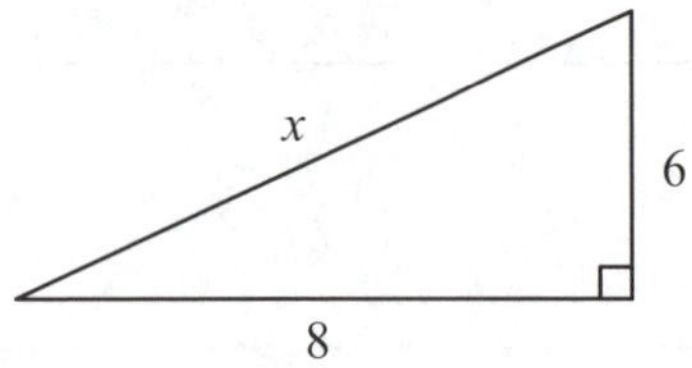


Pythagoras' theorem gives $x^2 = 6^2 + 8^2$
Square the sides $6^2 = 6 \times 6 = 36$
$8^2 = 8 \times 8 = 64$
ADD the answers $36 + 64 = 100$ so $x^2 = 100$
Square root $\sqrt{100} = 10$
Answer $x = 10$

**Type II** to find a shorter side

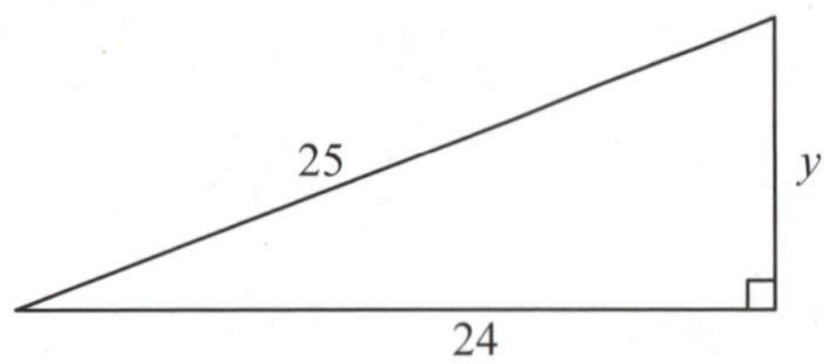


Pythagoras' theorem gives $25^2 = y^2 + 24^2$
Square the sides $25^2 = 25 \times 25 = 625$
$24^2 = 24 \times 24 = 576$
SUBTRACT the answers (ie. take 576 from both sides of the equation)
$625 - 576 = 49$ so $49 = y^2$
Square root $\sqrt{49} = 7$
Answer $y = 7$

1. Find the sides marked with a letter.

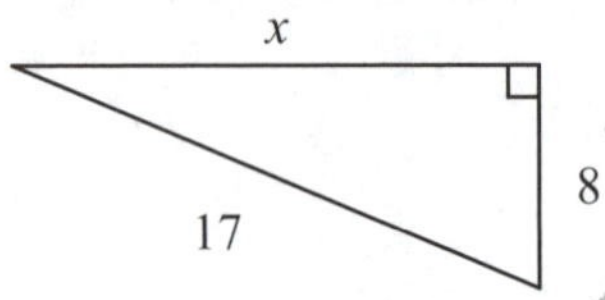


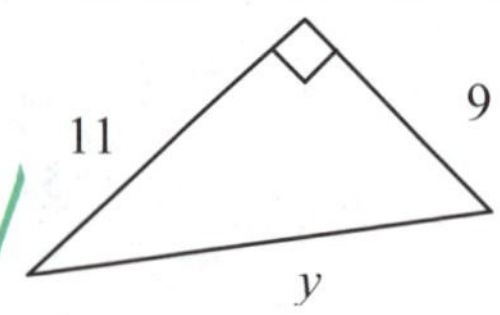


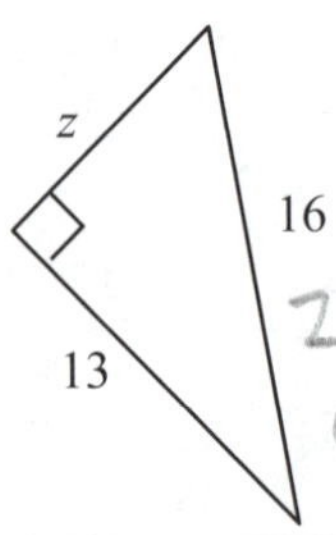


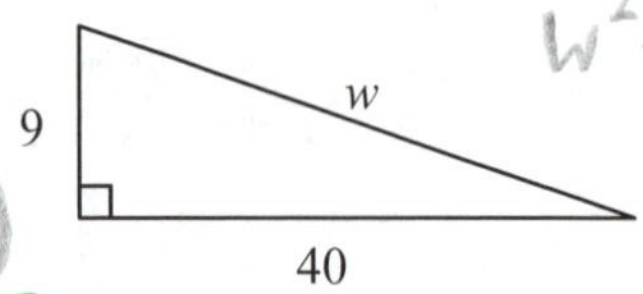


*Square the given sides.*
*Add and square root to find the longest side.*
*Subtract and square root to find a shorter side.*

*Give the answers for y and z to 3 sig. fig.*

2. Find the length of the diagonal of this rectangle to 3 significant figures.

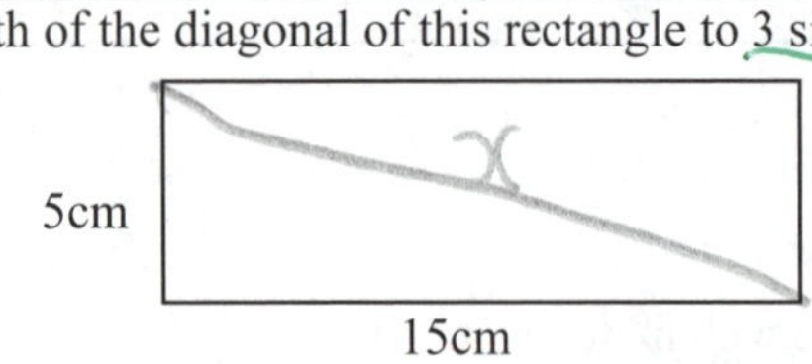


*Draw in a diagonal and you can see that you have a right-angled triangle.*
*Use Pythagoras' theorem.*

3. A triangle has sides of length 7 m, 24 m and 25 m. Is this a right-angled triangle? Give a reason showing your working.

*If it is a right-angled triangle then:*
*the two shorter sides squared and added will equal the longest side squared.*

*You must then state that it is a right-angled triangle or it is not a right-angled triangle.*

4. An equilateral triangle has side lengths as shown. Find the perpendicular height, h, of the trian[illegible] significant figures.

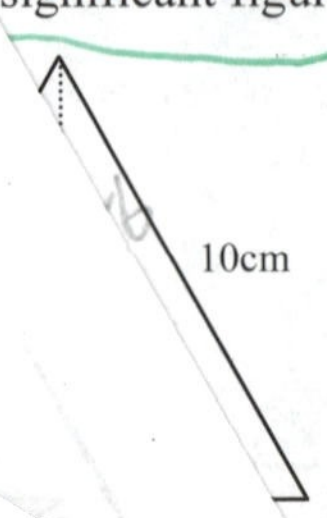


*This is not a right-angled triangle. But half of it is!*
*So just use half of it (redraw it if you wish) - be careful, the length of the lower side will not be 10cm.*

5. Find the area of the shape shown below.

Semicircle diameter 8 cm
AP = BP

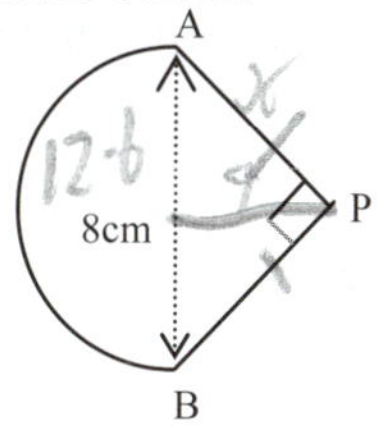


*Use Pythagoras to find the length of the sides of the triangle.*
*Hint: The triangle is isosceles.*

6. Work out the perimeter of this right angled triangle to one decimal place.

**Distance between two points:**
Find the distance between the points ( 7 , 6 ) and ( 1 , 4 )

Plot and join the points with a straight line.
This is called a **line segment** i.e. part of a line that stretches infinitely in both directions.

Draw in a right angled triangle.

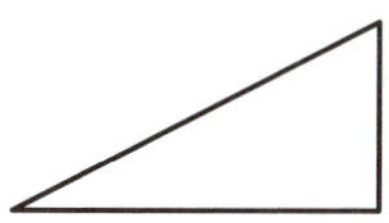

Use Pythagoras to work out the length of the line joining the two points.
Remember for a right-angled triangle: Square the known sides Add and square root to find the longest side. (Subtract and square root to find a shorter side)

length = √

length = to 3 sig fig

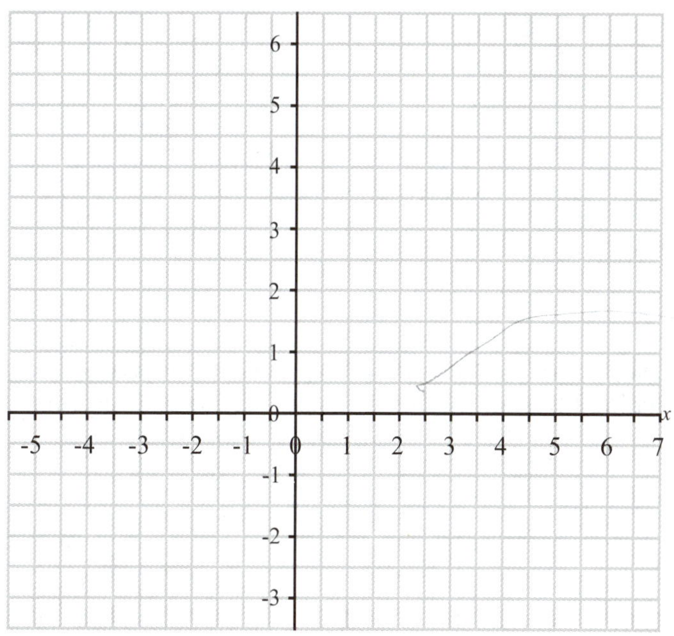


Using the same grid to help you work out the length of the lines joining these points:

1. ( 3 , -1 ) and ( 6 , 3 )

2. ( - 4 , -1 ) and ( 1 , -3)

3. ( -1 , 3 ) and ( 2 , -2 )

4. ( -3 , 1 ) and ( -2 , 5 )

5. ( -3 , -3 ) and ( -2 , 2 )

6. Write an expression for the distance between the points ( $x$ , $y$ ) and ( $a$ , $b$ )

**Trial and improvement:**

Some equations are difficult to solve algebraically. You can use trial and improvement to help you find a solution.

Example: Find the value of $x$ correct to one decimal place for the equation $x^3 + 2x = 9$

| $x$ | $x^3 + 2x$ | | |
|---|---|---|---|
| 1 | $1^3 + 2\times1 = 3$ | too small | So $x$ is between 1 and 2 |
| 2 | $2^3 + 2\times2 = 12$ | too big | |
| 1.5 | $1.5^3 + 2\times1.5 = 6.375$ | too small | |
| 1.7 | $1.7^3 + 2\times1.7 = 8.313$ | too small | So $x$ is between 1.7 and 1.8 |
| 1.8 | $1.8^3 + 2\times1.8 = 9.432$ | too big | |
| 1.75 | $1.75^3 + 2\times1.75 = 8.859$ | too small | So $x$ is nearer to 1.8 $\therefore$ $x = 1.8$ to 1 decimal place. |

1. a) Evaluate $x^3 - 2x$ when $x = 3$ and $x = 4$
   b) Find the value of $x$ correct to one decimal place for the equation $x^3 - 2x = 28$.

*a) Substitute x = 3 into the equation.*
*Substitute x = 4 into the equation.*
*b)Try 3.5. Too big or too small? etc.*

*Write x = ...... to one decimal place*

2. Use trial and improvement to find the positive solution of the equation $2x^2 - 3x = 40$ to one decimal place. The first line has been done for you.

| $x$ | $2x^2 - 3x$ | comment |
|---|---|---|
| 5 | $2\times5^2 - 3\times5 = 35$ | too small |
| | | |
| | | |
| | | |
| | | |
| | | |
| | | |

$x =$

3. Use trial and improvement to find a solution between 4 and 5 of the equation $4x^2 + 5x = 100$ to one decimal place. The first line has been done for you.

| $x$ | $4x^2 + 5x$ | comment |
|---|---|---|
| 4 | $4\times4^2 + 5\times4 = 84$ | too small |
| | | |
| | | |
| | | |
| | | |
| | | |
| | | |

$x =$

**Drawing non linear graphs.**

Example: Draw the graph of $y = x^2 - 4x + 3$

First you need some points to plot. The table may be given to you and you have to fill in the missing values.

| $x$ | -1 | 0 | 1 | 2 | 3 | 4 | 5 |
|---|---|---|---|---|---|---|---|
| $y$ | | | 0 | -1 | | | |

Working: $x = 1 \quad y = 1^2 - 4 \times 1 + 3 = 0$
$x = 2 \quad y = 2^2 - 4 \times 2 + 3 = -1$
$x = 3 \quad y =$
$x = 4 \quad y =$
$x = 5 \quad y =$
$x = 0 \quad y =$
$x = -1 \quad y =$

Complete the working and hence the table of values.

Careful with the $x = -1$.
When you plot the points you will be able to tell if you get it correct - the finished curve should be smooth and ∪ shaped.

Plot the points and join them with a smooth curve.

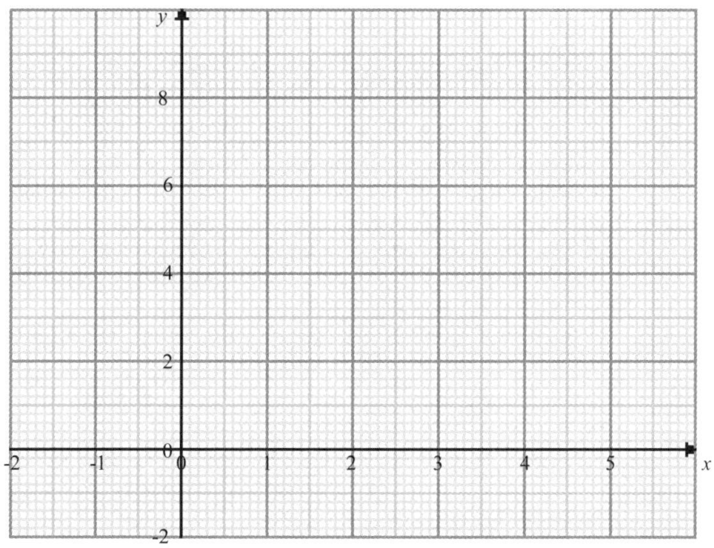


The curve **MUST** go through the plotted points and be smooth.

Use the graph to solve the equation $x^2 - 4x + 3 = 0$

Solution $x =$ or $x =$

Look at the equation. To make it the same you need to replace $y$ with 0.
What are the $x$ coordinates when the $y$ coordinate is 0. This is where the curve cuts the $x$ axis.
Write your answers as accurately as you can.

1. Draw the graph of $y = x^2 - 2x + 1$

Complete the table below:

| $x$ | -2 | -1 | 0 | 1 | 2 | 3 | 4 |
|---|---|---|---|---|---|---|---|
| $y$ | | 4 | | | | | |

Plot the points and join them with a smooth curve.

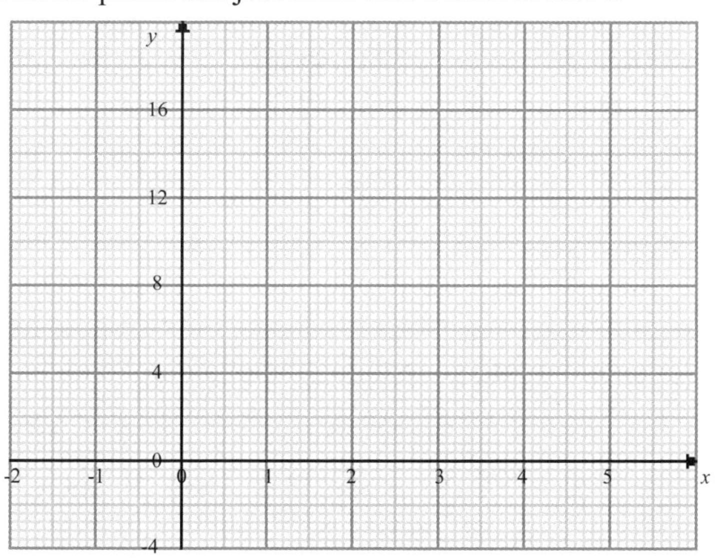


Use the graph to solve the equation $x^2 - 2x + 1 = 8$
( This is when y = 8 )

Solution $x =$ or $x =$

**Simultaneous equations:**

To find the value of two unknowns in a problem, two different equations must be given/found containing the two unknowns. These two equations are called **simultaneous equations**.

There are two main methods for solving simultaneous equations: elimination and substitution. Learn both methods so that you can choose the most suitable one for a particular problem.

**Method 1 – Elimination**

With this method you multiply the equations by suitable amounts to **make the same amount of one of the letters in both equations.**

Example 1:

Solve: $3x + 2y = 16$ (i)
$5x - 4y = 12$ (ii)

$3x + 2y = 16$ (i)×2 gives

$6x + 4y = 32$ (i)
$5x - 4y = 12$ (ii)
(i)+(ii) gives

$11x = 44$

So $x = 4$

Using (i) with $x = 4$ we get

$12 + 2y = 16$

So $y = 2$

Check in (ii) $20 - 8 = 12$

> Always start by numbering the equations. This will allow you to explain your working which is essential for higher level questions.
>
> If necessary, rearrange the equations so that they both look like:
> $x$s … $y$s = numbers
> It is easier to make the same amount of $y$s in both equations.
> To do this multiply equation (i) by 2
>
> Once you have the same amount of one of the letters you eliminate that letter by:
>
> **Adding the equations if the signs are opposite.** ( eg. $3y$ and $-3y$)
> **Subtracting the equations if the signs are the same.** ( eg. both $4x$)
>
> In this case the $y$s are $4y$ and $-4y$ so add the equations.
>
> Solve the equation to find the value of one of the letters.
> Use this value in one of the original equations to find the value of the other letter.
> Always check your answer using the other equation to make sure it works with both values. You will always know when you have solved the equations correctly if this final check works.

Example 2:

Solve: $2x - 3y = 13$ (i)
$6x + 4y = 26$ (ii)

$2x - 3y = 16$ (i)×3 gives

$6x - 9y = 39$ (i)
$6x + 4y = 26$ (ii)
(i)-(ii) gives

$-13y = 13$

So $y = -1$

Using (i) with $y = -1$ we get

$2x + 3 = 13$

So $x = 5$

Check in (ii) $30 + -4 = 30 - 4 = 26$

> This time it is easier to make the same amount of $x$s in both equations.
>
> To do this multiply equation (i) by 3.
>
> Here we have $6x$ in both equations.
>
> Same sign so we subtract the equations.
> Always take special care with signs when subtracting.
>
> $-9y$ subtract $+4y$ gives $-13y$ ie $-9y -4y$ is $-13y$
>
> $y = -1$ so $-3y$ is 3 ( not -3 since $-3×-1 = 3$ )
>
> NB: If you had wanted to eliminate the $y$s instead you would need to multiply equation (i) by 4 and equation (ii) by 3.
> This would give $-12y$ and $12y$ so you would add the equations to eliminate the $y$s.

Now try to solve these equations using the elimination method:

1.a) $2x + 3y = 23$
$4x - 2y = 6$

b) $2x - 3y = 12$
$5x + 9y = -3$

c) $2x + 3y = 11$
$x + 4y = 18$

**Method 2 – Substitution**

With this method you get make one letter the subject of one of the equations and substitute this value into the other equation to produce a single equation with just one letter in it.

Making a letter the subject of an equation means rearranging the equations so that it looks like $x =$ ….. or $y =$ ….. with non of that letter on the other side of the equation.

Use this method if one of the equations has $x$ or $y$ in it ( not $2x$, $3x$ … or $2y$, $3y$ …).

Example 1:

Solve: $x + 2y = 9$ (i)
$3x - 4y = 7$ (ii)

$x = (9 - 2y)$ (i) with $x$ the subject

$3(9 - 2y) - 4y = 7$ (ii) substitute for $x$

$27 - 6y - 4y = 7$ (ii)

$27 - 10y = 7$ (ii)

$-10y = -20$ (ii)

So $y = 2$

Using (i) with $y = 2$ we get

$x + 4 = 9$

So $x = 5$

Check in (ii) $15 - 8 = 7$

> Always start by numbering the equations. This will allow you to explain your working which is essential for higher level questions.
>
> As there is just $x$ in equation (i) use the substitution method and make $x$ the subject. To do this subtract $2y$ from both sides
>
> Always put the substitute in brackets.
>
> Multiply out the bracket, collect like terms and solve to find $y$.
>
> Use this value in the other original equations to find the value of the other letter.
>
> Always check your answer using the other equation to make sure it works with both values. You will always know when you have solved the equations correctly if this final check works.

Example 2:

Solve: $2x - 3y = -5$ (i)
$3x + y = 9$ (ii)

$y = (9 - 3x)$ (ii) with $y$ subject

$2x - 3(9 - 3x) = -5$ (i) substitute for $y$

$2x - 27 + 9x = -5$ (i)

$11x - 27 = -5$

$11x = 22$ so $x = 2$

Using (ii) with $x = 2$ we get

$6 + y = 9$

So $y = 3$

Check in (i) $4 - 9 = -5$

> This time equation (ii) has a single $y$ in it so it is easier use substitution.
>
> To do this make $y$ the subject of equation (ii).
>
> Substitute into equation (i)
> Multiply out the bracket - Careful with the signs. $-3 \times +9 = -27$ and $-3 \times -3x = +9x$
>
> Collect like terms and solve to find $x$.
>
> Use this value in the other original equations to find the value of the other letter.
>
> Check your answer.

Now try to solve these equations using the substitution method:

1.a) $x + 3y = 18$
$4x - 2y = 2$

b) $2x - 3y = 5$
$5x + y = 21$

c) $2x + y = 16$
$x + 3y = 18$

Solve these equations using either method:

1a) $5x + y = 17$
$4x - 2y = -6$

b) $4x - 3y = 0$
$8x + 2y = 32$

c) $2x + 4y = -2$
$2x + 3y = -3$

d) $x + 2y = 19$
$4x - 4y = 4$

e) $2x - 3y = 12$
$5x + 4y = 7$

f) $4x + y = -2$
$2x + 3y = 4$

You may also be asked to draw the graphs of the two equations and find the solution which will be where the graphs intersect (cross each other).

2. Solve $6x + 7y = 42$
$x - y = 2$ by drawing graphs

You can rearrange these equations to give $y = \ldots$ and draw the two graphs.

*OR*

Quick method

For $6x + 7y = 42$

$x = 0 \quad y =$

$y = 0 \quad x =$

This finds two points - join them up and extend them in both directions for the line.

For $x - y = 2$

$x = 0 \quad y =$

$y = 0 \quad x =$

As these points are close together it is a good idea to find another point, say $x = 6$ $y = \ldots$

Point of intersection gives the solution.
Read the values as accurately as you can.

Solution: $x =$ $\quad y =$

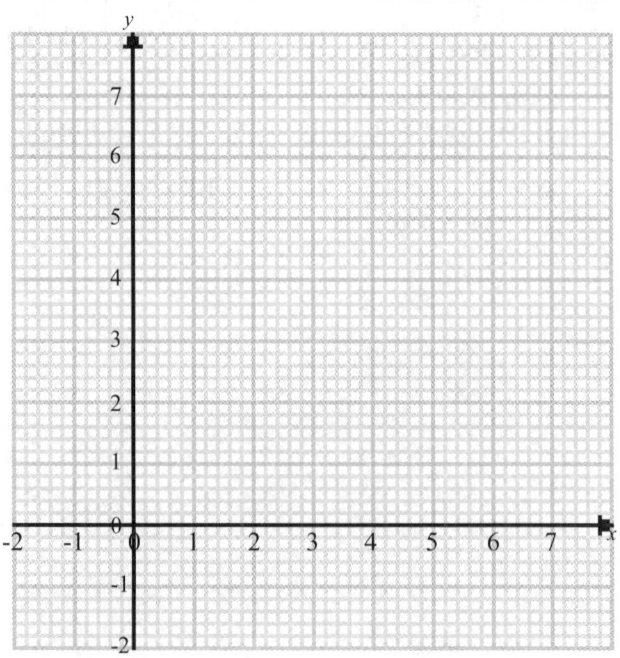

# ANSWERS

Page3

1. Seven hundred and twenty thousand, two hundred and eight
2. 40057
3. 2 thousand
4. (a) Even (b) Odd (c) Odd (d) Even (e) Odd (f) even
5. 7, 14, 21, 28, 35, 42, 49, 56
6. 13, 26, 39, 52, 65
7. 63, 72
8. 1, 2, 3, 5, 6, 10, 15, 30
9. 1, 2, 5, 10, 25, 50
10. 3, 9, 18, 1
11. 23, 17, 19, 79
12. 83, 89
13. (a) 65, 81, 97, 25, 39 (b) 97, 2 (c) 60, 24 (d) 100, 25, 2

Page4

14. 53, 59

15.a) 9764 (b) 4679 (c) 4796

1.

| | | OR | |
|---|---|---|---|
| 2 | 300 | | 300 |
| 2 | 150 | | 2 × 150 |
| 3 | 75 | | 2 × 2 × 75 |
| 5 | 25 | | 2 × 2 × 3 × 25 |
| 5 | 5 | | 2 × 2 × 3 × 5 × 5 |
| | 1 | | |

So $300 = 2 \times 2 \times 3 \times 5 \times 5 = 2^2 \times 3 \times 5^2$

2. $450 = 2 \times 225 = 2 \times 3 \times 75 = 2 \times 3 \times 3 \times 25 = 2 \times 3 \times 3 \times 5 \times 5 = 2 \times 3^2 \times 5^2$
3. $200 = 2 \times 100 = 2 \times 2 \times 50 = 2 \times 2 \times 2 \times 25 = 2 \times 2 \times 2 \times 5 \times 5 = 2^3 \times 5^2$
   a = 3 b = 2
4. 420 = 2 × 2 × 3 × 5 × 7 196 = 2 × 2 × 7 × 7
   The HCF is 2 × 2 × 7 = 28
5. 30 = 2 × 3 × 5 36 = 2 × 2 × 3 × 3
   The LCM is 2 × 2 × 3 × 3 × 5 = 180
6. 54 = 2 × 3 × 3 × 3 36 = 2 × 2 × 3 × 3
   The HCF is 2 × 3 × 3 = 18
   The LCM is 2 × 2 × 3 × 3 × 3 = 108

Page5

1. 1 × 1 = 1 2 × 2 = 4 3 × 3 = 9
   4 × 4 = 16 5 × 5 = 25 6 × 6 = 36
   7 × 7 = 49 8 × 8 = 64 9 × 9 = 81
   10 × 10 = 100 11 × 11 = 121 12 × 12 = 144
   13 × 13 = 169 14 × 14 = 196 15 × 15 = 225
2. $\sqrt{1} = 1$ $\sqrt{4} = 2$ $\sqrt{9} = 3$ $\sqrt{16} = 4$ $\sqrt{25} = 5$
   $\sqrt{36} = 6$ $\sqrt{49} = 7$ $\sqrt{64} = 8$ $\sqrt{81} = 9$
   $\sqrt{100} = 10$ $\sqrt{121} = 11$ $\sqrt{144} = 12$ $\sqrt{169} = 13$
   $\sqrt{196} = 14$ $\sqrt{225} = 15$
3. 1 × 1 × 1 = 1 2 × 2 × 2 = 8 3 × 3 × 3 = 27
   4 × 4 × 4 = 64 5 × 5 × 5 = 125
   10 × 10 × 10 = 1000
4. $\sqrt[3]{1} = 1$ $\sqrt[3]{8} = 2$ $\sqrt[3]{27} = 3$
   $\sqrt[3]{64} = 4$ $\sqrt[3]{125} = 5$ $\sqrt[3]{1000} = 10$

5.a) 2 × 2 × 2 × 2 = 16 b) 5 c) 4 × 4 = 16
d) 10 e) 9×9 = 81 f) 10 000
g) 1 000 000 h) 20 × 20 × 20 = 8000

6.a) 4×4×4 = 64 b) 10 c) 5×5×5×5 = 625
d) 3 e) 9 + 16 = 25 f) 25 - 16 = 9

Page6

1. (a) 7 × 6 = 42 (b) 19 + 121 = 140
   (c) 72 + 56 = 128 (d) 15 × 15 = 225
   (e) 20 × 25 = 500 (f) 100 - 36 = 64
   (g) 12 ÷ 3 = 4 (h) 5 + 2 = 7
   (i) 8 + 7 = 15 (j) 9 × 5 = 45
   (k) 20 + 12 = 32 (l) 21 ÷ 1 = 21
   (m) 2 × 9 = 18 (n) 6000 - 4000 = 2000
   (o) 5600 ÷ 400 = 14 (p) 3 × 8 = 24
   (q) 2 × 121 = 242 (r) 81 + 27 = 108
   (s) 225 - 169 = 56
2. (a) 16 × 58 = 928 (b) 459 + 441 = 900
   (c) 152 + 119 = 271 (d) 503 × 42 = 21126
   (e) 32 × 169 = 5408 (f) 7870 - 2736 = 5134
   (g) 2562 ÷ 280 = 9.15 (h) 489 + 218 = 707
   (i) 19 × 207 = 3933 (j) 2940 + 783 = 3723
   (k) 641 ÷ 25 = 25.64 (l) 690 × 172 = 118680
   (m) 2484 - 1085 = 1399 (n) 13770 ÷ 500 = 27.54
   (o) 35 × 938 = 32830 (p) 28 × 1849 = 51772
   (q) 1728 × 625 = 1080000 (r) 676 + 225 = 901

Page7

1. -5 , -3 , -1 , 3 , 7
2. (a) -1 (b) 8 (c) -5
3. (a) - 6 (b) -7 (c) 4
4. (a) -1 (b) -10 (c) 8
5. (a) -35 (b) -8 (c) 48 (d) 9
6. (a) 21 + - 10 = 11 (b) -11 + -15 = -26
7. (a) -21 - - 10 = - 21 + 10 = -11 (b) 7 + - 7 = 0

8.i) 4 × (-2) = -8 (ii) 3 × 4 = 12
(iii) 2 × 4 + 3 × (-3) = 8 - 9 = -1
(iv) 5 × 4 - 3 × (-2) = 20 + 6 = 26
(v) 4 × (-2) × (-3) + (-3) × (-3) = 24 + 9 = 33
(vi) 4 ÷ (-2) = -2
(vii) 2 × (-2) × 6/(-3) = (-24) ÷ (-3) = 8
(viii) 4 - 2 × 6/2 × (-2) = (-8) ÷ (-4) = 2
(ix) $(4 + -2)^2 = 2^2 = 4$
(x) 16 + 4 = 20
(xi) $4^2 - (-3)^2 = 16 - 9 = 7$

Page8

1. 3472 2. 13104 3. 48035 4. 463
5. 857 6. 172.6 7. 7713 8. 21575
9. (a) 229 (b) 85 (c) 122
   (d) 169 (e) 27 (f) 120
   (g) 20 (h) 3 (i) 8

Page9

1. a) 7 × 9 = 63 then £63 + £42 = £105
   b) 150 - 42 = 108 then 108 ÷ 9 = 12 days
2. Missing numbers 3 , 7 , 6 , 10
3. Missing numbers 7 , 27 , 7 , 9
4. a) 6 (b) 8 (c) 7
5. a) i ) 120 miles (ii) 260 miles
   b) 170 + 210 + 60 = 440 miles

Page10

1. 4.7 , 3.699 , 3.65 , 3.649 , 3.6 , 2.152
2. 8.095 , 8.9 , 9.10 , 9.9 , 9.999 , 12.5
3. 2.07 4. 0.33 5. 21.35
6. 8.95

Page11

7. 12.76 8. 4.44
9. 6.76 10. 12.63 11. 0.5868
12. 0.3064 13. 348.65 14. 587.5
15. 67987.1 16. 34000 17. 5.483
18. 85.327 19. 4.56 20. 3.4565
21. 0.0684 22. 5900 23. 69.6
24. 2 900 25. 201 000 26. 68 000
27. 2.7 28. 28.441 29. 1.51
30. 3.2282 31. 0.0228

Page12

1. 12 × 6 = 72 1.2 × 0.6 = 0.72
2. 1 × 3 = 3 0.1 × 0.3 = 0.03
3. 34 × 2 = 68 0.34 × 0.2 = 0.068
4. 12 × 12 = 144 1.2 × 1.2 = 1.44
5. 2 × 2 × 2 = 8 0.2 × 0.2 × 0.2 = 0.008
6. 11 × 12 = 132 1.1 × 1.2 = 1.32
7. 565 × 1 = 565 5.65 × 0.1 = 0.565
8. 25 × 5 = 125 25 × 0.5 = 12.5
9. 5 × 6 = 30 0.5 × 0.6 = 0.30 = 0.3
10. (a) 86.3 (b) 8.6 (c) 0.8
11. (a) 1.248 (b) 0.124 (c) 0.012
12. (a) 3.5 (b) 0.35 (c) 0.03
13. (a) 9.25 (b) 0.925 (c) 0.0925
14. 385×62 = 23870 38.5 × 0.62 = 23.870 = 23.87
15. 25 × 76 = 1900 2.5 × 7.6 = 19.00 = 19
16. 275 × 12 = 3300 27.5 × 1.2 = 33.00 = 33
17. 5.87125

Page13

18. 86.28 ÷ 1.2 = 862.8 ÷ 12 Answer 71.9
19. 0.225 20. 3.876 ÷ 0.06 = 387.6 ÷ 6 = 64.6
21. 86.32 ÷ 0.2 = 863.2 ÷ 2 = 431.6
22. 2
23. 25
24. 55.5 ÷ 7.5 = 7.4
25. 2 × 0.12 = 0.24
26. 32.25 ÷ 7.5 = 4.3
27. 7.128 ÷ 5 = 1.4256
28. 11.55 ÷ 5.5 = 2.1
29. 3.33 ÷ 5 = 0.666
30. 9.396 ÷ 4.35 = 2.16
31. £8.23
32. 3 × £2.24 = £6.72 then £20 - £6.72 = £13.28
33. a) 20 × £9 = £180 (b) £72 ÷ £9 = 8 so 8 hours
34. 2 × 13.25 = 26.50 and 3 × 7.15 = 21.45
    £26.50 + £21.45 = £47.95
35. a) £21.20 (b) £41.05
36. £137.60 + £146.76 = £284.36

Page14

1. (a) $\frac{2}{5}$ (b) $\frac{12}{25}$ (c) $\frac{19}{20}$ (d) $\frac{33}{250}$ (e) $\frac{307}{2500}$
2. (a) 0.8 (b) 0.875 (c) 0.15 (d) 0.325 (e) 0.08
3. Answers given in question
4.
   a) $0.8\dot{3}$ recurring b) 0.875 terminating
   c) $0.\dot{2}\dot{7}$ recurring

Page15

1. a) 23 b) 46 c) 177
2. a) 350 b) 8750 c) 1 000
3. a) 600 b) 4 000 c) 945 600
4. a) 50 000 b) 30 000 c) 240 000
5. a) 3 000 000 b) 35 000 000 c) 45 000 000
6. a) 2 600 b) 800
   c) 256 900
7. a) 25.6 25.55
   b) 67.50 67.5
   c) 34.3 34.34
   d) 24.58 24.583
   e) 6.3 6.350

Notice for 7(b) and 7(e) you keep the zero to show the answer is correct to the required number of decimal places.

8. a) 50 000 46 000 b) 20 000 23 000
   c) 500 520 d) 2 000 1 980
   e) 6 000 000 6 185 000 f) 50 45.0
   g) 60 57 h) 0.005 0.0053
   i) 0.1 0.13

Page16

1. 8 × 100 × 3 × 1000 = 2 400 000
2. 50/0.5 = 50×10/0.5×10 = 500/5 = 100
3. 180 000 4. 630 000 5. 2 000 6. 12
7. 900/30 = 30 8. 8000/40 = 200
9. 5000/0.5 = 50000/5 = 10000
10. 30/0.02 = 3000/2 = 1500
11. a) 5 × 100 = 500 b) 100 × 8 = 800
    c) 300 × 50 = 15 000 d) 3000 × 8 = 24 000
    e) 800 × 0.1 = 80.0 = 80 f) 0.6 × 9 = 5.4
12. a) 80 ÷ 2 = 40 b) 80000 ÷ 400 = 200
    c) 600 ÷ 0.1 = 6000/1 = 6 000
    d) 5000/800 = 6.25 ≈ 6

13.a) 200 × 40/4 = 2 000 b) 30 × 900/300 = 90
c) 8000 × 60/0.2 = 4800000/2 = 2 400 000
d) 50 × 0.4/(10 × 0.02) = 20.0/0.2 = 100

14. a) 3000 × 7p = 21000p = £210
    b) 20 × £10 = £200 or 20 × £12 = £240
    or 22 × £10 = £220
    c) 800 × 80p = 64000p = £640

Page17

1. $3 \times 3 = 9$ too big so the answer is between 3 and 4

$2.5 \times 2.5 = 6.25$ too small

$2.6 \times 2.6 = 6.76$ too small

$2.7 \times 2.7 = 7.29$ too big so the answer is between 2.6 and 2.7

$2.65 \times 2.65 = 7.0225$ too big

Answer $\sqrt{7} = 2.6$ to 1 decimal place.

2. $7 \times 7 = 49$ too small

$7.1 \times 7.1 = 50.41$ too big so the answer is between 7.0 and 7.1

$7.05 \times 7.05 = 49.7025$ too small

All numbers between 7.05 and 7.1 round to 7.1

Answer $\sqrt{50} = 7.1$ to 1 decimal place

3. a) $10^{5+6} = 10^{11}$

b) $10^{7-4} = 10^3$

c) $10^{6+-2} = 10^8$

d) $10^{9-5} = 10^4$

4. a) $2^{3+4+3} = 2^{10}$

b) $2^{8-5} = 2^3$

c) $2^{6+2+5} = 2^{13}$

5. a) $8 + 25 = 33$

b) $9 \times 16 = 144$

c) $25 \times 1000 = 25\,000$

d) $2^5 = 32$

Page18

1. $\frac{14}{18} = \frac{7}{9}$ 2. $\frac{9}{20}$ 3. $\frac{18}{51} = \frac{6}{17}$

4. $\frac{21}{24} = \frac{7}{8}$ 5. $\frac{30}{42} = \frac{15}{21} = \frac{5}{7}$

6. $\frac{9}{30} = \frac{3}{10}$ 7. $\frac{36}{84} = \frac{18}{42} = \frac{9}{21} = \frac{3}{7}$

8. $\frac{28}{168} = \frac{14}{84} = \frac{7}{42} = \frac{1}{6}$ 9. $\frac{33}{99} = \frac{3}{9} = \frac{1}{3}$

10. $\frac{16}{36} = \frac{8}{18} = \frac{4}{9}$ 11. $\frac{24}{60} = \frac{12}{30} = \frac{6}{15} = \frac{2}{5}$

12. $\frac{108000}{232000} = \frac{108}{232} = \frac{54}{116} = \frac{27}{58}$

13.

$\frac{1}{3} = \frac{10}{30}, \frac{2}{5} = \frac{12}{30}, \frac{3}{10} = \frac{9}{30}$

Answer $\frac{3}{10}, \frac{1}{3}, \frac{2}{5}$

14. $22/7 = 3.142857$ $\pi = 3.14159$

Answer 3.1, 3.14, $\pi$, 22/7

Page19

15. $\frac{7}{12}, \frac{2}{3}, \frac{3}{4}$ 16. $\frac{11}{16}, \frac{5}{8}, \frac{13}{24}$

17. False 18. 0.45 19. 90

20. £117 21. 4957m 22. £345.60

23. £520.20 24. 319.5km 25. £202.30

26. 4 out of 12 shaded

27. $\frac{6}{15} = \frac{2}{5}$ 28. 10 out of 16 shaded

29. 14 shaded 30. $\frac{5}{6}$

Page20

1. $\frac{12+10}{15} = \frac{22}{15} = 1\frac{7}{15}$ 2. $\frac{35-12}{40} = \frac{23}{40}$ 3. $\frac{4\times2}{5\times3} = \frac{8}{15}$

4. $\frac{5}{6} \times \frac{4}{3} = \frac{20}{18} = \frac{10}{9} = 1\frac{1}{9}$

5. a) $3\frac{1}{4} = \frac{13}{4}$ (b) $5\frac{2}{3} = \frac{17}{3}$ (c) $4\frac{3}{5} = \frac{23}{5}$

d) $\frac{20}{3} = 6\frac{2}{3}$ (e) $\frac{34}{8} = 4\frac{2}{8} = 4\frac{1}{4}$

6. a) $\frac{32+5}{40} = \frac{37}{40}$

b) $\frac{3}{10} + \frac{7}{4} = \frac{12+70}{40} = \frac{82}{40} = \frac{41}{20} = 2\frac{1}{20}$

c) $\frac{3}{9} + \frac{2}{9} = \frac{5}{9}$

d) $\frac{21-16}{24} = \frac{5}{24}$

e) $\frac{9}{4} - \frac{1}{3} = \frac{27-4}{12} = \frac{23}{12} = 1\frac{11}{12}$

f) $\frac{23}{5} - \frac{15}{8} = \frac{184-75}{40} = \frac{109}{40} = 2\frac{29}{40}$

g) $\frac{5}{1} \times \frac{2}{3} = \frac{10}{3} = 3\frac{1}{3}$ (h) $\frac{4}{5} \times \frac{12}{1} = \frac{48}{5} = 9\frac{3}{5}$

i) $\frac{3\times2}{4\times3} = \frac{6}{12} = \frac{1}{2}$ (j) $\frac{3}{4} \times \frac{3}{4} = \frac{9}{16}$

k) $\frac{7}{5} \times \frac{11}{4} = \frac{77}{20} = 3\frac{17}{20}$ (l) $\frac{3}{8} \times \frac{7}{6} = \frac{21}{48} = \frac{7}{16}$

m) $\frac{5}{9} \div \frac{10}{3} = \frac{5}{9} \times \frac{3}{10} = \frac{15}{90} = \frac{1}{6}$

n) $\frac{27}{10} \div \frac{5}{4} = \frac{27}{10} \times \frac{4}{5} = \frac{108}{50} = \frac{54}{25} = 2\frac{4}{25}$

Page21

7. a) 72 b) 450 c) 504 d) 0.06

8. $\frac{5}{12}$

Page22

1. a) 2.25 hours b) 8.2 hours c) 6.3 hours

2. a) 4 h 45 min b) 6 h 12 min c) 3 h 24 min

3.a) 0.6 (b) 0.35 (c) 0.03 (d) 0.3 (e) 0.27

f) 0.09 (g) 0.25 (h) 0.8 (i) 0.666..= $0.\dot{6}$ (j) 0.625

4.a) 20% (b) 84% (c) 7% (d) 73.5%

e) 70% (f) 9% (g) 27% (h) 87.5%

5.

$a)\frac{6}{10} = \frac{3}{5}$ $b)\frac{2}{100} = \frac{1}{50}$ $c)\frac{95}{100} = \frac{19}{20}$ $d)\frac{165}{1000} = \frac{33}{200}$

$e)\frac{5}{100} = \frac{1}{20}$ $f)\frac{16}{100} = \frac{4}{25}$ $g)\frac{12.5}{100} = \frac{125}{1000} = \frac{1}{8}$

Page23

1. $5 \times £540 \div 100 = £27.00$

2. $12 \times 240 \div 100 = 28.8$kg

3.i) VAT £24

Total Cost = 160 + 24 = £184

ii) VAT £32

Total Cost = 160 + 32 = £192

iii) VAT 16+8+4 = £28

Total Cost = 160 + 28 = £188

4. $1.15 \times £6780 = £7797$

5. $0.88 \times £1765 = £1553.20$

6. $1.175 \times £1250 = £1468.75$

7. $1.05 \times £76.60 = £80.43$

Page24

8. $£9500 \times 0.92 \times 0.92 = £8040.80$

9. $£600 \times 1.04 \times 1.04 = £648.96$

10. $£16000 \times 1.03 \times 1.03 \times 1.03 = £17483.63$

11. $3400 \times 1.042 \times 1.042 = £3691.60$

1. $\frac{4}{125} \times 100 = 3.2\%$

2. Reduction £40 $\frac{40}{320} \times 100 = 12.5\%$

3. $33.\dot{3}\,\%$

4. (a) ½ (b) 2 (c) 4/3 (d) 5/6 (e) 2/5

(f) 4/15 (g) 9 (h) 1/9 (i) 1/15 (j) 15

Page25

1.a) 1 : 8 b) 2 : 5 c) 30 : 36 = 5 : 6

2. 1 : 5 ÷ 4

1 : 1.25

3. 5 + 7 = 12 £4800 ÷ 12 = £400

Suresh 5 × £400 = £2000

Laura 7 × £400 = £2800

4. 2 + 3 + 5 = 10 £7650 ÷ 10 = £765

A 2 × £765 = £1530

B 3 × £765 = £2295

C 5 × £765 = £3825

5. £84 ÷ 2 = £42 £42 × 5 = £210

6. a) 1 litre 320 ÷ 50 = 6.4miles

12 litres 6.4 × 12 = 76.8 miles

b) 1mile 50 ÷ 320 = 0.15625

100miles 0.15625 × 100 = 15.625 litres

7. 1 can 4.5 ÷ 9 = 0.5

5 cans 0.5 × 5 = 2.5 litres

8. 28.95 ÷ 1.62 = £17.87037 = £17.87 to the nearest penny

Test Yourself P26

1. 41, 43, 47

2.a) 3, 4, 18 b) 18, 24, 54, 450

3. 440 = 2×220 = 2×2×110 = 2×2×2×55

= 2×2×2×5×11 = $2^3$×5×11

4. 108 = 2×54= 2×2×27 = 2×2×3×9 = 2×2×3×3×3

60 = 2×30 = 2×2×15 = 2×2×3×5

HCF = 2×2×3 = 12

LCM = 2×2×3×3×3×5 = 540

5. a) 7 b) 12×12 = 144 c) 5×5×5 = 125

d) 0.6×0.6 = 0.36 e) 10 (as10×10×10 = 1000)

6. 2.5 × 2.9 = 7.25 6.3 + 2.2 = 8.5

7.25 ÷ 8.5 = 0.85294 = 0.85 to two dec. places

7. a) 4 + (-3) = 1 b) 4 - (-3) = 7

c) 2 × 6 = 12 d) 5 × (-3) = -15

e) 4 × (-3) = -12 f) 4 × (-3) × 6 = -72

g) (-3) × (-3) = 9

h) 2 × 4 - 3 × (-3) = 8 - -9 = 8 + 9 = 17

i) 24 ÷ (-3) = -8

8.a) 36.7 b) 347 800 c) 0.04592 d) 3.4

9.a) 17612 b) 1350.8 c) 16302 d) 136

10.a) 13.6 b) 1.944 c) 8.22÷0.03 = 822÷3 =274

11.a) 40 000 b) 0.05 c) 34.5

12.a) 3 × 8 = 24 300 × 80 = 24 000

b) 40 × 40 = 1600

c) 600 ÷ 0.3 = 6000 ÷ 3 = 2000

d) 4 ÷ 0.005 = 4 000 ÷ 5 = 800

Page27

13.a) 400 × 40 = 16 000 b) (300 × 600)/90 =2000

c) (30×80)/0.2 = 2400÷0.2 = 24000÷2 = 12 000

14. a) 3 × 9 = 27 b) 0.2 × 3 = 0.6

15. a) 14.49 ÷ 4 = 3.6225 b) 3.6 ÷ 2.25 = 1.6

c) 29.76 ÷ 7.75 = 3.84

16. a) 4 × 4 × 4 = 64 b) 2 × 2 × 2 × 2 × 2 × 2 = 64

17. a) 12 b) 4

18. $x$ = 5 or -5

19. 4 × 4 = 16 5 × 5 = 25

4.1 × 4.1 = 16.81 4.2 × 4.2 = 17.64

4.15 × 4.15 = 17.2225

All numbers between 4.1 and 4.15 round to 4.1

Answer 4.1

20. a) $10^{18}$ b) $10^6$ 21. 143 22. 10817.39

23. a) 1770000 b) 16800000

c) 1620000 d) 80

24.a) $\frac{3}{8}$ b) $\frac{128}{440} = \frac{64}{220} = \frac{32}{110} = \frac{16}{55}$

25. $\frac{2}{5} = \frac{28}{70}, \frac{4}{7} = \frac{40}{70}, \frac{3}{10} = \frac{21}{70}$ or as decimals

$\frac{3}{10}, \frac{2}{5}, \frac{4}{7}$

26. £378 ÷ 5 = £75.60 £75.60×3 = £226.80

27.a) $\frac{8+15}{20} = \frac{23}{20} = 1\frac{3}{20}$ b) $\frac{9}{4} - \frac{7}{5} = \frac{45-28}{20} = \frac{17}{20}$

c) $\frac{2}{9} \times \frac{7}{4} = \frac{14}{36} = \frac{7}{18}$ d) $\frac{5}{6} \div \frac{3}{10} = \frac{5}{6} \times \frac{10}{3} = \frac{50}{18} = \frac{25}{9} = 2\frac{7}{9}$

28. a) 0.265 b) 4.5% c) 35/100 = 7/20

d) 0.075 e) 35% f) 24/100 = 12/50 = 6/25

29. $0.\dot{8}5714\dot{2}$

30. 15 × 425 ÷ 100 = £63.75

Page28

31. £268 × 1.24 = £332.32

32. £9800 × 0.9 × 0.9 × 0.9 = £7144.20

33. reduction £51.75 $\frac{51.75}{345} \times 100 = 15\%$

34. 90%

35. 25%

36. a) $\frac{1}{10}$ b) $\frac{1}{5}$ c) $\frac{1}{4}$ d) $\frac{3}{4}$ e) $\frac{1}{3}$

37. $\frac{1}{8}$ 38. $\frac{3}{2}$ 39. $\frac{4}{17}$ 40. 3:4

41. 12480 ÷ 8 = 1560

1560 × 3 = £4680

1560 × 5 = £7800

42. Chris £21 Ivan £15

43. 247: 290 44. £5.67 45. 25.08€ 46. £81.50

Page29

1. mean 51÷10 = 5.1 median (4 + 5)÷2 = 4.5

mode 4

2. 4 × 5.5 = 22

3. 7 × 12 = 84 84 + 6 = 90 90 ÷ 8 = 11.25

4.a) 133 ÷ 6 = 22.16666… = 22.17

b) (22 + 23) ÷ 2 = 22.5 c) 23

5. 36 ÷ 6 = 6 Ans 106

6. 4 × 55 = 220 6 × 45 = 270

220 + 270 = 490 490 ÷ 10 = 49

7. 0.8kg 8. 131 9. 7 10. 4

Page30

1. Rent 156° Food 96° Savings 24°

Entertainment 48° Other 36°

360° ÷ 150 = 2.4°

Page31

2. Tea 126° Coffee 90° Orange 54°
   Lemon 18° Water 72°
3. 154 ÷ 44 = 3.5    3.5 × 360 = 1260

Page32

1. a) 35    (b) 145    (c) Cola
2. North
   East
   South
   West
   Centre

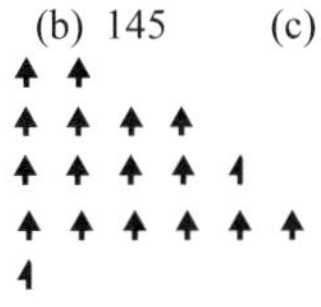

Key ▲ = 20

Page33

1. 9 + 12 + 6 + 4 + 3 + 2 = 36
2. a) 82  b) 63 - 38 = 25
   c) 36/63 × 100 = 57.1%
   or 36/64 × 100 = 56.25%

Page34

1. Mean = 78 ÷ 20 = 3.9
   Mode = 4   Median = 4   Range = 6 - 2 = 4
2. Total 36   Mean = 36 ÷ 24 = 1.5   Mode = 1
3. a) 6    b) mean = 132 ÷ 32 = 4.125
   c) Spin it a large number of times. If fair then the frequency for each score will be roughly the same.

Page35

4. a) 90 + 45 = 135
   b) 50 + 80 + 55 + 65 + 65 + 90 + 95 = 500
   c) 500 ÷ 7 = 71.42857 = 71.4 to 1 d.p.

Page36

1. a) 24   b) 10/24 = 5/12   c) 7 and under 8
2.a) 60-80mm   b) 6+12+18+22+20+16+4 = 98
   c) 6×10 = 60
   12×30 = 360
   18×50 = 900
   22×70 = 1540
   20×90 = 1800
   16×110 = 1760
   4×130 = 520
   total = 6940

Est of mean = 6940 ÷ 98 = 70.81632 = 70.8mm

Page37

1. a) As the mark for Paper 1 increases the mark for Paper 2 increases.
   b) Positive correlation
   c) Accept answer between 42 and 46
   d) Accept answer between 66 and 68

Page38

2. a) As the petrol consumption increases the engine size decreases.
   b) negative correlation
   c) Accept answer between 12.8 and 14.8
3. a) As the father's height increases the son's height increases.
   b) Positive correlation
   c) Accept 175 to 180cm
   d) No. This height is outside the values given and you do not know how the graph behaves in this region.

Page39

The journey started at 9 o'clock a.m. Jane travelled at a speed of 30÷2 = 15km/h for 2 hours covering a distance of 30km. She then stopped for an hour. She then continued at a speed 30÷0.5 = 60km/h for ½ hour covering a distance of 30km.
John's graph: Join (0930,0) to (1000,20) then to (1100,20) then to (1230,60)

1. a) 128 km   b) 25 miles   c) 106 km
   d) 56 miles   e) 50 km   f) 91 miles
2. a) (i) £80   (ii) £90   (iii) £104
   b) (i) 38 $m^3$   (ii) 88 $m^3$   (iii) 114 $m^3$

Page40

1. The crosses should be marked on the number line
   at A 0.2   B 0.5   C 0.8   D 0

Page41

1. a) ½  (b) ¼  (c) ⅔  (d) ⅝  (e) 3/5
   f) 0.3  (g) 0.9  (h) 0.65  (i) 0.29  (j) 0.73
   k) 1 - 0.6 = 0.4  (l) 1 - 0.75 = 0.25
   m) 1 - ⅜ = ⅝
2. 1 - 0.68 = 0.32
3. 1 - 0.03 = 0.97
4. 1 - 1/5 = 4/5
5. a) 1 - (0.7 +0.2) = 1 - 0.9 = 0.1
   b) 0.2 + 0.1 = 0.3    c) 0.3
6. a) $\frac{26}{52}=\frac{1}{2}$  b) $\frac{13}{52}=\frac{1}{4}$  c) $\frac{4}{52}=\frac{1}{13}$
   d) P(king) + P(ace) = $\frac{4}{52}+\frac{4}{52}=\frac{8}{52}=\frac{2}{13}$
   e) 60 × ¼ = 15
7. $\frac{15}{50}=\frac{3}{10}$

Page42

8. H1, H2, H3, H4, H5, H6, T1, T2, T3, T4, T5, T6
   a) $\frac{1}{12}$  b) $\frac{4}{12}=\frac{1}{3}$
9. HHH, HHT, HTH, HTT, THH, THT, TTH, TTT
   a) $\frac{1}{8}$  b) $1-\frac{1}{8}=\frac{7}{8}$  c) $\frac{3}{8}$
10. a) 36  b) $\frac{2}{36}=\frac{1}{18}$  c) $\frac{4}{36}=\frac{1}{9}$  d) $\frac{9}{36}=\frac{1}{4}$
11. a) $\frac{1}{8}$  b) $\frac{2}{8}=\frac{1}{4}$
12. a) 40  b) $\frac{1}{40}$  c) $\frac{5}{40}=\frac{1}{8}$  d) $\frac{20}{40}=\frac{1}{2}$

Page43

1.a) 50 b) 18 c) 32 d) $\frac{26}{50}=\frac{13}{25}$  e) $\frac{13}{25}\times 1200 = 624$

2.a) 188  b) 102  c) $\frac{102}{188}=\frac{51}{94}$  d) $\frac{37}{188}$

Page44 Test Yourself

1. mean = 66 ÷ 12 = 5.5  mode = 5
   median = (5 + 5) ÷ 2 = 5
   range = 9 - 3 = 6
2. mean = 169 ÷ 50 = 3.38  mode = 5
   median = (3 + 4) ÷ 2 = 3.5
3. 360° ÷ 24 = 15
   angles 0 is 60° 1 is 120° 2 is 90° 3 is 60° 4 is 30°
4. 360° ÷ 40 = 9
   angles Red - 54° Black - 126° Silver - 90°
   White - 72° Blue - 18°
5. Bar graph - see page 35 for this type.
   a. 127  b. 60  c. extra bar height 140

Page45

6. a) 29  b) 11  c) 4  d) $\frac{9}{29}\times 100$ = 31.0%
7. a) Positive correlation
   b) Accept 18 - 20  c) $y$ increases as $x$ increases
8. a) 0.54  b) 0.46 × 50 = 23
9. 36 outcomes (1,1) (1,2) (1,3) (1,4) (1,5) (1,6)
   (2,1) (2,2) (2,3) (2,4) (2,5) (2,6)
   (3,1) etc
   P(score 7) = $\frac{6}{36}=\frac{1}{6}$
10.

|  | 1 | 2 | 3 | 4 |
|---|---|---|---|---|
| 1 | 2 | 3 | 4 | 5 |
| 2 | 3 | 4 | 5 | 6 |
| 3 | 4 | 5 | 6 | 7 |
| 4 | 5 | 6 | 7 | 8 |

P(5) = 4/16 = ¼

Page46

1. Obtuse 130° to 150°
   Acute 70° to 85°
   Reflex 210° to 230°
   Reflex 320° to 340°
   Acute 20° to 40°

Page47

2. $a = 180° - 130° = 50°$
   $d = 28°$  $b = 180° - 28° = 152°$  $c = 152°$
   $110° + 105° = 215°$  $e = 360° - 215° = 145°$
3. $65° + 10° = 75°$  $p = 180° - 75° = 105°$
   $112° + 75° + 78° = 265°$  $q = 360° - 265° = 95°$
   $t = 80°$  $r = 80°$  $s = 180° - 80° = 100°$
4. $s = 180° - 112° = 68°$  $t = 68°$
   $u = 180° - 98° = 82°$  $w = 98°$  $x = 82°$
5. $a = 180° - 165° = 15°$
   $162° + 86° = 248°$  $b = 360° - 248° = 112°$
   $c = 110°$  $d = 70°$  $e = 180° - 75° = 105°$  $f = 75°$
6. $5x = 180°$  $\therefore x = 36°$
   $5y = 360°$  $y = 72°$
   $6z = 180°$  $z = 30°$

Page48

1. $x = 180° - 95° = 85°$  $a = 180° - 112° = 68°$
   $b = 180° - 133° = 47°$  $d = 180° - 81° = 99°$
   $e = 180° - 154° = 26°$
2. $p = 180° - 144° = 36°$  $q = 150° \div 2 = 75°$
   $180° - 148° = 32°$  $2 \times 32° = 64°$
   $r = 180° - 64° = 116°$
3. $b = 23°$  $a = 180° - 140° = 40°$
   $180° - 90° = 90°$  $3c = 90°$  $\therefore c = 30°$  $2c = 60°$
   $2d + 2d + d = 5c$  $5d = 180°$
   $\therefore d = 36°$  $2d = 72°$
4. $180° - 130° = 50°$  $a = 50°$
   $180° - 120° = 60°$  $50° + 60° = 110°$
   $b = 180° - 110° = 70°$
   $2 \times 82° = 164°$  $c = 180° - 164° = 16°$
   $180° - 56° = 124°$  $124° \div 2 = 62°$
   $d = 180° - 62° = 118°$
5. $112° + 45° + 76° = 233°$  $p = 360° - 233° = 127°$
   $r = 180° - 85° = 95°$  $100° + 85° + 95° = 280°$
   $q = 360° - 280° = 80°$
   $360° - 70° = 290°$  $3x + 2x + 5x = 10x$
   $10x = 290°$  $\therefore x = 29°$

Page49

1. $p = 141°$  $q = 154°$  $r = 53°$
2. Rectangle - two lines of symmetry
   Parallelogram - no lines of symmetry
   Equilateral triangle - three lines of symmetry
3.

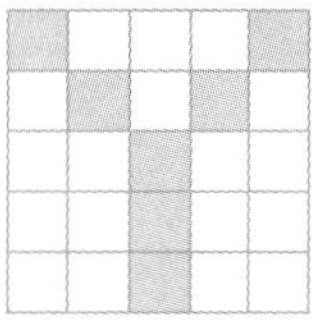

4.

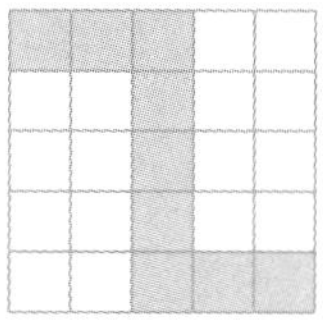

Page50

5. Exterior angle add up to 360°
   Exterior angle = 360 ÷ 5 = 72°
   Interior angle = 180 - 72 = 108°
6. Exterior angle = 360 ÷ 8 = 45°
   Interior angle = 180 - 45 = 135°
7. $a = 360 \div 8 = 45°$
8. Exterior angle add up to 360°
   Exterior angle = 360 ÷ 20 = 18°
   Interior angle = 180 - 18 = 162°
9. Exterior angle = 180 - 150 = 30°
   360 ÷ 30 = 12 sides
10. Exterior angle = 360 ÷ 6 = 60°
    Interior angle = 180 - 60 = 120°
11. Exterior angle = 360 ÷ 9 = 40°
    Interior angle = 180 - 40 = 140°

Page51

Cube
An example

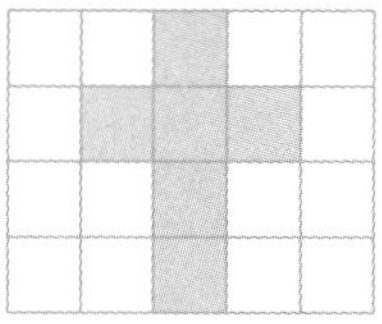

Here
1 square = 1cm

Triangular prism

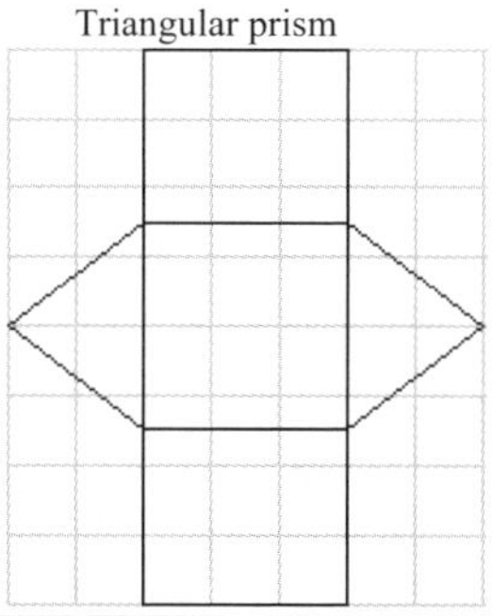

cuboid
An example

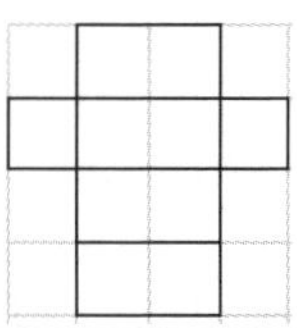

Page52

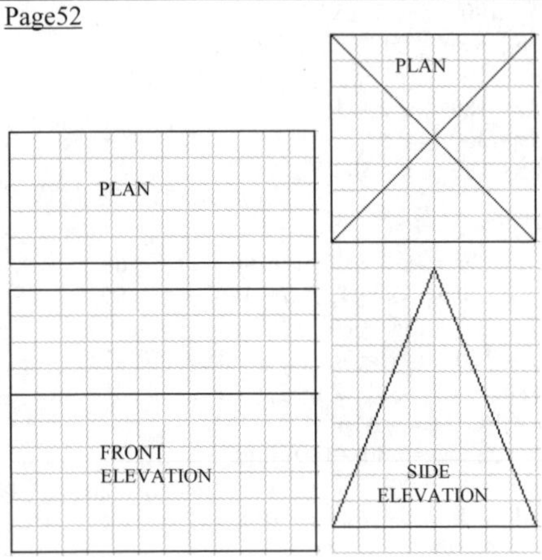


Page53

1. 

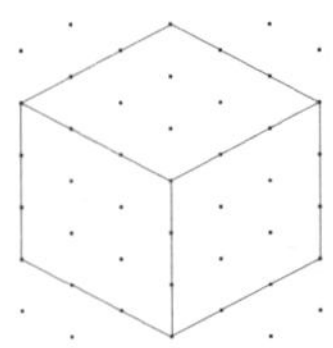

2. an example

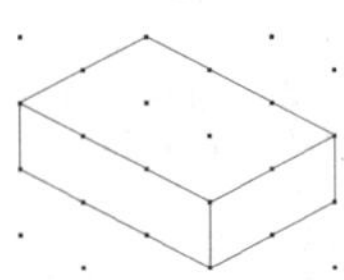

3. 4. Examples
a) b)

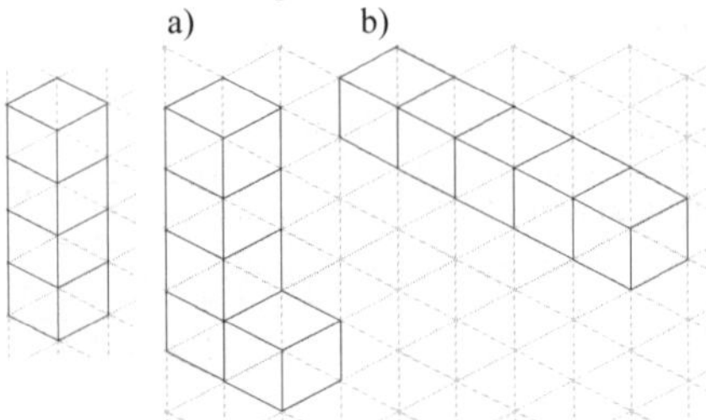

5. 6. a) b)

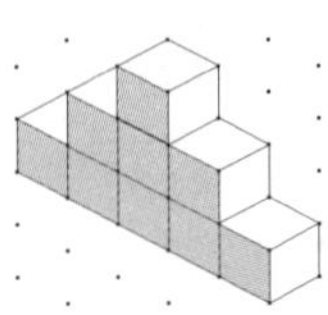

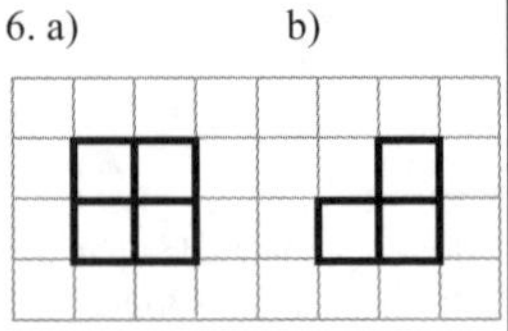

Page54

1. a) Perimeter 12 cm Area 9 $cm^2$
   b) Perimeter 14 cm Area 10 $cm^2$
   c) Perimeter 20 cm Area 16 $cm^2$
2. a) Perimeter 20 cm Area 18.75 $cm^2$
   b) Perimeter 12 mm Area 6 $mm^2$
   c) Perimeter 26 m Area 32 $m^2$
   d) Perimeter 18 cm Area 12 $cm^2$

Page55

3.a) $\frac{1}{2} \times 8 \times 3 = 12cm^2$ b) $\frac{1}{2} \times 3 \times 3 = 4\frac{1}{2}\ cm^2$
   c) $6 \times 2.5 = 15m^2$ d) $\frac{1}{2} \times (9+3) \times 2 = 12cm^2$
   e) $\frac{1}{2} \times (6+5) \times 4 = 22m^2$ f) $10 \times 1.5 = 15cm^2$
4. a) $7 \times 6 = 42$ $5 \times 3 = 15$ $42 + 15 = 57cm^2$
   b) $6 \times 12 = 72$ $\frac{1}{2} \times 12 \times 4 = 24$
   $72 + 24 = 96m^2$
5. a) Volume = $4 \times 4 \times 4 = 64\ cm^3$
   b) Area of end = $\frac{1}{2} \times 4 \times 3 = 6$
   Volume = $6 \times 9 = 54\ mm^3$
   c) volume = $6 \times 2 \times 3 = 36cm^3$
   d) Area of end = $(3 \times 2) + (\frac{1}{2} \times 3 \times \frac{1}{2}) = 6.75$
   Volume = $6.75 \times 4 = 27m^3$
   e) Area of end = $\pi\ 3^2 = \pi \times 3 \times 3 = 28.27433$
   Volume = $28.2743 \times 8 = 226.19$
   $= 226cm^3$ to 3 sig.fig.
6. a) $30 \div 4 = 7.5$ m
   b) $2 \times 7 = 14$ $36 - 14 = 22$ $22 \div 2 = 11$cm
7. a) $\sqrt{64} = 8$ cm b) $54 \div 6 = 9$ cm

Page56

8. a) $\sqrt[3]{27} = 3$cm b) $4 \times 2 = 8$ $96 \div 8 = 12$cm
9. a) $C = \pi \times 10 = 31.4$cm
   $A = \pi \times 5 \times 5 = 78.5cm^2$
   b) $C = \pi \times 8 = 25.1$cm
   $A = \pi \times 4 \times 4 = 50.3cm^2$
10. a) C 28.3cm A $63.6cm^2$
   b) C 9.42cm A $7.07cm^2$
11. a) C 47.1cm A $177cm^2$
   b) C 75.4mm A $452mm^2$
12. a) C 9m A $6m^2$
   b) C 27cm A $58cm^2$
13.C $10\pi$ cm A $25\pi\ cm^2$
14. 30.8cm to 3 sig fig
15. $\pi d = 24\pi$ d = 24 r = 12cm
16. a) $\pi \times 30 \times 20 = 1884$ cm
   = 18.8 m to 3 sig fig
   b) $471 \div (3.14 \times 30) = 5$
17. $500\ 000 \div 10\ 000 = 50m^2$
18. $10 \times 10000 = 100\ 000\ cm^2$

Page57

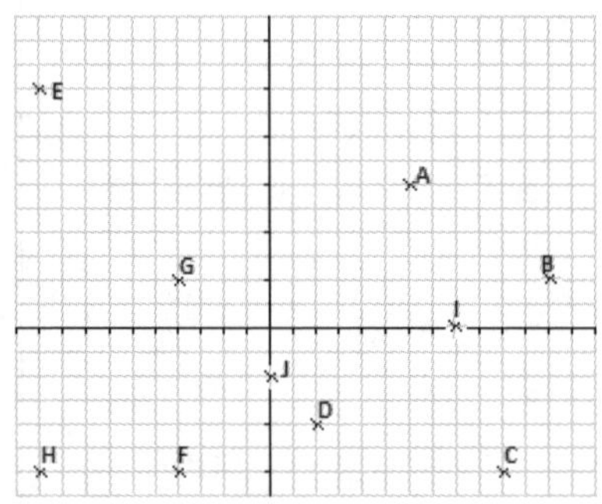


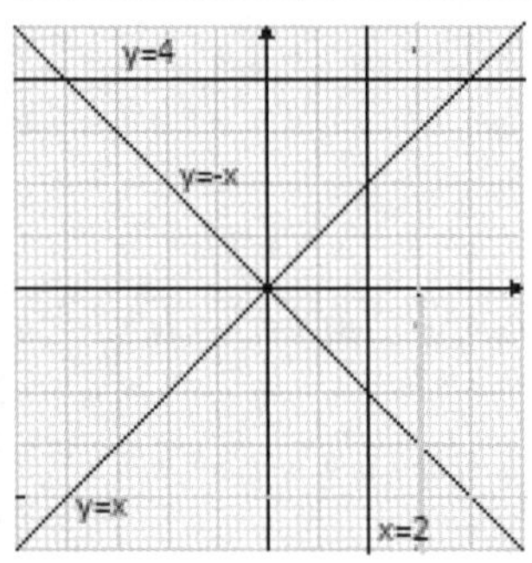


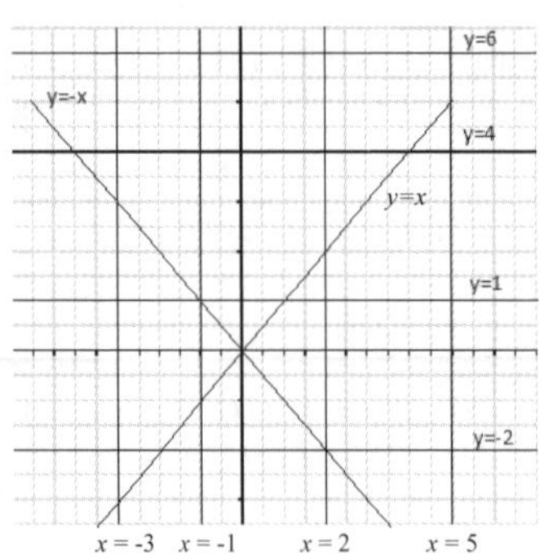


Page58

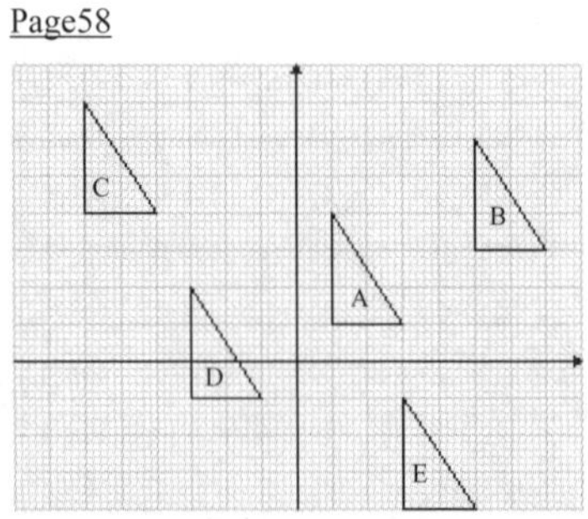


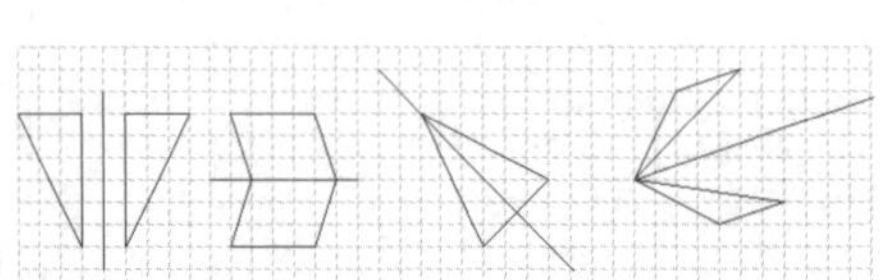

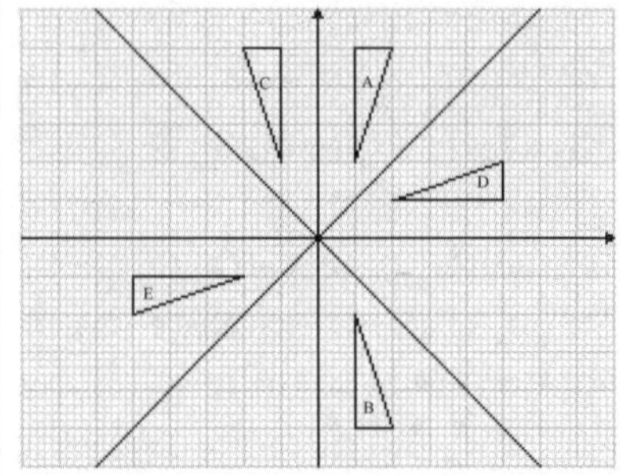


Page59

Rotations

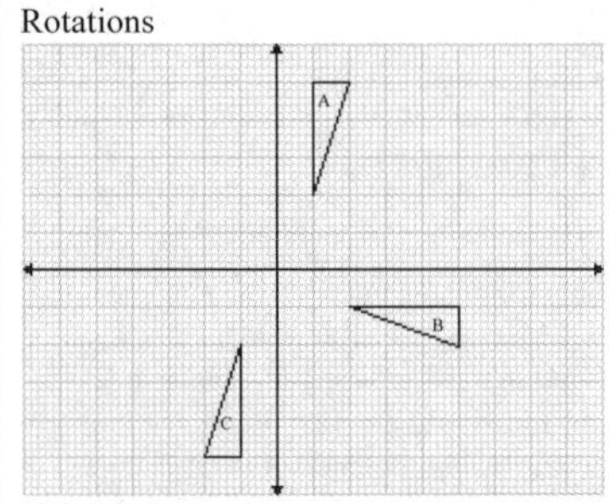


Enlargements

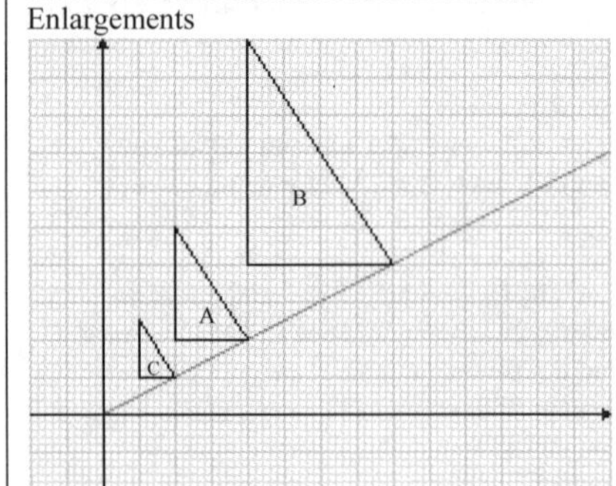


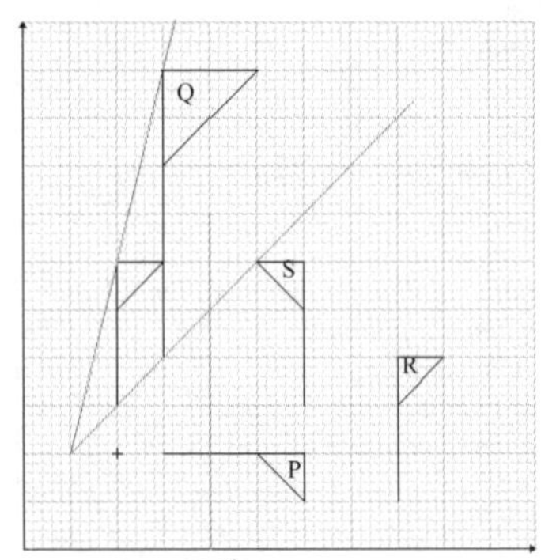


Page60

1. A and C 2. C and E
3. D and B, D and C, D and A, B and C, B and A
4. C and F, A and F
5. A to C $\begin{bmatrix} -3 \\ 1 \end{bmatrix}$ C to E reflect in *x=1*

D to B 180° rotation about (-3,-1)
D to C 90° clockwise rotation about (-2,0)
D to A 90° clockwise rotation about (0,-3)
B to C 90° anti-clockwise rotation about (-4,0)
B to A 90° anti-clockwise rotation about (-1,2)
C to F Enlargement Factor 2 centre (0,2)
A to F Enlargement Factor 2 centre off grid

Page61

1. a) $8 \times 50000 = 400\ 000$cm = 4000m = 4km
   b) $9 \times 1000 \times 100$cm = 900000
   $900\ 000 \div 50\ 000 = 18$cm
2. $6 \times 125 = 750$cm = 7.5m
   $4.5 \times 125 = 562.5 = 5.625$m
   i.e. 7.5m by 5.625m
3. a) $30 \times 500 = 15000$ mm = 15m
   b) 2.5m = $2.5 \times 1000 = 2500$mm
   $2500 \div 500 = 5$mm

Bearings - Answers are approx.
bearing 280° distance 7.4km

Page62

8.2km
1. i. 065° ii. 223°
2, i. 231° ii. 051°
3. a. 323° b. 6km

Page63

4. a. 356° b. 24.5km
5 a. 100° b. 2530m

Page66

1. (4.5,1) 2. (-1.5, -2) 3. (0.5, 0.5) 4. (-2.5, 3)
5. a is 27 b is 43 c is 46 d is 55 e is 76
f is 115 g is 140 h is 50 i is 160
j is 185 k is 120 l is 170 m is 32.4
n is 32.75 o is 7.2 p is 7.35 q is 40.4
r is 41.3 s is 6.2 t is 6.7 u is 41.5

Page67

6. a is 20.25 b is 21.5 c is 8.05 d is 8.35
e is 30.5 f is 33.5 g is 60.6 h is 61.7
i is 0.4 j is 1.2 k is 1.9 l is 2.8 m is 3.1
1. a) 3 m b) 6000 g c) 24 inches
d) 5000 m = 500000 cm e) 2 litres
f) 16 km g) 24 ÷ 8 = 3 3 × 5 = 15 miles
h) 2 × 2.2 = 4.4 lb i) 4 × 2.5 = 10 cm
j) 1 lb 4 oz k) 7 litres
2.a) 54 m b) 2600 g c) 36 inches
d) 3100 m = 310000 cm e) 6.4 litres
f) 80 km g) 184 ÷ 8 = 23 23 × 5 = 115 miles
h) 3 × 2.2 = 6.6 lb i) 8 × 2.5 = 20 cm
j) 3 lb 5 oz k) 58.9 litres

Page68

1. 2hours 33min 2. a) 3.3h b) 6.85h c) 12.55h
3. a) 5h 39min b) 8h 42min c) 13h 55min
4. 2h 46min 5. 65 × 3 = 195 miles

Page69

6. 5 / 2 = 2.5 km / h
7. 25 / 4 = 6.25 seconds
8. speed = 150 ÷ 3 1/3 = 45mph
9. t = 80 ÷ 35 = 2.2857 = 2h 17min
10. 12km 11. 72m 12. 24 km/h
13. 13.5 seconds 14. 32 km/h

Test Yourself Page70

1. see pages 48
2. Infinite
3. 97 + 48 = 145°
$a$ = 180 - 145 = 35°
$b$ = 360 - 280 = 80°
$c$ = 90 - 73 = 17°
4. $x$ = 30° $y$ = 180 - (65 + 30) = 85°
$m$ = 77° $n$ = 180 - (2 × 77) = 26°
$p$ = 55° $q$ = 55+25 = 80° $r$ = 180-(80+62) = 38°
5. 360 ÷ 10 = 36 180 - 36 = 144°
6.

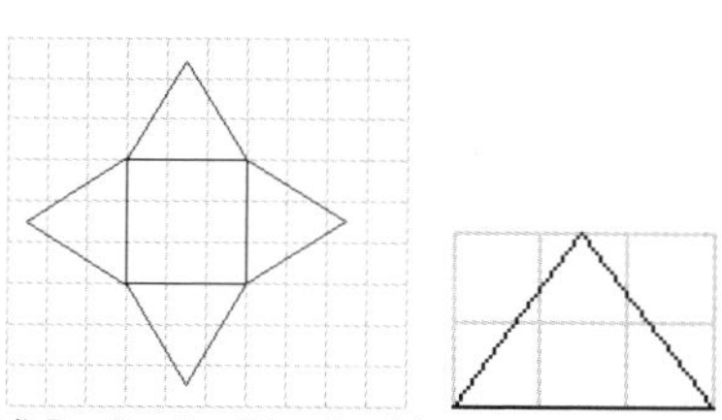

7.a) i) P = 9 + 5 + 15 + 5 = 34cm
A = ½ (9 + 15) × 4 = 48cm²
ii) P = Circumference = π×4 = 12.6cm to 3sig.fig
A = π × 2 × 2 = 12.6cm² to 3 sig.fig.
b) V = 48 × 20 = 960cm³

Page71

8.

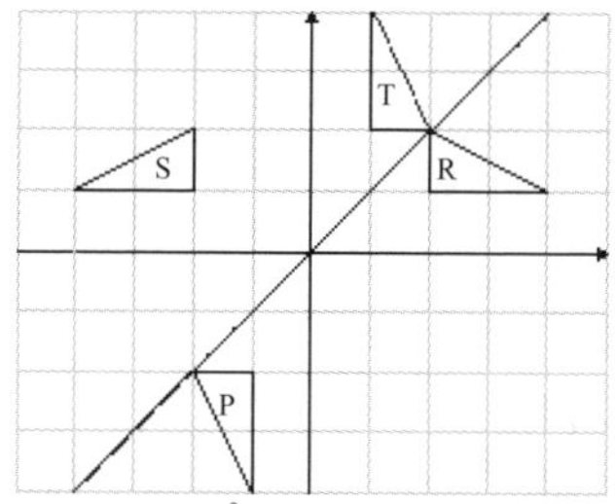


Rotation of 180° clockwise, with the origin. as the centre of rotation.
9. AP = 3.95km scale drawing
10. (3,1)
11. see P51 S.A =52 unit² Volume 24 unit³
12. see P51 S.A =22 unit² Volume 6 unit³

Page72

13. Not to scale

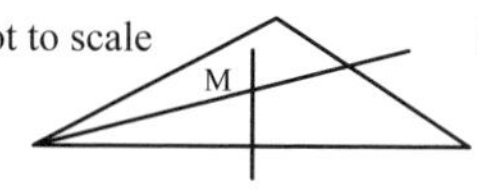


14.

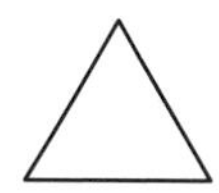

15.a) 3.568km b) 32700g c) 3.5 × 2.2 = 7.7lb
d) 65 ÷ 5 = 13 13 × 8 = 104km
16. 43m and 4h and 29min total 5h 12min
17. Time = 80 ÷ 64 = 1.25h = 1h 15min
18. 112 km

Page73

1. i. $x^9$ ii. $y^4$ iii. $x^4$ iv. $p^8$ v. $x^5$
vi. $x$ vii. $x^3$ viii. $z^4$ ix. $8x^5$ x. $15x^3$
xi. $12k^5$ xii. $3q^2$ xiii. $\frac{3h}{2}$ xv. $\frac{2p^2}{r}$ xvi. $\frac{2y^3}{3h^3}$

Page74

1. (i) $-2x + 9y$
(ii) $3x^2 - 7x$
2. (i) $3y$
(ii) $5x$
(iii) $6m$
(iv) $2p$
(v) $r^2$
(vi) $2pq$
3. i) $3x + 4$
(ii) $-2x + 6$
(iii) $6x - 3$
iv) $x^2 + 2x - 6$
(v) $m^2 + 4m + 8$
1. (i) 3a + c = (3 × 4) + (-2) = 12 - 2 = 10
(ii) 2ab - c = 2 × (4 × 5) - (-2) = 40 + 2 = 42
2. (i) 3ab + 3c = (3×4×5) + 3×(-2) = 60 - 6 = 54
(ii) 2b + c² = (2×5) + (-2)² = 10 + 4 = 14
(iii) a - c² = 4 - (-2)² = 4 - 4 = 0
(iv) a(c - b) = 4×( [-2] - [5] ) = 4 × (-7) = -28
(v) a(b - c) = 4×( [5] - [-2] ) = 4 × (7) = 28

Page75

3. a) $10 - x^2 = 10 - (-4)^2 = 10 - 16 = -6$
b) $(2x)^2 - 3y^2 = (2×(-4))^2 - 3×9 = 64 - 27 = 37$
c) $xy^2 = (-4) × 9 = -36$
d) $-7-2x = -7 - 2×(-4) = -7 + 8 = 1$
e) $4xyz - \frac{xy}{4z} = 4×(-4)×3×2 - \frac{-4×3}{3×2} = -96 - -2$
$= -94$
(f) $\frac{(4y - z^2)}{(4y - z\ )^2} = \frac{12-4}{(12-2)^2} = \frac{8}{100} = \frac{2}{25}$
4. P = 4$x$ + 6$y$
a) P = 4 × 7 + 6 × 2 = 28 + 12 = 40
b) 56 = 4$x$ + 6 × 4 ∴ 32 = 4$x$ ∴ $x$ = 8
5. P = 3$x$ - 2$y$ + 6$y$ + 3$x$ + 2$y$ = 6$x$ + 6$y$
P = 6 × 3 + 6 × 2 = 18 + 12 = 30
6. a) q = 7 × 8 = 56 (b) 36 = 4r ∴ r = 9
7. 7 × 6 × 3 = 126cm³
8. C = $\frac{5}{9}$(86 – 32) = 30
9.a) $(-2)^2 + 5×(-2) = 4 + -10 = -6$
b) $(-2)^2 - 3×(-2) - 2 = 4 + 6 - 2 = 8$

Page76

1.(i) $2y + 2$ (ii) $5m - 10$ (iii) $4x + 12$
(iv) $x^2 - 2x$ (v) 2p - 10q (vi) -5p + 6
(vii) $-12p^2 - 2p^2q + 4p$
2. a) 8(3c - 10) = 24c - 80
b) - (7 - 3d) = -7 + 3d
c) 4f - 2(3f + 7) = 4f - 6f - 14 = -2f - 14
d) $g(2g - 4) - (3g - 5) = 2g^2 - 4g - 3g + 5$
$= 2g^2 - 7g + 5$
e) $3j(4j + 5hj - 2) = 12j^2 + 15hj^2 - 6j$
3. a) $5(2x + 1)$ (b) $4(2x - 3)$ (c) $x(x - 2)$
d) $x(x + 5)$ (e) $2x(x + 5)$ (f) $3x(x + 3)$
g) $x(x - 3)$ (h) $2(3x + 2)$
4. a) $5x(3y + 1)$ b) $6(x - 2)$ c) $6ab(5a - 2b)$
d) $5xy(y + 4)$ e) $2bc(2a + 3d)$ f) $9x(y - 3)$
g) $2pq(4p - 3q)$ h) $y(y - 1)$

Page77

1. a) $(x – 5)$ cards
b) £9$y$
2.(a)£( $x$ + 20)
(b) £3$x$
(c) $x + x + 20 + 3x = 100$ ∴ $5x + 20 = 100$
3. a) £45$x$ (b) £78$y$ (c) $45x + 78y = 1680$
4. $2x + 4y = 8$ $3x + 3y = 9$
Lines cross at $x = 2$ $y = 1$

Page78

1. $x = 3$ 2. $x = 7$ 3. $4t = 32$ ∴ $t = 8$
4. $3p = 15$ ∴ $p = 5$ 5. $y = 4$ 6. $x = 6$
7. $3x = 12$ $x = 4$ 8. $-2x = 6$ $x = -3$
9. $5x = 2x + 6$ $3x = 6$ $x = 2$
10. 4q + 4 = 2q + 11 ∴ 2q = 7 ∴ q = 3.5
11. $2x - 2 = 5x + 20$ ∴ $-22 = 3x$ ∴ $x = -22/3$
12. $10×6 = x$ ∴ $x = 60$

Page79

13. $20 = 2x$ ∴ $x = 10$
14. $x = 2$
15. $5 × x = 3 × 4$ $5x = 12$ ∴ $x = \frac{12}{5} = 2\frac{2}{5}$
16. $3x = 12$ ∴ $x = 4$
17. a) $3x = 39$ ∴ $x = 13$
b) $x + 8 = 25$ ∴ $x = 17$
c) $x - 14 = 39$ ∴ $x = 53$
d) $3x + 4 = 31$ ∴ $3x = 27$ ∴ $x = 9$
18. $x + 4x + x + 4x = 60$ ∴ $10x = 60$ ∴ $x = 6$
Length = 24
19. $x × 2x = 98$ ∴ $2x^2 = 98$
∴ $x^2 = 49$
∴ $x = 7$ (or -7 which is not possible)
Length = 14
20. $x + x + 10 + x + 20 + x + 30 + x + 40 = 360$
$5x + 100 = 360$ ∴ $5x = 260$ ∴ $x = 52°$

Page80

21. 180 - 90 = 90 $y + 2y = 90$
∴ $3y = 90$ ∴ $y = 30°$
22. $x + 8 = 3$ ∴ $x = -5$
∴ Temperature at 3am is -5°C
1. The area of a circle equals pi times the radius squared
2. The perimeter equals $a$ plus h plus r
The area equals a half of $a$ multiplied by h
3. C = 25 + 8d
4. S = $\frac{d}{t}$

Page81

1.a) $x > 4$
b) $2x \le 8$ ∴ $x \le 4$
c) $15 > 5x$ ∴ $3 > x$ normally written $x < 3$
d) $x < -5$
2. a)

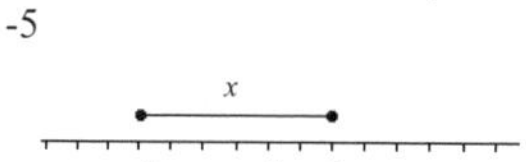


b)

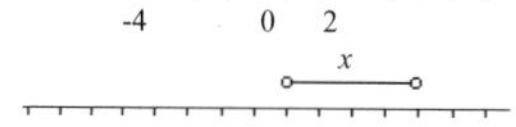


c)

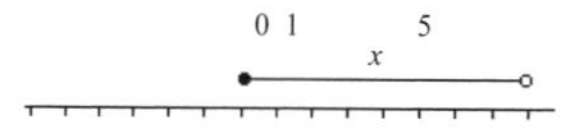


d)

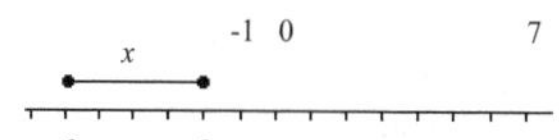


3. -1, 0, 1, 2, 3

Page82

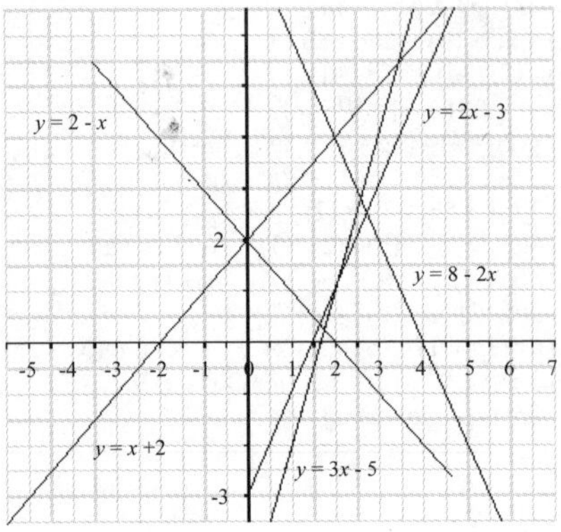


Lines through (0, 6) and (6, 0)
(0, 4) and (6, 0)
(5, 0) and (0, 2.5)

Page83

1. $x = 7$ or $-7$
2. $x = 13$ or $-13$
3. $x^2 = 4$ $\therefore$ $x = 2$ or $-2$
4. $x^2 = 16$ $\therefore$ $x = 4$ or $-4$
5. $x^2 = 81$ $\therefore$ $x = 9$ or $-9$
6. $3x^2 = 27$ $\therefore$ $x^2 = 9$ $\therefore$ $x = 3$ or $-3$
7. $2x^2 = 128$ $\therefore$ $x^2 = 64$ $\therefore$ $x = 8$ or $-8$
8. $x^2 = 88$ $\therefore$ $x = 9.38$ or $- 9.38$
9. a) $x^2 = 16$ $\therefore$ $x = 4$ (or - 4 which is not possible) $\therefore$ side length is 4 cm
b) $x^3 = 125$ $\therefore$ $x = 5$ $\therefore$ side length is 5 cm

1. a) 14 , 17 , 20
(b) 21 , 25 , 29
(c) 2 , -3 , -8
(d) 1 , 8 , 15
(e) 25 , 36 , 49
(f) 18 , 29 , 47
(g) 2 , -1 , - 4
(h) -2 , 1 , 4
(i) 1/5 , 1/6 , 1/7
(j) 32 , 64 , 128

Page84

1. a)

| *Position of term* | *1* | *2* | *3* | *4* | *5* | *6* |
|---|---|---|---|---|---|---|
| Sequence | 1 | 4 | 7 | 10 | 13 | 16 |
| *Difference* | | 3 | 3 | 3 | 3 | 3 |
| Position ×3 | 3 | 6 | 9 | 12 | 15 | 18 |

The n[th] term is 3n - 2

b)

| *Position of term* | *1* | *2* | *3* | *4* | *5* |
|---|---|---|---|---|---|
| Sequence | -3 | 2 | 7 | 12 | 17 |
| *Difference* | | 5 | 5 | 5 | 5 |
| Position ×5 | 5 | 10 | 15 | 20 | 25 |

The n[th] term is 5n - 8

c)

| *Position of term* | *1* | *2* | *3* | *4* | *5* |
|---|---|---|---|---|---|
| Sequence | 5 | 7 | 9 | 11 | 13…. |
| *Difference* | | 2 | 2 | 2 | 2 |
| Position ×2 | 2 | 4 | 6 | 8 | 10 |

The n[th] term is 2n + 3

d) The n[th] term is -2n + 15
e) The n[th] term is -5n + 43
2. 3, 7, 11, 15
20[th] term 79
3. -3, 0, 5, 12, 21
4. 5, 14, 29, 50, 77

Page85

14white tiles for 4 grey tiles
26white tiles for 10 grey tiles
2n + 6 white tiles for n grey tiles

1.

| S | 1 | 2 | 3 | 4 | 5 | n |
|---|---|---|---|---|---|---|
| P | 2 | 3 | 4 | 5 | 6 | n + 1 |
| R | 2 | 4 | 6 | 8 | 10 | 2n |

2.

| T | 1 | 2 | 3 | 4 | 5 | t |
|---|---|---|---|---|---|---|
| A | 3 | 5 | 7 | 9 | 11 | 2t + 1 |

For example:
Each additional triangle requires 2 arrows.
If we take the first triangle as 2 arrows then for t triangles we need 2t matches plus one more to finish off the first triangle.
3. a) four squares in a row
b) 16 (c) $10 \times 3 + 1 = 31$ d) 3n + 1

Test Yourself Page86

1.a) $x^{3+4} = x^7$
b) $y^{8-2} = y^6$
c) $5z^{8-2-3} = 5z^3$
2. $y = x - 1$ line through ( 0,-1) and (1,0)
$2x - y = 4$ line through (0,-4) and (2,0)
Lines intersect at (3,2)
3.

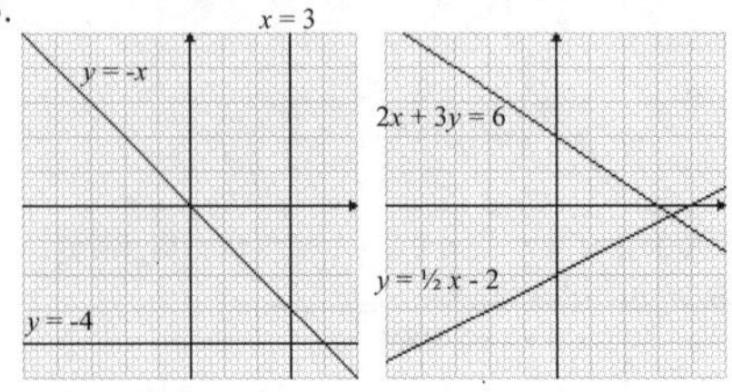


4. a) 4- (-2) = 6
b) 5×4 + 8×(-2) = 20 + -16 = 4
c) (4-8)÷(-2) = 2
d) $\sqrt{\frac{16}{4}} = \sqrt{4} = 2$
e) $2\times(-2)^2 = 8$
5. a) $5x - x - 2 = 4x - 2$
b) 4p - 4q +3p + 6q = 7p + 2q
c) $2x^2 + 10x - x^2 + 3x = x^2 + 13x$
6. a) 2n + 14
b) 16e + 18
c) -2h + 21

Page87

7.(a) $6x - 9 = 3(2x - 3)$
(b) $6ab^2 + 2ab = 2ab(3b + 1)$
(c) $15pqr - 3pr^2 = 3pr(5q - r)$
8. i) $3x = 24$ $\therefore$ $x = 8$
ii) $3x + 2x - 10 = 40$
$5x = 50$ $\therefore$ $x = 10$
iii) $5x + 5 = 4 - x + 2$
$6x = 1$ $\therefore$ $x = \frac{1}{6}$
iv) $x = 25.5$ v) $x = 51$ vi) $x = 36$
vii) $x = 16$ viii) $x = -10$
9. Perimeter (4x -4) x=5
10.

| *Position of term* | *1* | *2* | *3* | *4* | *5* |
|---|---|---|---|---|---|
| Sequence | 1 | 5 | 9 | 13 | 17 |
| *Difference* | | 4 | 4 | 4 | 4 |
| Position ×4 | 4 | 8 | 12 | 16 | 20 |

The n[th] term is 4n - 3
11. 8, 13, 18, 23 10[th] term 53
12. 4n < 24 $\therefore$ n < 6

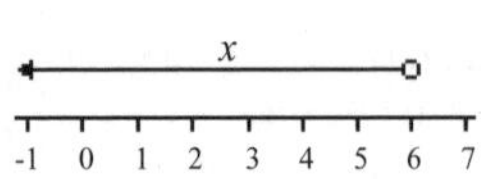


13. n < 6
a)

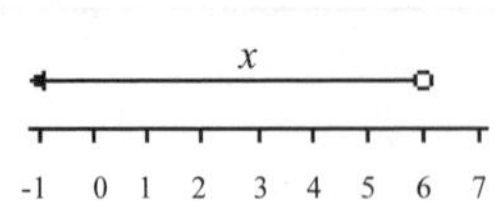


b) 2, 3, 5

Page88

1. $17 \times 17 = 289$ $8 \times 8 = 64$ $289 - 64 = 225$
$x = \sqrt{225} = 15$
$11 \times 11 = 121$ $9 \times 9 = 81$ $121 + 81 = 202$
$y = \sqrt{202} = 14.2$ to 3 sig. fig.
$16 \times 16 = 256$ $13 \times 13 = 169$ $256 - 169 = 87$
$z = \sqrt{87} = 9.33$ to 3 sig. fig.
$40 \times 40 = 1600$ $9 \times 9 = 81$ $1600 + 81 = 1681$
$w = \sqrt{1681} = 41$
2. $15 \times 15 = 225$ $5 \times 5 = 25$ $225 + 25 = 250$
*diagonal* = $\sqrt{250}$ = 15.8cm to 3 sig. fig.
3. $25 \times 25 = 625$ $24 \times 24 = 576$ $7 \times 7 = 49$
$625 = 576 + 49$ $\therefore$ It is a right-angled triangle
4. $10 \times 10 = 100$ $5 \times 5 = 25$ $100 - 25 = 75$
h = $\sqrt{75}$ = 8.66cm to 3 sig. fig.

Page89

5. Sides of triangle $\sqrt{32}$ $\therefore$ area triangle 16cm$^2$
Area semicircle 25.1cm$^2$
$\therefore$ Area shape 41.1cm2 to 3 sig. fig.
6. 37.9cm
length$^2 = (6 - 4)^2 + (7 - 1)^2 = 4 + 36 = 40$
length = $\sqrt{40}$ = 6.32 to 3 sig.fig.
1. length = $\sqrt{(16 + 9)} = \sqrt{25} = 5$
2. length = $\sqrt{(4 + 25)} = \sqrt{29} = 5.39$ to 3 sig.fig.
3. length = $\sqrt{(9 + 25)} = \sqrt{34} = 5.83$ to 3 sig.fig.
4. length = $\sqrt{(1 + 16)} = \sqrt{17} = 4.12$ to 3 sig.fig.
5. length = $\sqrt{(1 + 25)} = \sqrt{26} = 5.10$ to 3 sig.fig.
6. length = $\sqrt{((x - a)^2 + (y - b)^2)}$

Page90

1.a) $x = 3$, $x^3 - 2x = 3^3 - 2 \times 3 = 21$
$x = 4$, $x^3 - 2x = 4^3 - 2 \times 4 = 56$
b) $x = 3.5$, $x^3 - 2x = 3.5^3 - 2 \times 3.5 = 35.875$ too big
$x = 3.2$, $x^3 - 2x = 3.2^3 - 2 \times 3.2 = 26.368$ too small
$x = 3.3$, $x^3 - 2x = 3.3^3 - 2 \times 3. = 29.337$ too big
$x = 3.25$, $x^3 - 2x = 3.25^3 - 2 \times 3.25 = 27.828$ too small
Answer $x = 3.3$ to 1 d.p.
2. $x = 6$, $2x^2 - 3x = 2.6^2 - 3 \times 6 = 54$ too big
$x = 5.2$, $2x^2 - 3x = 2.(5.2)^2 - 3 \times 5.2 = 38.48$ too small
$x = 5.3$, $2x^2 - 3x = 2.(5.3)^2 - 3 \times 5.3 = 40.28$ too big
$x = 5.25$, $2x^2 - 3x = 2.(5.25)^2 - 3 \times 5.25 = 39.375$ too small
$x = 5.3$ to 1 decimal place
3. $x = 4$ gives 84 too small
$x = 5$ gives 125 too big
$x = 4.5$ gives 103.5 too big
$x = 4.4$ gives 99.44 too small
$x = 4.45$ gives 101.46 too big
$x = 4.4$ to 1 decimal place

Page91

Plot points
(-1,8) (0,3) (1,0) (2,-1) (3,0) (4,3) (5,8)
Solutions $x = 1$ or $x = 3$
1. Plot points
(-2,9) (-1,4) (0,1) (1,0) (2,1) (3,4) (4,9)
Approximate solution $x = -1.8$ or $x = 3.8$

Page92

1 .a) $x = 4$ $y = 5$
b) $x = 3$ $y = -2$
c) $x = -2$ $y = 5$

Page93

1 .a) $x = 3$ $y = 5$
b) $x = 4$ $y = 1$
c) $x = 6$ $y = 4$

Page94

1 .a) $x = 2$ $y = 7$
b) $x = 3$ $y = 4$
c) $x = -3$ $y = 1$
d) $x = 7$ $y = 6$
e) $x = 3$ $y = -2$
f) $x = -1$ $y = 2$
2. $x = 0$ $y = 6$ $y = 0$ $x = 7$
$x = 0$ $y = -2$ $y = 0$ $x = 2$
Point of intersection gives the approximate solution $x = 4.3$ $y = 2.3$